Dear Mr. Potter

LETTERS of LOVE, LOSS, & MAGIC

compiled & edited by Lily Zalon

designed by Chris Ritchie, Coa Design

Visit us on the Web at www.dearmrpotter.org

Book designed by Chris Ritchie, Coa Design
Cover lettering by Ross MacDonald

ISBN: 978-0-615-47931-6

PRINTED IN THE UNITED STATES OF AMERICA

June 2011

10 9 8 7 6 5 4 3 2 1

To Jo Rowling,

from those who stuck with Harry until the very end.

Foreword by Andrew Slack

EXECUTIVE DIRECTOR *of the* HARRY POTTER ALLIANCE

Dear Professor Dumbledore,

After you died, I made a vow.

At first, I just lay there, my horrified eyes transfixed to the page in shock. Everything that had ever made me feel mirthful was destroyed before my eyes. Hogwarts had been invaded by Voldemort and I, a lightning struck reader immobilized on a lightning struck tower, could not get the image out of my mind: again and again, the wisest man I ever knew was forced to kneel before hoodlums and transfigured into a "rag doll" of a corpse, then cast off one of the buildings of his own school under the perverse light of the Dark Mark.

I didn't know if Snape was actually guilty. I didn't know what would become of Harry. I didn't know what would happen in the war against Voldemort. I only knew that despite the many traumas and losses that I have seen in my own life; despite my loved ones' many traumas and losses, for which I am humbled to serve as a secret keeper; despite the many traumas and losses that overwhelm me when seeing video footage of genocide and poverty; and despite the many traumas and losses I had shared with Harry through these amazing books, there was still no preparation for seeing you here, spread-eagled, broken: the greatest wizard that I and that Harry had ever, or would ever, meet .

The story of your death changed the story of my life. When you died, I lost the person that I wanted to grow up to be, who represented all of my greatest teachers, and who not only gave me a feeling of childlike wonder and spontaneity, but a feeling of safety. When someone I loved was suffering, whether amongst my relatives, friends, or my family at Hogwarts, I looked to your strength, wisdom, and your humor for solace. And then it was over. You begged Snape and he answered you with the killing curse. For a few moments, the hope and faith I had in kindness and trust had dissaparated. Suddenly Fawkes had stopped singing... the phoenix had gone, had left Hogwarts for good, just as Dumbledore had left the school, had left the world... had left Harry... and had also left me.

But even amidst these ashes of despair, something was reborn inside of me. A vow. A vow inspired by something that Harry had said at your funeral. When Harry replied to Scrimgeour's insensitive, politically motivated questions by explaining that their answers were private between he and his Headmaster, Scrimgeour chided him: "Such loyalty is admirable of course... but Dumbledore is gone, Harry. He's gone." Conjuring from his heart something you had said in his second year Harry replied, smiling in spite of himself, "He will only be gone from the school when none here are loyal to him." Confused, Scrimgeour ended by saying "I see you are—" and Harry interrupted, "Dumbledore's man through and through...that's right."

Minutes later, my astonished eyes had taken in the last words of *Half-Blood Prince*. I closed the book and walked outside; it was a warm summer evening. The world was alive and vibrant as I took a silent walk. Perhaps you'll remember, for in that walk I made a vow that Harry would not be the only one who would remain loyal to you, for I would, too.

Just five weeks before watching you die, I told the band Harry and the Potters (you've heard of them, yes? They sing indie rock punk music from Harry's perspective and inspired hundreds of Wizard Rock bands to emerge. Professor, you would LOVE them!) an idea I felt very passionate about: a Dumbledore's Army for the real world called "The Harry Potter Alliance." The two members of the band, brothers Paul and Joe DeGeorge, loved it. Paul and I began brainstorming. As a traveling sketch comedian with several projects on his plate, I was certainly struggling to make ends meet and the HPA was only an exciting possibility. But as I walked that July night, something changed within me. My greatest teacher had just died. And so I made a vow to help ensure that you wouldn't be gone. I made a vow to be Dumbledore's man through and through. And I would do it through the Harry Potter Alliance.

Though I have certainly paused and stumbled along the way, my walk that night in the summer of 2005 has not stopped. In the years that followed, I have been joined by close friends, family, Wizard Rock bands, the leaders

of *Harry Potter* fan sites, an army of HPA volunteer staff and chapters, leaders of the fan fiction community, actors in the *Harry Potter* movies, the International Quidditch Association, donors, experts in human rights and social organizing, a long list of cutting edge nonprofit groups, Nerdfighters, YouTubers, best-selling young adult authors, scholars, and many more—all fighting together, vowing to stay loyal to your spirit.

Together we have sent five cargo planes full of medical supplies to Haiti (each named after a different *Harry Potter* character), donated over 70,000 books across the world, started a constructive dialogue with the CEO of Warner Brothers to make all *Harry Potter* chocolate Fair Trade, and made significant strides for the LGBTQ, anti-genocide, and media reform movements. Somewhere in the midst of this journey, I was stunned when J.K. Rowling talked about us in *Time* Magazine before writing on her web site: "I am honoured and humbled that Harry's name has been given to such an extraordinary campaign, which really does exemplify the values for which Dumbledore's Army fought in the books." And then in a personal letter, "The HP Alliance is, without doubt, the purest expression of 'the spirit of Albus Dumbledore' yet to emerge from the *Harry Potter* fandom..." Professor, I hope that you agree, would smile and say "you did do the thing properly."

But there is much work still to be done. As your bravest student, Severus Snape, declared, Dark Arts are a "many headed monster, which each time a neck is severed, sprouts a head even fiercer and cleverer than before." Indeed, the Dark Arts move at speeds and volumes far faster and louder than the slow, soft lullabies that Lily Potter sang to Harry as a baby. But the odds are in our favor, for as you demonstrated in the war against Voldemort, it is the quiet, subtle, intimate, and vulnerable force of love which Dark Lords, Death Eaters, and dementors know not:

"Of house-elves and children's tales, of love, loyalty, and innocence, Voldemort knows and understands nothing. Nothing. That they all have a power beyond his own, a power beyond the reach of any magic, is a truth he has never grasped."

Just as you gave Hermione Granger a children's storybook to arm her with the knowledge required to defeat Voldemort's horcruxes, we look to the story of *Harry Potter* as our own weapon in fighting our real-world horcruxes. We in the Harry Potter Alliance are part of a generation that grew up with the "children's tale" of *Harry Potter*, and we have allowed its stories of love, loyalty, and innocence to transform us. The depth and significance of that transformation is what you will find sir, in the contents of this book, *Dear Mr. Potter*. I feel very grateful to the sixteen-year-old heart-powered genius named Lily Zalon, who created and directs this project (where people may continue to enter their letters at dearmrpotter.org), and who chose to donate its proceeds to the HPA. Her vision of the project and each of these letters demonstrate that you will not be gone any time soon sir. There are so many of us who remain loyal to you.

The authors of the letters that follow include a five-year-old fan dictating to his mother, best-selling authors, a star of the *Harry Potter* films, fandom leaders, and many who have endured depression, bullying, and indescribable loss—the loss of their children, their siblings, their parents, and friends. These letters share a common thread: they have been written by the bravest of souls whose journeys have been inspired by our dear Mr. Potter to love in spite of, and because of, loss. As you say to Harry in his sixth year, "Yes, Harry, you can love...which, given everything that has happened to you, is a great and remarkable thing. You are still too young to understand how unusual you are, Harry." Indeed, professor. But may I be so bold as to add that these brave individuals who have internalized Harry's steadfast ability to love, make "the Boy Who Lived" a bit less unusual.

Thank you for our frequent visits and your continual guidance, sir. Thank you for helping me discover that strength, love, and childlike spontaneity are more powerful than magic, status, or material wealth. As members of the Harry Potter Alliance and as *Harry Potter* fans who have written our dear Mr. Potter, we have all taken a vow to be loyal to your spirit. To be Dumbledore's men and women through and through.

LOVE,

—Andrew Slack, 31, Gryffindor

Introduction

Dear Ms. Rowling,

I think, perhaps, you owe us an apology. After all, was it not the world you created that ruined this one for us? Was it not your world that made us long for something with a little more magic, that made us insist that we couldn't be Muggles? We're not very pleased with you, Jo. This can be resolved quickly, don't worry; just admit that you didn't make any of it up, send us our letters (enjoy the owls!), and let Hogwarts know they'll simply have to accept a few foreigners and a few older-than-eleven-year-olds. We'll put down our dungbombs, lower our wands, and go off to pack our trunks. We know your secrets, Jo, you're not fooling anyone. It's too real to not be real.

Of course, I kid. I know your world isn't real, although I admit it reluctantly. We all knew, as September 1st of our eleventh years came, that there was no scarlet steam engine leaving King's Cross without us. We knew that there was no separate world just beyond our reach, more magical and more fantastic than our own. This knowledge was buried very far down, and we fought for years to keep it there. We've come up with crazy theories to fight it—perhaps you were really Hermione Granger in disguise, documenting the events of your school years? Maybe the American school of magic didn't accept students until much later, and I'd get my letter at eighteen? And yet despite these theories, we have finally embraced what we always knew we must: the wizarding world is not real. Magic, in all its glory, is not real. This is the first essential thing every *Harry Potter* fan must realize.

The second, of course, is how very untrue that is.

If I retain only one lesson from my experience as a *Harry Potter* fan, I hope it will be the knowledge that magic will always be real. Your books are about two types of magic. The first, the magic of wand-waving and potions and Hogwarts School of Witchcraft and Wizardry, is a fantasy. But this is not the only powerful magic in your books; you taught me that. The

powerful magic is something you have given me and millions more, something that we will always be able to carry with us. This is the magic of humanity, of bravery, of compassion, of acceptance, of love, and it is more real than anything.

That is what these letters are about. They are thank-you letters, yes, but above all they are proof of what you have taught us and what you have given us. What you have given us, Jo, is the ability and confidence to love, to feel passion, and to fight for what is right and not give in to what is easy.

I don't think you created a world. I think you created two. The wizarding world is yours, no one can argue that. But what of our own world – the Muggle world? For your fans, you created that, too. You designed Harry, Ron, and Hermione, but you also designed us. Not a single one of us would be the same without your world. Are we also your characters? If so, you crafted us well. We can love. We can sacrifice. We can laugh. We can read. We can create magic, not with our wands, but with our hearts.

The magic documented within these pages is wholly yours, Jo. We have trapped that which you have given us in hopes that we can give some small part of it back to you. We have struggled to make the words meaningful enough, for you taught us that there is nothing words cannot do. Each of these stories is different. You created different memories for us all. Each picture shows a different face, each copy of *Harry Potter* is uniquely dog-eared and, although they hold the same story within their pages, all of these copies have their own stories as well. You have millions of fans, and we are all distinctly different, but we are bound together through a love of your world and a profound appreciation for what you have given us.

You have created a generation, Jo. Let this book serve as proof.

Thank you, from the bottom of my heart, and on behalf of everyone who you have touched so deeply.

LOTS OF LOVE,

Dear Mr. Potter

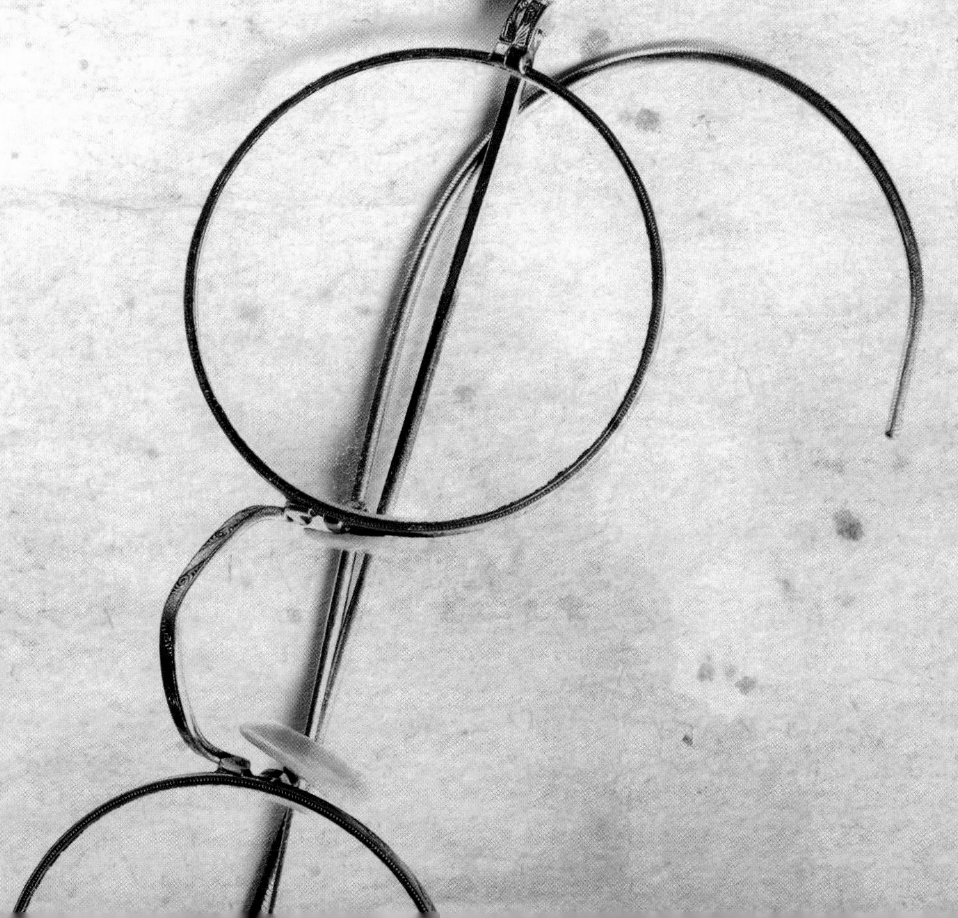

I'm happiest when I'm dressed as Harry Potter.

Caitlin C., 17, Gryffindor

When the dementors were surrounding me, you were my patronus. Thank you from the bottom of my heart. –Anita E.

Jordon B., 21

I'm 22 now.
HARRY POTTER AND THE SORCERER'S STONE
THIS Book Belongs to
12 years later, I'm still reading. It just never gets old.
HARRY POTTER

Kimberly S., 16, Gryffindor

Emma S.

Some things never change.
–Victoria W., 15

Dear Mr. Potter,

In third grade, my teacher decided to do something different and read a couple of pages from a novel to the class every day. The first book she chose was *Harry Potter and the Sorcerer's Stone.* I remember thinking how amazing it was to truly get lost in a book. Even though I absolutely hated my teacher, I was eager to go to school every day so I could hear what happened next. That year I reread the first book, finished the second one and went out and bought the third and the fourth, which were the only other books out at the time.

THEN TRAGEDY STRUCK MY FAMILY in the form of disease and loss and I tucked the series away in a box in the back of my closet where they lay, forgotten. From that day until the summer after eighth grade, I didn't read another book. Not a single one. I, too, lay tucked away inside myself, until one day, out of boredom, I was digging through my closet and found the box where I kept all of the books from my childhood. *Harry Potter and the Prisoner of Azkaban* was on top. I don't know what it was, but something about seeing that book switched on a part of myself I thought had died. I sat down on my bed and began to read. I didn't stop until the last page. The feeling from the third grade was brought back and I couldn't get enough. I went out and bought the fifth and the sixth one that day. By the end of the week, I had finished them all.

When the final installment came out, I was first in line at midnight. I called into work the next day and my sister and I stayed in my room the whole day as I read it aloud. We didn't stop once. My voice was hoarse for the rest of the week from speaking so much.

The third book has always been my favorite, because I feel like it saved me. It reintroduced me to the joy of reading and I made a ton of friends at school through a mutual love of *Harry Potter*. It restored that eagerness I once felt. I cannot express the impact *Harry Potter* has had on my life. For me, it's a necessity right up there with oxygen.

– Cora V., 19

Jenny

Dear Mr. Potter,

Thank you for saving me. It's been ten years now; more than half of my life. You've allowed me to live, to be myself and to open up. I grew up with you just as you grew up with me. You and your books were there throughout the fighting, throughout the depression, throughout the bad times. You were there through sunny summers and bitter winters. Thank you for letting me grow. Thank you for being there.

– Jenny G., 16

Gryffindor
HARRY POTTER TAUGHT ME WHAT KIND OF PERSON I WANT TO BE.

Heather C.

Dear Mr Potter,

I was lucky enough to recieve a copy of Harry Potter and the Philosopher's Stone in the mail from an aunt in England before it became popular in Australia. I remember being so proud of myself upon reading it at age 7, because the Smarties award sticker said "ages 9 and up". If I think back to my childhood, I cannot imagine one without Harry.

Lunchtimes at Primary school were filled with roleplay adventures at Hogwarts. I had a birthday party where guests had to be sorted before they sat down for the feast, house colours tacked to the walls and stars hanging from the ceiling. We played Quidditch on the trampoline. We had family boardgame nights with the Harry Potter "Cluedo" game. I had all the Lego sets.

My copies of the books are loved and care-worn. Every time a new one came out I would re-read the series in preparation. But also, every time I was feeling sad or despondent, I would curl up and retreat into the magical world JK Rowling created. My friends at Hogwarts were there for me when my Dad was serving in East Timor and again when he was in Iraq. They were there when I needed a break from studying, they have been there for me more times than I can count. I went to Hogwarts. I went to the library with Hermione. I laughed with Ron. I fought battles with Harry.

I learned that it's OK to ask for help, that you don't have to cope by yourself. I learned that there is no black and white, but infinite shades of grey. I learned that love is the greatest magic of all.

I am forever in JK Rowling's debt for giving me such a wonderful world to grow up in.

Alison H.
18
Australia

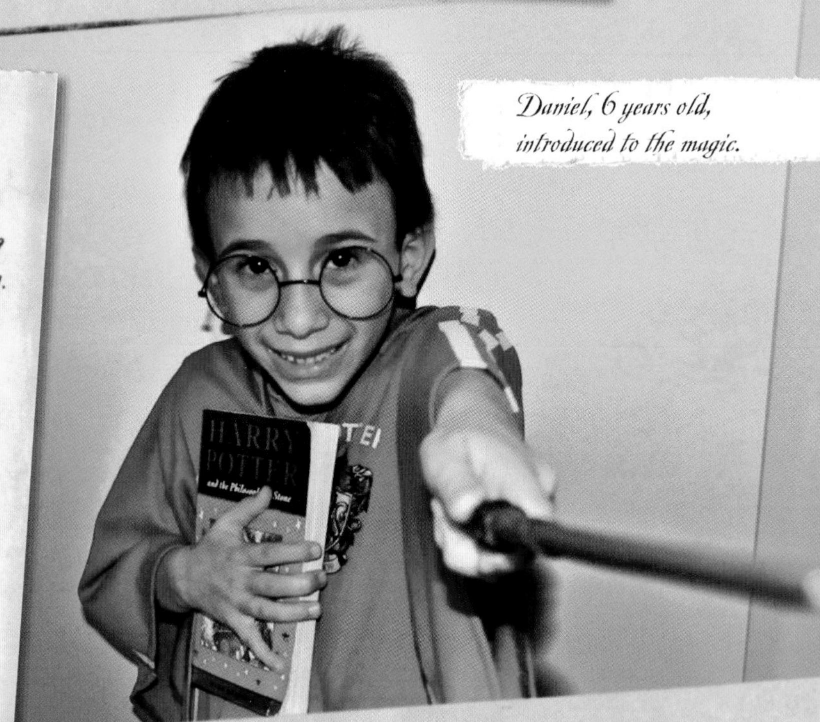

Daniel, 6 years old, introduced to the magic.

Claire

Dear Mr. Potter,

I was seven years old when I first encountered *Harry Potter*. I would sit at our white tiled breakfast table and eat my eggs and toast while my mother read aloud from the book with the boy and the broomstick on the cover. She was reading from the book that would forever change the way that I saw reading. It was our first year at Hogwarts and, in a fitting way, *Harry Potter* and I conquered many firsts together.

After my mother finished reading *The Sorcerer's Stone* to me, I attacked reading like my life depended on it. I began to read voraciously. I now knew that whole other worlds were out there, just within my reach, far beyond the boundaries of library shelves and yet accessible every time I picked up a book. And, now that I look back on it, *Harry Potter* taught me this.

Thank you for creating a world that I can hide in when I'm sick of my own. –Lucy G.

In middle school, I was teased for being a nerd. Though there was that one sliver of a time where being a "nerd" was considered cool, I still didn't escape some teasing. Thankfully, it never had much of an effect on me. I was chubby when I was younger – a chubby, blond haired, glasses-wearing girl whose only solace was imaginary worlds. And I loved it that way. I read. And I read a lot. Because of *Harry Potter*, I wanted to read everything. For most of seventh and eighth grade, I would lay stomach down on my bed with *Harry Potter* in my hands and Norah Jones on my Walkman. During middle and high schools I struggled with the constant battle of putting the book down, and getting homework done.

The world that J.K Rowling created was a place that felt like home. I fell so easily into the ways of Harry, Ron, and Hermione, that I often times hoped with all my might that it was real. Hearing the crack of the books spine opening always brings back the same warm feeling, like walking into my bedroom after having gone on a long trip. While I never forgot about the magic of *Harry Potter*, it was nice to be reminded that it still existed. That it hadn't all been in my head.

I've always felt a strong connection with J.K. Rowling. My mother was also a single parent raising a daughter. Recently, a family friend told me a story about one of his co-workers. She is a single mother with a son who loves *Harry Potter*. Just after the release of the second book, when her son was about nine, Jo was giving a book reading in a town near where they lived. The day of the book reading came and went – in her haste, the boy's mother had written down the wrong date. Feeling horrible, she decided to write to J.K. Rowling. In the letter, she explained how she had messed up and was a single mother raising a child. A few weeks later, a parcel arrived for the boy. It contained a copy of the first two *Harry Potter* novels, signed and annotated by Jo. She also wrote the boy a letter explaining that sometimes mothers mess up, but that you should always love them, and that being a single parent is especially hard. This story made me cry because, at some point or another, I had felt like that young boy. I will forever view my mother as strong and courageous, just like Lily when she sacrificed her life. I, too, have the power of love running through my veins. *Harry Potter* taught me this.

I have tried many times to write J.K Rowling a letter of deepest gratitude. I didn't know quite how to summarize my feelings poignantly and intelligently when what I really wanted to do was just give her a big hug. I know J.K. Rowling didn't write these books for me, but they helped me get through some times that needed the distraction of a fantastic tale. They taught me the beauty of words, plots, and characters. But, above all else, I learned that loving and living go hand in hand. With that, I will forever live my life like I am fighting the Dark Lord. Taking a deep breath, I will take my life one day at a time.

– Claire M., 20, Gryffindor

Tara

Three years ago, my older sister was hit by a drunk driver. We were shocked and angry. Everything seemed to be fine for a short time after her recovery, but then she began passing out. These fainting spells transformed into small seizures and then into violent fits. I never will forget seeing my sister in these fits. It is something that cannot be erased.

The doctors had no idea what was wrong with her. She went to the emergency room so often that the nurses knew her by name. The stress of constantly fearing that she would fall and crack her head tore at the rest of my family. Sometimes I thought it would be better if she just died than to face another day of waiting.

The fear that her illness put on my family began to show itself. My father contracted a deadly bacteria that began to eat away at his organs. I remember sitting in his hospital room, my father in his bed, looking pale and scared, and my sister in a chair, twitching and crying in another fit. I had never felt so hopeless.

WHAT DOES THIS HAVE TO DO WITH HARRY POTTER? **Everything**. The world that J.K. Rowling created is my escape. When I open the books, I am transported to a world of magic and wonder. I feel that each character is a part of me. Good and bad, they each taught me something.

Ron Weasley represents my feelings of worthlessness in this situation. He never felt good enough or brave enough. However, he put aside his insecurities and fought and loved better than any other. He never failed to put smiles on his companions' faces. He represents true courage.

Hermione Granger is the most beautiful and determined character I have ever known. Even though she is looked down upon and shunned, she never lets it get to her. She looks at the good in every situation and she sees the good in every person. She is the "brightest witch of her age" in more ways than one.

Harry Potter never, ever gave up. He had so many hardships that kept piling up on top of him but they did not stop him from being hopeful. He lived through unimaginable pain only to over come it.

I won't go on, but I could, because every character and theme in the *Harry Potter* series gave me something that helped me through my dark situation. Without *Harry Potter*, I would feel worthless and hopeless. He saved me from a dark and hopeless future. He gave me light when I thought there was none. Every time I opened a book, I was on the Hogwarts Express, eating Chocolate Frogs with Harry, Ron, and Hermione, laughing as we journeyed home.

– Tara B., 16

Dear Mr. Potter, 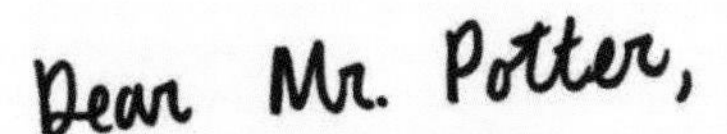

Every night from ages 5-11 my Dad would read me a chapter from the Harry Potter series. At the time I didn't really understand the books but every night I could expect to hear a little more of Mr. Potter's story. I didn't always pay attention to my Dad reading. Sometimes I would be too caught up in my 4th grade drama to care about Harry Potter. Then going into middle school I told my Dad to stop reading the books to me. I wanted to be cool and Harry Potter wasn't. I took down my chamber of secrets movie poster + removed the books from my room. Those first 2 years of middle school are the ones I regret the most. I became a copy of every other pre-teen brat. I compromised my beliefs just to get a guy to like me. I became this mindless drone who stood for nothing + believed in nothing. Going into 8th grade I found Harry Potter again. He was still waiting for me. He's taught me so much since then. I don't want to be anyone but myself. with love, Georgia K.

Fiana M.

dear ms. rowling:

it's because of you that i don't suck.

love,

lily, 15, Ravenclaw

Dear Mr. Potter,

Hi! It's so nice to finally write to you. I feel like I've been keeping this letter in my heart for 10 years.

Jaime, 6, as Ron, Joaquin, 6, as Harry, and Gaby, 7, as Hermione

We're the same age, you know. You have kids now, like I do, and you know how it is to have your own family to love, learn and grow up with. It's an amazing experience, and I'm glad you're living a dream.

I read your stories back when I was in college. I suppose it's a bit funny for a "grown up" to still read children's books, but I'm a child at heart, and your story introduced me to a world that was magical to be in. It dawned on me while reading the books that I was living in a time when a children's classic was being published. How many people do you know lived within the time when a Lewis Carroll or C.S. Lewis book was published? Not many, I suppose, and I knew that now was the time to cherish, document, and be a part of history.

Since the moment I picked up the books, my life has changed and grown, just like yours. Today, I'm happily married to my best friend, and together we have 5 children – a princess, and two sets of twins! Molly Weasley would be proud.

This year marks the year that my kids fully understood and appreciated your story. They've watched the movies, but my eldest daughter is now reading through the first book by herself. I am so proud to share with her something that I know she will hold as a classic – a story about courage, friends, family, and love. She will go through her own journey with you, and I am excited to watch her slowly discover your magical world.

Because of your stories, I am able to impart the love of reading and books to my children, a legacy that I hope they in turn will teach their own children. And you are a big part of it, Mr. Potter. For that I thank you immensely.

My youngest daughter is tugging at my shirt, so I must bid you goodbye for now. The real world calls, and I suppose you'll go back to yours. But until the next time I open one of your books, I wish you, your family, and friends, and Ms. J.K. Rowling much happiness, joy and peace.

From Monica, 30, Philippines

hank you for making
n feel like Potions class.
-Kelsie U. (15)

Alex

I realized something recently. The first time I opened the pages of *Harry Potter and the Sorcerer's Stone* was a few weeks after I began the first grade.

I will be a sitting in a theater watching *Harry Potter and the Deathly Hallows: Part Two* shortly after I graduate from high school.

Thank you, Mr. Potter, for growing up with me.

Love, Alex T.

Shaemarie M.

Dear Mr. Potter,

I won't say the *Harry Potter* novels were my childhood, because they're more than that. I've grown up with you and will continue to carry you in my heart wherever I go. You are my inspiration and my motivation.

You've taught me a myriad of invaluable lessons, but above all else, you made it okay to be me. You made me realize it was okay to be the "smart girl." In fact, you showed me that I can be a smart girl, a beautiful girl, a witty girl, a loving girl. I can be whatever I want, and I will be. I can never thank you enough for showing me that.

Forever indebted,

– Rebecca K., 18, Canada

Emily G., 15

Dear Mr. Potter,

I am not an author.

Please, make no mistake. You have given me that dream, too. Your books, first and foremost, have set me free in such a way that my dearest ambition is to return that same feeling to new generations of readers. But I am not an author.

How do you credit the woman who has made you who you are? How do you say thank you to the person who has given you the tools you needed to shape who you will be in the future? And how do you show your gratitude to the real-life hero who created the adventure that makes your life worth living every single day?

I don't know that many outside the *Harry Potter* phenomenon have been faced with the challenge of explaining how their lives came to be eternally tied to seven books. It will make sense only to these people, perhaps, that as I sit with my fingers to keys, the task of saying what *Harry Potter* means to me seems insurmountably daunting, and that somehow words might never be enough. But words are enough. You taught me that, Jo. Your words were more than enough to ensnare me at the age of five, as I sat surrounded by the existing books and tore through *Harry Potter*'s story in a trance of exhilaration. Indeed, I brought the copies that held his journey upon them to virtual ruin, as again and again I turned their pages.

Your words were more than enough to grow up with. Like so many others, the steps of my own journey are marked by pages rather than time.

Lauren

I walk parallel to *Harry Potter*, and it is this that may explain why I simply cannot imagine the person I would have grown to be without him.

Your words were more than enough to shape the values and beliefs that I truly attempt to uphold each day. It is because of you, Jo, that I believe in the indomitable power of the human spirit, and that we can do anything we desire. I believe that love conquers all obstacles. I believe that our true person takes place far outside race or gender or House or past mistakes; that no one can be defined completely. I believe that we are all capable of change, and that there is no good or evil without the power of choice. And I firmly believe that no matter what, we always, always have a choice.

> *Most people are saved by religion or love or change. I was saved by Harry Potter.*
> *–Hannah C.*

I believe that we are powerful beyond our imagination. Your words were more than enough to save me, when, years ago, I battled my own dementors. You taught me that we need never be hopeless, that there is always a means to fight. You showed me that there is never a reason not to grapple my fears; you taught me to walk calmly into the tumult of reality not because it is easy, but because it is right. Your words save me every day.

Your words inspired an entire generation to read, to do the unthinkable and truly, fully give themselves over to the freedom that exists in falling headfirst into a book. You sparked the making of posters and toys and banners and scarves, yes, but something else. Your words founded Wizard Rock and charity organizations; forums, web sites, and friends. These are the venues in which those who might not be understood fully can finally exist freely, to experience within themselves the emotions you inspire within us. Your words have freed us to laugh and sob and scream unashamedly in the name of *Harry Potter*. You've taught us to feel passion, an all-consuming passion for something only *Harry Potter* fans can say they can truly access within themselves—to feel so completely for the thing they love.

> The 7 books are our horcruxes
> We are the-generation-that-shall-not-be-named.

This is the passion that leaves us stumbling over ourselves to tell you what an inherent part of us *Harry Potter* has become. This is the passion that leaves us breathless in book lines and movie queues. This is the passion we feel when we read long into the night, our red eyes drinking in the adventure time after time. This is the passion that has changed our adolescent desperation into brilliant, colored exuberance. *Harry Potter* is not a part of my life but a part of myself. My childhood, my future, and the way I am able to think and feel uniquely are owed to these books. You have instilled within me the knowledge that magic does exist, though not in a letter on the leg of an owl. Magic exists in the imagination, the acceptance, the community, and the strength you have given to me.

WORDS ARE ENOUGH. YOUR WORDS ARE EVERYTHING.

To you, Jo, I have two. Thank you.

–Lauren M., 16, Gryffindor

Emily W.

Mexican Fandom!

Dana T., 22, Ravenclaw

Sarah T., 16

MIDNIGHT MAGIC PARTY

JULY 21, 2007

3,440 PAGES READ, ONLY 784 TO GO!

BARNES&NOBLE
BOOKSELLERS

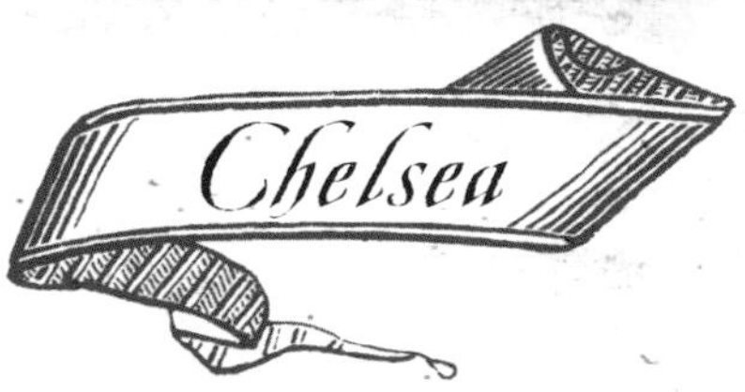

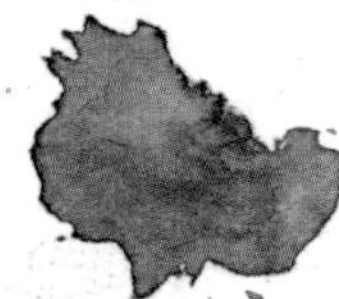

Chelsea M.

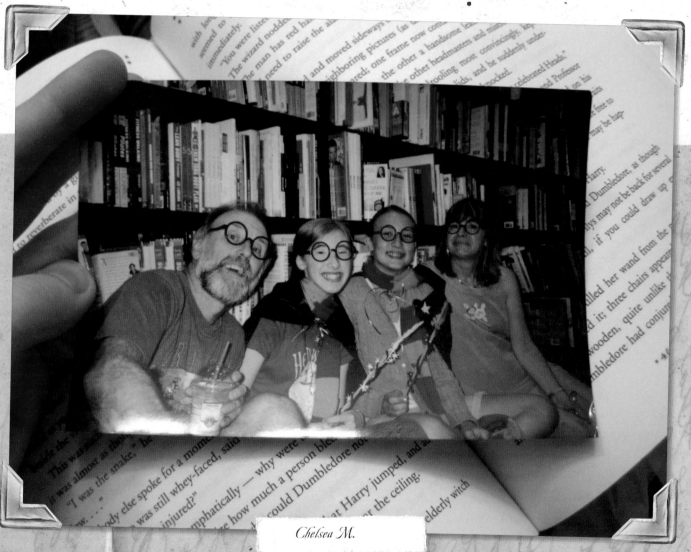

It's no secret to my friends and family that I'm a huge *Harry Potter* fan. Since the third grade, the books have been an immense part of my life. When they first came out in the US, they had already become wildly popular across the pond. My grandmother first gave the book to me as a Christmas present. I was completely uninterested at the time, only to be coaxed into listening to it read aloud by my mother, who threatened to read it without me if I didn't care enough to listen. At that age I already loved books, so eventually I caved. My mom and I became fans almost instantly.

We read through the rest of the series quickly as the years passed. We stayed up until all hours of the night reading, desperately trying to find out what happened next. Being read to by my mother was an important bonding experience for us. It wasn't until fifth grade that I decided I was ready to read one of the new books—the fifth one, and my favorite to this day—by myself. That also happened to be the year I met Christina.

Until this point, I was alone in my love of the *Harry Potter* books. The boys in my class made fun of me, and none of the girls I was friends with were readers. I had no one to talk to about what was going to happen in the next book or how many lines I had memorized from the movie. It was the sort of thing you couldn't understand unless you were a fan as well. I was alone—or so I thought. The first day of fifth grade came, and being a *Harry Potter* fan finally meant something, because I had met someone who was just as big a fan as I was.

Christina had gone to Catholic school before coming to my elementary school. Almost instantly upon meeting her in the line of 4th through 6th graders standing outside the building on that sunny September day, we discovered a mutual love of the books. She and I became best friends. We were in the same class and talked about the books relentlessly. We kept journals cataloguing the spells, foods and characters found in J. K. Rowling's world and raced each other to the end of the fifth book, comparing pages read when we came to school each morning.

Finding another fan was an incredible feeling of hope for me, despite our closeness being short-lived. As I found myself year after year without any other Potter-obsessed friends, Christina, who had become more interested in lip-gloss and boys than books, had begun to seem like my last hope. But I realize now that having another fan to talk to was well worth it, no matter how temporary it may have been. I still have those journals, locked up safe and sound with other precious things from my childhood, and I still have the memories of feeling what it was like share something so major with someone.

Harry Potter has had a major influence on what I want to do with my life. At the age of ten, it finally occurred to me that maybe I could become a writer of fantasy novels just like J. K. Rowling. It's been three years since *Deathly Hallows* was released, and despite the end of our boy wizard's journey, the past three years have been amazing. I've finished my first novel. I've made the friends I never thought I would in my senior year of high school, the nerdy, dorky, book-obsessed friends I was deprived of since elementary school. And over a decade later, I still attribute my happiness and who I am to J.K. Rowling's books. *Harry Potter* has been my everything since I was an 8-year-old girl anxiously awaiting the release of *Goblet of Fire*. It has defined me, comforted me, and instilled in me a hope and a drive that will never burn out. To the people who know me, I'm that *Harry Potter* girl, but to the fans, we know that we're that *Harry Potter* generation.

– Chelsea M.

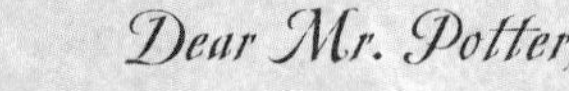

My journey with Harry, Ron, and Hermione began when I was in fifth grade. I received the first *Harry Potter* book from my mother and grandmother. I had no idea that I was about enter this magical world, or that it would have such an impact on my life.

I always loved reading, but I had never heard of *Harry Potter*, so I just tossed the book on my shelf. It wasn't until I needed a new book for a class report that I finally pulled Harry off my shelf and cracked its spine for the first time. I couldn't put it down. My mother had to yell at me to put my lights out and go to sleep the first night. Soon I was searching for the books that followed.

My grandmother, in particular, fueled my love for *Harry Potter*. She often reminds me of Dumbledore, from her larger-than-life personality to her quirky ways. We saw the films together, and devoured any *Harry Potter*-related reading we could find. Our love of Harry gave us a connection and a bond. Every summer when I visited my grandmother, we would stay up late and read together. She even went to the *Harry Potter* book releases with me.

It has been many years since I received the first *Harry Potter* book. My grandmother now has Alzheimer's and lives next door to my parents. She remembers few things about our times spent together, and it makes me sad sometimes. But each time she watches a *Harry Potter* movie, she asks my mom what I am up to. She never forgets how much I love *Harry Potter*.

I learned so much from reading the *Harry Potter* books: how to be brave and loyal, the meaning of friendship, and how to love with my whole heart. They helped me learn about my grandmother. She always stressed how important it is to use your imagination. Without *Harry Potter*, I may never have gotten to know my grandmother in the ways that I did. She loved to read and write. She lived far away, and each of her letters showed up in my mailbox with an owl on the stationary.

I still have every letter my grandmother ever wrote to me. I am so grateful to *Harry Potter* for giving me so many wonderful memories with my grandmother. I have developed closer bonds to my friends and family throughout my journey with Harry. I have shared my love of Harry with my sister, brother, and my fiancé. To this day, we love to discuss *Harry Potter* at the dinner table. So thank you, Harry, and thank you, J.K. Rowling.

– Amanda D., 23, Gryffindor, Florida

Dear Mr. Potter,

I want to say thank you for making my childhood what it was, but more importantly to thank you for giving me something that my daughter can grow to believe in, too.

Harry Potter will show her that there is magic in the simplest things, that friendship and love are the most powerful bonds, and that no matter what your differences may be, we all have the ability to band together and do something great. I hope that Malorie will grow up knowing that even though she may be just an ordinary girl, she can grow up to do extraordinary things, just as many of the characters in these books have.

Already she enjoys dressing up and playing with wands and books, and her imagination and laughter are magic enough.

Thank you on behalf of my daughter and myself. Thank you, thank you.

Jessica C., 21,
Slytherin
(and Malorie W.,
7 months old)

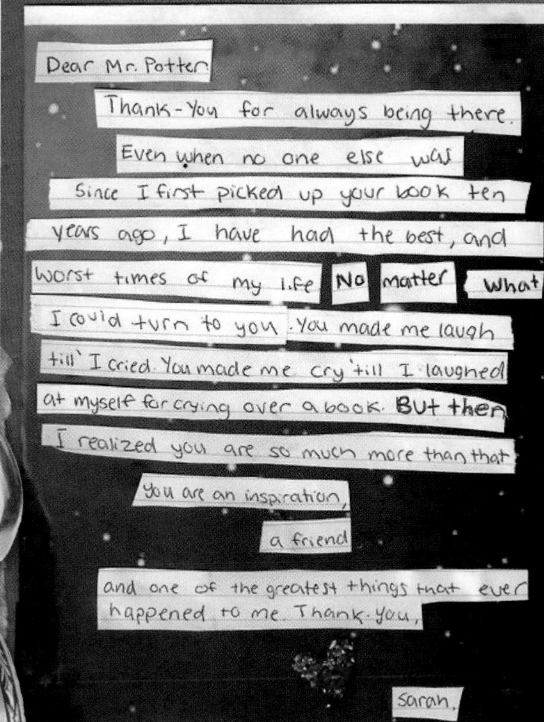
Dear Mr. Potter
Thank-You for always being there.
Even when no one else was
Since I first picked up your book ten
years ago, I have had the best, and
worst times of my life No matter what
I could turn to you. You made me laugh
till I cried. You made me cry 'till I laughed
at myself for crying over a book. But then
I realized you are so much more than that
You are an inspiration,
a friend
and one of the greatest things that ever
happened to me. Thank-You,
Sarah.

Kara J., 17

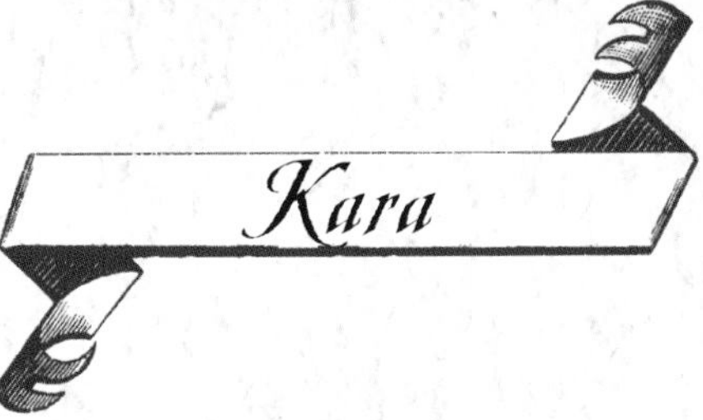

Kara

Dear Mr. Potter,

On July 21st, 2007 I was wearing a long black skirt, a witches hat, a cheap black cape, and a Lord Voldemort shirt I bought for twenty dollars at Hot Topic. I had been sitting on the steps waiting for UPS to show up with my pre-ordered copy of *Harry Potter and the Deathly Hallows*. I was practically shaking with anticipation. I had been waiting for close to five hours for that book to arrive and when it finally did I wouldn't let it out of my sight for days. I read straight through the night and devoured all 759 pages. I took brief breaks to get another Diet Dr Pepper, go to the bathroom, or get a snack, but I made sure the break never lasted more than five minutes. I cried throughout the night, quite a few times... Oh, who am I kidding? After Snape died I had to go in the closet to make sure I did not wake up my parents with my sobbing. Over the years I had developed a huge connection to all of the characters in the story, and the years of anticipation I went through before *Deathly Hallows* only made the end even harder to bare.

During the months before that amazing 2007 summer, I had discovered many things: Wizard Rock, Mugglecast, and all the other wonders of the Potter fandom. Like many, I became engrossed and fully devoted to all of it. It was then that *Harry Potter* made its strongest impact on my life. During my freshman year of high school, I was not very talkative, and did not have many friends. My best friend Alex was the only person in my life who shared my love for Harry. I would spend hours with her, discussing what J.K. Rowling could be planning for the last book, or the true identities of certain characters. Together, and alone, we immersed ourselves completely into the world of *Harry Potter*. In that period of time my walls became adorned *Harry Potter* posters and Potter memorabilia constantly lay scattered around my room. I painted my walls green, in honor of Slytherin—but don't get me wrong, I have Gryffindor in me, too! During the beginning of my sophomore year was when the huge change came. I met one of my best friends, Kate, and we immediately bonded over our love for Harry. My connection with her brought me to my current group of best friends, and we

Whenever I feel down, I just pick up one of the books and I feel completely reconnected. I feel like I've gone home. I'm a wizard girl, stuck in a Muggle world. –Cierra R.

still bond over Harry all the time. Over the years I've gone through some tough times, I found Harry as a way to escape from the chaos of normal life. If at any time I feel upset, I'll go over to my *Harry Potter* shelf, grab a random book, turn to a random page, and start reading whatever scene I find there. It never fails to calm me and give me a sense of peace.

From my immense passion for the *Harry Potter* series, and my experience with it, emerged the person I am today. The characters and situations in these stories have taught me how to be strong through rough situations and as a result, I have gained a greater sense of self confidence. The passion I have for *Harry Potter* has brought me the friendships and relationships that I treasure so dearly. As a person, I have no doubt that my creative and imaginative mind has to give a lot of credit to all that I've learned from the stories I've read. In a few short months, the *Harry Potter* series will come to a theatrical end. I have given myself the irrevocable duty of doing everything in my power to keep the series, and its messages, alive. Have no doubt, my children will read these books, as will my grandchildren, and, if I'm lucky, my great-grandchildren. *Harry Potter* has always been there for me, and I will always be there for him. It will always remain my strongest conviction that the easiest way to find happiness is by simply opening up a book.

– Kara J., 17

Dear Ms. Granger,

From one bushy-haired, brunette bookworm to another, I salute you! Thank you for reminding me that being myself is a wonderful thing.

Tiffany G., 23

Dear Mr. Potter,

This was my 8th birthday party—of course it was *Harry Potter* themed. Seven years later, I'm just as excited about the wizarding world as I was while this photo was being taken. *Harry Potter* changes lives, and it certainly changed mine.

THANK YOU SO MUCH.

– Bailey R. 15, Gryffindor

Dear Mr. Potter,

To my old friend, Harry,

How are you? I hope you are doing well. I hope you and Ginny and the kids are happy. I have no doubt in my mind that you are a great father. I know we haven't talked in a while, but I wanted to let you know how much I miss you and that I feel much better now. My life is great and I'm finally happy. I've found closure in my hectic life, as you have in your own.

I was sad, even angry, when you left. I cried, I wallowed, but mostly, I remembered. I remembered every one of the adventures we went on together. I remembered *Sorcerer's Stone*, *Chamber of Secrets*, *Prisoner of Azkaban*, *Goblet of Fire*, *Order of the Phoenix*, *Half-Blood Prince*, and *Deathly Hallows*. I remembered living without a family, enduring a horrid aunt and uncle, getting the letter to Hogwarts, being sorted, looking into the Mirror of Erised, fighting a basilisk, playing Quidditch, riding Buckbeak, encountering Dementors, winning the Triwizard Tournament, guessing who the *Half-Blood Prince* might be, and living in a tent for what seemed like ages. I remember meeting Ron and Hermione, bonding with Hagrid, listening to the wise (and sometimes ridiculous) words of Dumbledore, meeting my beloved godfather Sirius, and falling so in love with the people that soon became my new family.

Not all of our memories were so sweet. I remember fearing for my life and the lives of my friends, being called a liar, enduring excruciating pain, being rejected, watching my loved ones die, seeing the person I loved kiss somebody else, fighting with my best friends, watching the last of my family disappear through a mysterious curtain, and watching my father figure and biggest influence lose the twinkle in his eye.

There are also the memories I hold dear to my heart. I remember laughing with my best friends, actually having a real Christmas, feeling like I had a family, and finally feeling like I had a home.

Harry, you understood me. You lacked certain family members, as did I. You experienced depression and loss, as did I. Sometimes you felt completely and utterly alone, as did I. You knew exactly how I felt and you were there for me whenever I needed you. Together we went through both hard times and good times. You were my best friend.

I hated you for leaving me, Harry. I wanted you to stay with me forever. I realize now how selfish I'd been. I realize that you had to leave. It was for the better. Harry, you finally found closure. You finally found peace within yourself, as well as in the outside world. You lead by example. When you found closure, I did the same.

When you left, I finally had to face the world on my own. I didn't have you to lean on anymore. When you left, I had no choice but to start living. And for that, I thank you. You showed me how to be happy, and then you made me do it.

I know you'll always be there for me, Harry, because that's what you stand for. You stand for loyalty, courage, hope, good, and love. Above all, you stand for love. And so, I stand by your side. And I, too, stand for love above all.

THANK YOU, HARRY. YOUR OLD FRIEND,

– Elina R.

Fiona

Dear Mr. Potter,

I was eleven when I discovered *Harry Potter*. At the time, both of my parents were suffering from severe depression and I, in turn, became a grievously withdrawn child. Through my childhood and into my teens, I used the books as an escape to something better. Finally, when I left high school, I knew what I wanted to do: I wanted to be a writer. More so, I wanted to write something where others could find the same sanctuary that I found, and still do find, in *Harry Potter*. Now, three years later, I am a third-year in university, studying Creative Writing, and getting ready to graduate. So, thank you to J.K. Rowling, the woman who single handedly kept me grounded, and to you, Mr. Potter, for everything you have done for me.

– Fiona S., 20

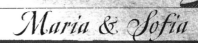

Maria & Sofia

Dear Mr. Potter,

You've bridged a gap between generations.

My sister and I are 12 years apart, yet our love for *Harry Potter* couldn't be more equal. Your books are something we share.

I grew up with your stories, and now the trio is returning to grow up with my sister.

Thank you for everything. So much love,

–Maria R., 18, Ravenclaw, and Sofia R., 6, Gryffindor

ACCIO!
MOBILARBUS!
RICTUMSEMPRA!
EVANES
APARECIUM!
SILENCIO!
REDUCIO!
ENGORGIO!
FERULA!
SPECIALIS REVELIO!
CONFUNDUS!
MUFFLIATO!
STUPEFY!
MOBILICORPUS!
PORTUS!
LUMOS!
WINGARDIUM LEVIOSA!
Erised stra ehru

Kristen B.
SONOROUS!
EPISKEY!
AVIS!
ALOHOMORA!
SCOURGIFY!
FLAGRATE!
DELETRIUS!
EXPECTO PATRONUM!
FINITE INCANTATEM!
COLLOPORTUS!
REDUCTO!
PRIOR
catru opt on wohsi
us
or less
best,
rate
hearts.
”

Dear Mr. Potter,

I didn't understand what the whole *"Harry Potter* craze" was all about until I was thirteen. I had seen the first three movies and tried several times to read the first book, but never really got into it. The summer before my eighth grade year changed everything, though, when I decided it really was about time I tried the books out, seeing as I had spent many days of my childhood pretending to be a witch and writing stories about magic and whatnot in my notebooks at school. I poured over the series, reading the first four books in a week, the fifth in another few days, and the sixth book when it came out that summer, which, admittedly, brought me to tears. Yes, I locked myself in my room all weekend when *Harry Potter and the Deathly Hallows* came out, refusing to check my email or Facebook account for fear that someone would write the ending out as their Facebook status.

This past summer, my last summer before college, I passed the time by rereading the series. I found myself strangely emotional, crying at little parts, like when Harry and Ron met on the train to Hogwarts and became best friends, or when Neville earned 10 points to allow Gryffindor to win the House Cup. I began to worry that college was not going to be as amazing as Hogwarts, and I was saddened by the fact that a series that had defined my friendships in high school was coming to such a timely end.

When I was young I believed in adventure. Then I got older. Now I believe in magic, too.
—Holly W.

In college, I was itching to find friends as interested in *Harry Potter* as my friends from home, so I mentioned it a few times. The day I knew I would be happy in college was when my friend Jonah and I started to discuss *Harry Potter* in my tiny dorm room. Soon, half the hall was crowded into my room, discussing everything *Harry Potter*: how the books and movies differed, which aspects of the series we loved the most, our hopes for the seventh movies. We brought up going to see the midnight premiere of *Harry Potter and the Deathly Hallows, Part One*, and my roommate and I constantly checked online for movie tickets. A month before the premiere, tickets became available. We struggled to figure out how everyone would manage to get there—the metro and buses wouldn't run that late. One of us suggested renting a "party bus," and what started as a joke suggestion became the real deal — we rented the bus, and we assigned every friend and friend-of-a-friend a character to play. Our one rule: everyone who entered that bus on November 18th had to be dressed in costume, and well-dressed at that. We spent weeks hunting down costume pieces at thrift stores, figuring out obscure characters to fill up the 32-person bus, and counting down the days.

At the age of eighteen, I can officially say I have had my brush with fame. After three hours of hair and makeup, our 32-person crew was ready for action. We got off the bus in front of the movie theater, and the first thing I heard was a passerby yell "PROFESSOR TRELAWNEY!", pointing at my frizzy hair and giant red glasses. The movie theater was packed with fans, and all eyes were on us. Sitting in the theater, watching the beginning of the end of my childhood, brought out something crazy in me. My boyfriend turned to me in the middle of the movie, at a moment where Hermione and Harry were alone in the woods after Ron had left, and asked me,

"Are you CRYING right now?" I wiped my tears and shook my head. When he asked what was wrong, I told him that "Everything's just so sad, there's so much evil in the world, and they're so alone, and they're supposed to be best friends forever!" You can only imagine how much I cried at Dobby's death.

The fact that *Harry Potter* could strengthen my friendships at home and at school is impressive, but what's even more impressive are the life lessons I have learned from a children's fantasy book. *Harry Potter* has taught me that even though it is impossible to prevent young people from being exposed to evil, we are so much more powerful than people give us credit for. Sure, I can't defeat Voldemort, but *Harry Potter* thrives off of the idea that the young can accomplish anything. *Harry Potter* has taught me that it's okay to be a little ridiculous, that it's the Luna Lovegoods and the Fred-and-Georges that are the most remarkable and memorable people this world has to offer.

–Melia S., Gryffindor

Melia S., Gryffindor

Delia

Dear Mr. Potter,

It all started with a father reading a book to his two daughters. Slowly, all three grew to love you and your friends. Then cancer stole the father away from the girls, despite their wishes that perhaps a Saint Mungo's healer could save him as no Muggle doctor could.

The two girls grew up, but without their father, they slowly became enemies. However, on the days new *Harry Potter* books were released, the girls would get the book together and race to finish it. The older girl read first, insisting that she was the quicker reader, and would get through it so that the littler sister could read it by nighttime. The little sister never got to finish a book first, but she read long into the night, eventually falling asleep dreaming of playing Quidditch instead of soccer and casting spells in empty Hogwarts classrooms. When they began to make movies the sisters would go together and compare, though the little sister would often forget the differences.

I have you to thank for the shared moments of joy and laughter my sister and I had when we were little, and still experience occasionally when we try to explain something to our mother, who has just recently began to read your stories.

Mischief Never Managed,

–Delia C., 16, Slytherin

Jesse

Dear Mr. Potter,

I was fortunate enough to be introduced to you through a dear friend, she had told me of your brilliance, but I wasn't convinced yet. It didn't take long before I knew she was right. We would spend our days reading about your adventures in empty classrooms, between exams and on our beautiful sandy shores. From our teens into our early twenties we never strayed from your side.

It wasn't until early this year that the same dear friend and I had to say goodbye to one another, there was little I could think of to say to express my feelings, so I turned to you....

This is what I came up with. I can't finish this letter, as I'm not ready to say goodbye to you, so until I open the pages onto our next adventure: Mischief Managed.

–Jessie E., 23, Gryffindor

Jessie E., 23, Gryffindor

Karima

Dear Mr. Potter,

My sister and I at a wax figures exhibition in Doha, Qatar. Taken in 2002.

–Karima Y., 21, Indonesia

Karima Y., 21, Indonesia

Dear Mr. Potter, Miss Spinnet, Miss Johnson, and Miss Chang,

I am forever grateful to the group of you. As a Filipino-Portuguese racial mix, I have been judged and stereotyped as everything from Lebanese, Pakistani, Aboriginal, Indian or anything else "brown" or "Asian". Living in a predominately Caucasian small town in southern Ontario, Canada, looking different than the other girls and boys really took a hit on my confidence; I was convinced that I wasn't beautiful enough to have a boyfriend when grew older.

When I discovered *Harry Potter*, I was nine. I read through every book, wishing I could be a part of the wonderful wizarding world where everyone was beautiful and talented. I had the biggest crush on Oliver Wood and the Weasley twins. You cannot imagine my happiness when I found out that Alicia Spinnet and Angelina Johnson, two characters of minority descent, were dating two of my favourite characters. When *Harry Potter* began to date Cho Chang, I was proud to play her as the lone Asian in my group of friends. I lived the lives of these three lovely ladies for my entire elementary school career. For once, when we played *Harry Potter* during recess, I had characters to role play who actually looked like me. For once I was proud to be different – if *Harry Potter* and his friends loved people who were different, then nothing else mattered.

Thank you for making a brown Asian girl feel beautiful and special.

– Samantha, 19, Gryffindor

When I was thirteen years old, I aspired to collect the first installment of the series in as many languages as possible.

Although that goal faltered pretty quickly, I've got all these lovely books to brag about now, even if I can't actually read the majority of them.

-Kelly S., 16

Jessika

Dear Mr. Potter,

I turned ten on September 22, 1999. For my birthday, I got a cassette tape of Britney Spears' *Baby One More Time* and a copy of *Harry Potter and The Sorcerer's Stone*. In all honesty, I was more excited about Britney Spears than *Harry Potter*. This was before all the hype, so I really didn't know too much about who this Harry kid was, and at that age, fantasy books weren't really my thing.

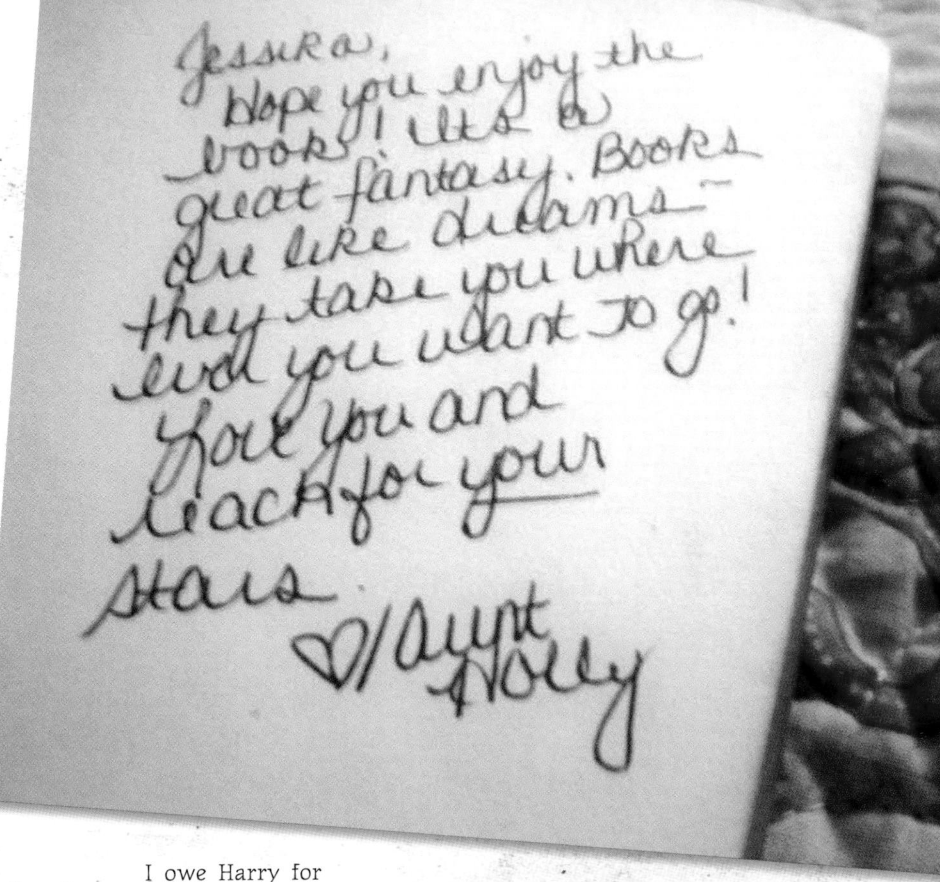

Jessika,
Hope you enjoy the book! It's a great fantasy. Books are like dreams – they take you where ever you want to go!
Love you and reach for your stars
♡/Aunt Holly

About a week later, I sat down with *Harry Potter*. I ate it up. And then ate it up again. And again. I loved Harry! Were there more books? I had to know. I went to school and found a Scholastic book order (I was big on those). I was so excited when I saw *Chamber of Secrets* for sale. It's been a love affair ever since. I bought the second and third books from the book order. I pre-ordered the fourth, fifth, sixth, and seventh books and I'll be sure to pre-order anything else J.K. Rowling ever puts out.

I feel bad for the kids who didn't have it like I did. I grew up with Harry. Literally. We remained roughly the same age every year after I discovered these great books. I feel bad for the kids who now have all seven books in their hands and don't have to wait in anticipation for the subsequent books to come out. For me, that was all part of the fun.

I owe Harry for helping me through many struggles in my life. I was teased quite a bit throughout elementary school and junior high. Where I come from, reading isn't "cool." Those who are avid readers often have to bear the brunt of juvenile meanness. Kids can be pretty mean, but with the *Harry Potter* books, there was another world I could retreat to, and be with the characters that I considered my dear friends.

I want to thank Jo Rowling for everything she's done for her readers, to Harry for keeping all of us wishing that our Hogwarts letter would hurry up and arrive already, and to my aunt for introducing me to these great books.

–Jessika M., 20, Gryffindor

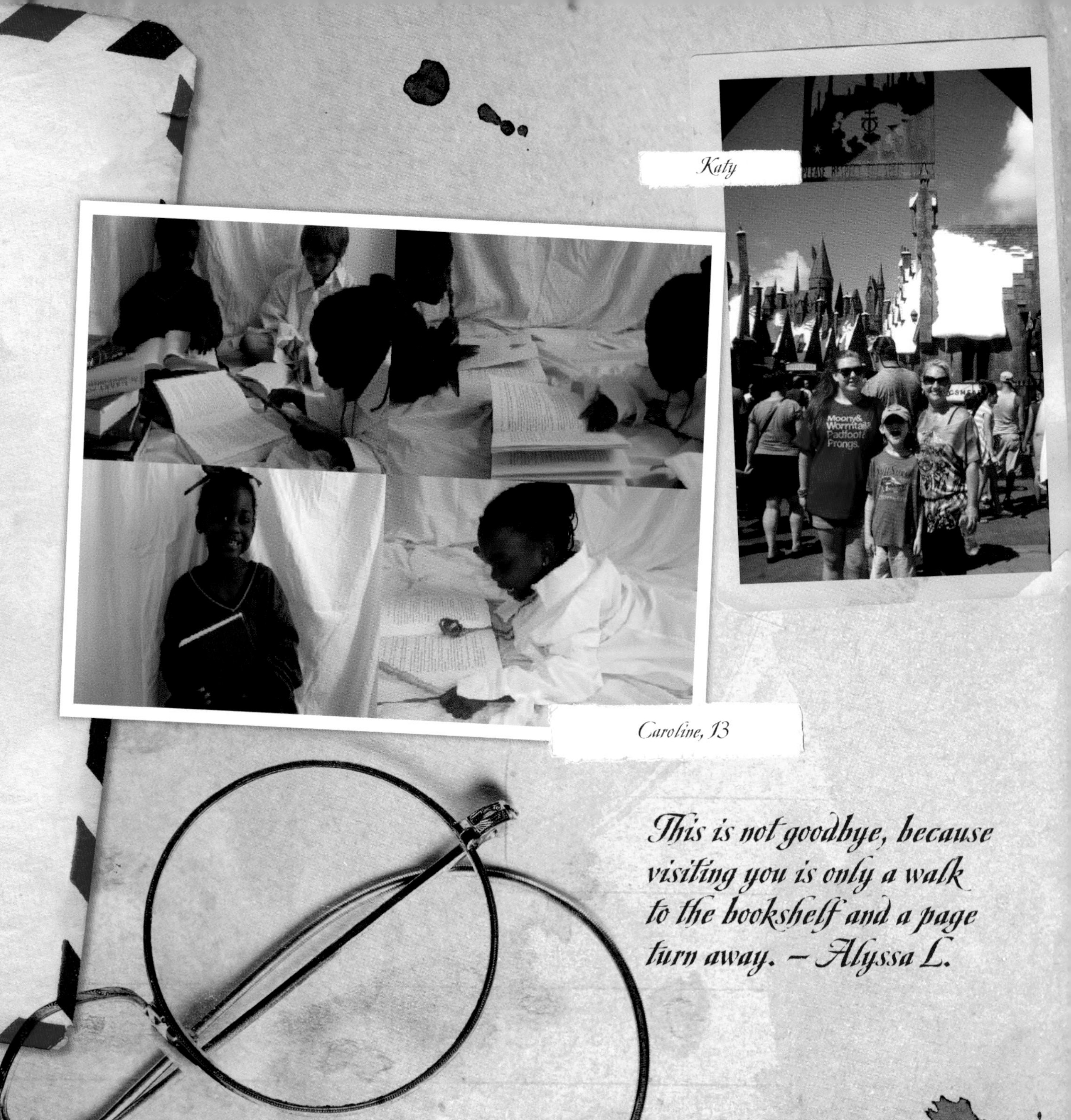

Katy

Caroline, 13

This is not goodbye, because visiting you is only a walk to the bookshelf and a page turn away. – Alyssa L.

Harry Potter was my first true addiction.
—Ana N.

Brooke M., 15

Dear Mr. Potter,

I'm the sixty-year-old father of two teenagers—one is a *Harry Potter* fanatic, and the other couldn't care less about *Harry Potter*.

I cannot adequately describe what the *Harry Potter* series has meant to me. My nineteen-year-old daughter is the fanatic, and the series has allowed me to bond and stay close with her when the typical teenage years are often met with distancing of the parent-teenager relationship. My daughter, Heather, and I read all of the books together. She would read, then I would read, and then we would sit and talk for hours about the characters and story lines. The time we spent together was magical. We both learned so much about each other without really realizing it. The story paralleled my daughter's experience growing up, as she dealt with a few close friends, bullying, loss, the importance of family, and the lesson that persistence in the face of challenges will yield incredible results.

Jo – your agent warned you that you'll never make money writing childrens' books. Good thing you wrote Harry Potter books instead. –Vincent D.

We saw all of the movies together. When the first came out, it was premiered in our community in mid-afternoon at a local theater. We were some of the first in line to get tickets and see the movie. Heather was even interviewed by a reporter from the local TV station. For all of the rest of the movies, we would attend the midnight premieres together. I'm a high school teacher; I would get home from teaching and coaching, take a nap, get up at about 11:00p.m. and then we'd go and get in line for the showing. Heather would not be able to sleep before the movie - she was too excited in anticipation of the event. We would get our popcorn and drinks and talk about what would happen and how it would mirror the events in the book. We were spellbound. Giving faces to the characters and structures to Hogwarts made the books come alive.

Jim K.

Attending the midnight premieres continued after Heather went away to college. She came back home and we continued our special tradition. Last summer, just after the Harry Potter attraction opened at Universal Studio, we had the opportunity to visit. Heather was excited beyond belief. We traveled the 100 or so miles to Universal, bought our tickets, and entered the park. Heather and I were both excited as we made our way to the

Harry Potter village. As we got closer, we could see the snow covered roofs of Hogsmeade and the tall spires of Hogwarts in the distance. Our pace quickened as we got closer. I will never forget the sight of Heather going a few paces ahead of me as we reached the bridge going into the village—she could not help herself. The sight was magical, as my daughter had a dream realized and was caught in the moment, actually able to visit the shops and Hogwarts. She paused on the bridge and stared at the sight ahead of her, and then turned back to me a few paces behind. She had tears of joy streaming down her face. That moment is forever etched in my memory. We spent the entire afternoon in the village, enjoying butterbeer and soaking up the atmosphere. It was truly an incredible and memorable experience. Seeing Heather so happy and getting to share the experience with her meant the world to me.

Of course Heather has all the staples of an obsessive *Harry Potter* fan. I would be remiss if I didn't mention her tattoos ("wit beyond measure" and a large Phoenix bird). I'm not thrilled about the tattoos, but they could be worse.

I love my daughter with all my heart. The *Harry Potter* experience has allowed me to stay close and even get closer to her. That is what life is all about: family relationships. My relationship with Heather would not be the same without *Harry Potter*. I am grateful to J.K. Rowling for the series, and for the timing. It has helped me to develop long and lasting memories with my daughter. There is nothing more important that a father could wish for.

—Jim K.

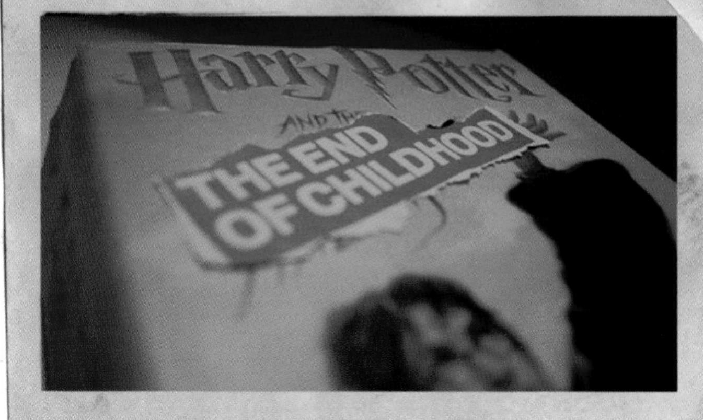

When Harry got his letter from Hogwarts, I wondered what it'd be like to get a letter of my own someday. When Harry had his first kiss, it wasn't long until I had mine. When Harry was learning to Apparate, I was learning to drive.

As I followed Harry on his journey, I was living my own. Though I wasn't consciously aware of it at the time, I was growing up with him. *Harry Potter* was my childhood. Harry was there for every awkward adolescent milestone and every growing pain. Harry was there the day I realized I wasn't a kid anymore. He was there the day I realized, somewhere along the way, while I was following his journey, that I'd grown up too.

Harry was there for that and I'm glad he was. So, Mr. Potter, thank you for being such a great companion and such an amazing childhood friend. It's been fun. I hope someday to tell my own children your story. I know you'll be as amazing a childhood friend to them as you were to me.

—Ashley A.

Dear Mr. Potter,

I remember when I was ten and my best friend talked my ears off about you until I finally asked my parents for the books for Christmas. I remember waking up that Christmas morning to find the first five books sitting under the tree. I remember reading and reading until I finished and wanted more. I remember how you were there for me when my friends were not. I remember all of that and so much more; I will never forget.

In *Sorcerer's Stone*, you taught me to have courage in the face of adversity. In *Chamber of Secrets*, you taught me that nobody is worth less than anyone else. In *Prisoner of Azkaban*, you showed me how tricky the truth can be. In *Goblet of Fire*, you showed me how to persevere through hardships and setbacks. In *Order of the Phoenix*, you taught me to fight bravely for good, to stand up for what is right no matter what. In *Half-Blood Prince*, you showed me that even the most evil of people can have miserable histories, and you taught me to treat the past with caution, because it is the key to the present. In *Deathly Hallows*, you taught me that love, truth, and light always conquer fear; that sacrifice is the purest form of love; and that there are much, much worse things in life than death.

Harry, I would not be the person I am today if it were not for you. I would never have learned to stand up for the things I believe in. I owe you so much because you taught me so much. You make me dare to be brave, to love, and to sacrifice for the people I care about. You taught me that no one deserves to live in a closet, that no one deserves to be tortured, and that love is the most powerful weapon there is.

Thank you, so much, Harry. Thank you for being there; thank you for teaching me all of this. Most importantly, thank you for giving me a reason to fight for what is right.

With great love,

– Nathan D., 16, Gryffindor

Sarah Jane

As an exchange student, I'm learning the German language as fast as I possibly can. *Harry Potter* was the first book I chose to tackle. No matter what language, these books have touched the hearts of children and adults all around the world. Thank you.

– Sarah Jane M., 16, Ravenclaw

Dear Mr Potter,

I have a lot to thank you for. The beginning of our friendship was bumpy, I'll admit. Sorcerer's Stone was given to me twelve years ago by a family friend who worked in publishing. "This is really big in England," she said. "You'll love it." I was an avid reader, but I was seven, and I didn't want to read about a boy. Eventually, reluctantly, I gave you a shot. And fell in love.

Thank you for always being there for me, for being a comfort, and for always being exactly what I need. When I would hide a flashlight under my covers to read about your adventures when my parents yelling would keep me up. When I needed an escape from a toxic home life. When I needed something familiar when everything else started to change. When I felt like an outcast. When I couldn't imagine that there were genuinely good people in the world. When I started struggling with depression and self injury.

Thank you for being fun, happy, poignant, depressing, funny and inspirational. Thank you for being a way to meet wonderful people and bond with existing friends. Thank you for helping me realize that even though your Wizarding World may not be real, magic most definitely is. And as dumb and cheesy as this may sound, thank you for being a friend.

Forever yours,

Samantha

Dear Mr. Potter,

Sometimes I'm a *Harry Potter*. We met when I was ten, so no wonder some of his personality has rubbed off on me! I always do my best to stand up and lead. I do what I must to protect my friends and family. In the end, I just want those I love to be happy and safe and I'm willing to go the distance to make that happen.

Sometimes I'm a **Hermione Granger**. I read and I read and I read and I read. I can research like a champion. I make a great trivia team member. I'm more than just a bookworm. While some people think I can't fend for myself, I always get myself out of sticky situations with a combination of smarts and resourcefulness.

Sometimes I'm a **Ron Weasley**. I'm loyal and dedicated to my cause. I do what I can to stand out, but I love being part of a team. While I sometimes get jealous, I know how to put that aside and do what needs to be done. Even though I'm afraid of spiders, I don't let fear hold me back from being a devoted friend and a hero in my own way.

Sometimes I'm a **Dumbledore**. I love teaching and helping my students find their way. I'm a natural leader. I like to be a support system for my friends and students. I don't always let people get close to me, but I always let them know that I care. If I could look in the Mirror of Erised, I would definitely see all of my loved ones...or maybe some socks.

Sometimes I'm a **Sirius Black**. I don't mean to cause trouble...it just happens. I'm mischievous and I like to figure out my way around rules. Despite all that, I'm a bit of a softy – my bark is definitely worse than my bite. I like to push people's buttons, but it's all in good fun. I would say that I have a pretty good sense of humor, even if it is sometimes at other people's expense.

To me, the real magic is the way you've opened my mind. –Lauren C.

Sometimes I'm a **Gryffindor**. I'll always fight to defend those that need my help. My good friends are always there for me in times of need. We've gone through some interesting issues together, but it has only made us stronger and braver. I know that I can face any obstacle with them by my side.

Sometimes I'm a **Ravenclaw**. I like to think things through and educate myself on important topics. I believe that it's extremely important to be well read and eager to share your knowledge. People often come to me for my advice, information, or a good riddle. Wit beyond measure is definitely man's greatest treasure!

Sometimes I'm a **Hufflepuff**. I'm misunderstood. I'm a hard worker, a dedicated friend, and a good finder... just ask anyone in my house that's misplaced their keys. While people don't always get me, I'm loving and fun to be around. Things just wouldn't be the same without me.

Sometimes I'm a **Slytherin**. I want to be successful and I want everyone to know that I want to be successful. I'm ambitious and I know how to get what I want. I love competition and I love it the most when I win.

Dani T., 22, Ravenclaw

Sometimes I'm a **Muggle**. I'm so focused on my own life that I can't see what is happening around me. I do things the hard way and don't always have the luxuries that others have. I know the function of a rubber duck.

Everything I am is thanks to J.K. Rowling. *Harry Potter* gave me the strength to leave my own cupboard under the stairs and journey into the beautiful world that was outside waiting for me. Without your amazing series, I wouldn't be the person I am today – a teacher, an artist, and a writer. Thank you for letting us into the world that you've created and, in doing so, letting us become more ourselves. You're an inspiration to us all. Thank you, thank you, thank you.

–Dani T., 22, Ravenclaw

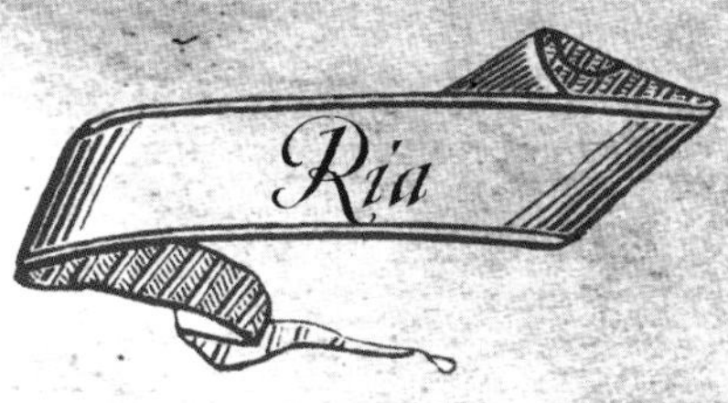

I do not know where I would be today without your story. I would not be the same person, the girl who bought her own wand at age eleven so she could have a sliver of hope that her letter from Hogwarts would come in the mail. I would not be the girl that wears her Ravenclaw scarf proudly all winter long. I would not be the girl who made it through her parents' divorce, three deaths in the family, and the teasing from other school children.

Starting when I was five, my mom would read the *Harry Potter* books to me every night before I would fall asleep. I fell in love with the series right away. The moments where I could just escape from the real world into the world of wizardry are the most precious. Those were the moments that got a little six year old girl through the roughest moments of her childhood. I'll never forget buying *Deathly Hallows* the night it was released. I put it next to all my other *Harry Potter* books and cried. I cried because it was over. It was finally over. It was like saying goodbye to a great friend.

Harry, I love you, your adventures at Hogwarts, and the wizarding world. I love what you and your story have done for me over the years. I really honestly do not know what I would've done if I did not have you, Ron, and Hermione. For that, I owe you the world and more.

LOVE,

– Ria T., 15, Ravenclaw

Aliya K, 18

It was a bittersweet moment when I turned the last page. But these three will always live on in my heart. ♥

Ready for Hogwarts, just waiting for a letter.

A long time ago, my brother dressed up as Harry for Halloween. Nobody outside our family knew who he was. We said to them, 'You will.'

–Aubrey B., 21

Jo, 17

Dear Mr. Potter,

I first read about you when I was eleven years old, the year your first book came out. I grew up with you.

When I read the first book, I was immediately attracted to the quirkiness of the wizarding world. I was a strange child. My mother and I were on two completely different levels of understanding, and my father and brother accepted me as just odd. I already loved to read, and found books that could take me away. Eleven years old and already I was searching for an escape. So when I found you, it changed the course of my life forever. You were an escape, yes, but you also showed me the way back to accepting my own reality and embracing the loss of my innocence with courage and a level head. As you grew up and faced all the magical wonders and battles and terrible adolescent years, I grew up and faced the challenges of accepting myself in a world that seldom did.

As we learned more about the people of your world – Ron's loyalty, Hermione's confidence, Dumbledore's machinations, Molly's fierceness, Snape's strength of purpose, Neville's courage, and your own ability to have humor in dire circumstances – all of these characters became like family to me. They taught me so much about the world. They taught me that people are rarely what they seem on the surface, that it's important to take joy in the little things, and that there is a confidence to be had in your loved ones. The life lessons I walk away with will always carry me. There's a quote I've seen recently, by Oscar Wilde: "It is what you read when you don't have to that determines what you will be when you can't help it." For all the *Harry Potter* believers out there, this is great news!

YOUR WORDS INSPIRED AN ENTIRE GENERATION TO READ, TO DO THE UNTHINKABLE AND TRULY, FULLY GIVE THEMSELVES OVER TO THE FREEDOM THAT EXISTS IN FALLING HEADFIRST INTO A BOOK. – LAUREN M.

And that's the crux of it all: the believers. You created millions of us. It is inexplicable, that feeling of being in a theater waiting for the next movie to begin, or in line waiting for the release of one of the books with hundreds of people who have faced their own battles by embracing the bravery you showed them. It's an instant knowing. The camaraderie of believers from all backgrounds, of all ages, who found the magic in their lives because of your story. **It's joy!**

I was able to convince my father to read about you before the first movie was released, and he loved you almost as immediately as I did. We started this tradition of always seeing the movies together at the midnight showings. I know that our father-daughter bond is stronger because you opened the way for us. And, over the years, my mother and I have also come to understand each other better. We've found strength in each other. Eternal debts of gratitude abound.

I cannot count the times I have acquired new friends based on a chance conversation with a stranger that starts with a Potter reference, followed by an enthusiastic, *"You like Harry Potter?!"* We talk about the characters, their lives and their choices as if we know them. It's because we do know them, some like the back of our hand, like mirror images of us. In a world of growing identity crises, you gave us a way to find the truth of ourselves. We are truly the Potter generation.

Mr. Potter, you have changed my life for the better. I can't wait to tell your story to my children and my grandchildren. To me, the excitement, the wonder, the joy of your books and your world, will never be over. And yes, Harry, I am with you, to the very end.

Always,

– Cait S., 24, Slytherin

Rachel & Elisa

Dear Mr. Potter,

Is it normal to build Harry and Voldemort snowmen on our days off from school? It certainly is for us.

Love,

– Rachel D. and Elisa C.

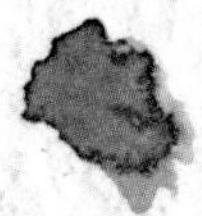

The end.
OUR BEST PREVIEW ISSUE EVER!
EMPIRE
POTTER 7
THE END BEGINS
I want to stay here forever.
DEAR MR. POTTER,
YOU'RE THE BOOK THAT SHOWED ME HOW STORIES COULD COME TO LIFE
(THANK YOU!)
-J.M.S.

Kate W., 17, Gryffindor

Caitlin C., 17, Gryffindor

Sylvia B., 16, Gryffindor

Dear Mr. Potter,

Let me begin with the blunt truth. I was afraid of you. More specifically, I was afraid of your world. When I was six years old, I saw *Harry Potter and The Sorcerer's Stone* at a friend's birthday party. I was little and I had no concept of fear. But when I saw that movie and saw the terrible aunt and uncle, the stormy night, the giant, the fiery sparks of magic, and the man with two faces, I was afraid. I could not grasp this mad world of evil and darkness. I left the movie in tears and had bad dreams for nights on end.

The fear lasted for five years, until it became less like fear and more like habit. Friends told me I was being stupid—the books are so good, it wasn't real, there was nothing to be afraid of! I thought they were liars. Nothing to fear? Please. You, at least, understand that. You faced the fear and saw that two-faced man for yourself. He had murdered your parents and sent your life spiraling. He had haunted your dreams for years. You saw a teacher that you thought you could trust and found your worst nightmare and more staring back. You were stunned, paralyzed with fear. You didn't know what to do.

And yet you fought him. You fought him and defeated him that day. He resurfaced and you thwarted him again—"thwarted, once again, by *Harry Potter*," he described to you derisively at the moment when he thought he held you in his grasp for good. But you possessed more bravery and more faith at eleven years old than I did. And you fought him again, face to face. You stared down your fear and knew that you had to rise above it—rise above it, or die its victim. I, on the other hand, grew accustomed to the presence of my fear. I was acclimated to the feeling of its eyes boring into my back when I went into the library, the movie theater, the toy store, a friend's house. I heard its condescending laugh when I saw the poster for *Sorcerer's Stone* in my local video store and immediately looked away. I did not try to fight it and I accepted it as unchangeable. I did not have faith that I could defeat it.

Late in my fifth grade year, when I was also eleven years old, I was perusing the school library with a friend. I have always been an avid reader and I would dive headfirst into any story that I could lay my hands on (except for your novel, of course). I was at a bit of a loss for reading materials and my friend held up *Sorcerer's Stone*. "Try it," she said casually. "You'll like it." I protested. She insisted, "What's not to like?" I protested more, saying, "Well, it's not that I didn't like it, but the movie was just so scary!" The clock was ticking and we had to be back in class. Never the type to break rules if it could be avoided, I sighed and brought the yellowy-orange book to the checkout desk. We returned to class and it was time for Sustained Silent Reading. The only book I had was the one I had never wanted to read. I reluctantly took a seat against the blue mat in the corner (I'll never forget it), removed the yellow stickie note that someone had been using as a marker, and opened to page one.

Gee L., 19

"Mr. and Mrs. Dursley, of number four, Privet Drive, were proud to say that they were perfectly normal, thank you very much." *Not so bad,* I thought, and read on. I read on to you, to the letters, to Hagrid, to Hogwarts. To Ron and Hermione and Malfoy. To your classes, your spells, your adventures, and your showdown with Lord Voldemort. I closed the book and flipped back to page one again. "Perfectly normal"—how could the Dursleys possibly believe that? They were so sheltered, so determined to shut out a world they didn't understand! Their close-minded fear seemed ridiculous to me. And then I realized why: because I wasn't like them anymore.

I'd thought my friends were liars when they tried to sell your story to me. They were, kind of. Saying that the books were good wasn't a lie. But saying that your world wasn't real? Lies. As Stan Shunpike told you, *"Muggles! Don' listen properly, do they? Don' look properly either. Never notice nuffink, they don'."* To me, your world is as real as my own. In fact, your world is part of my own. And saying there was nothing to be afraid of? That's the biggest lie of all. Your story is full of everything that I have ever feared: monsters, villains, bullies, injury, death, loss. But, when I read about my fears, I fight alongside you. I am your ally and you are mine. We conquer our fears together, no matter the stakes, no matter how much safer it would be to turn and run. We do not hide crouched behind gravestones. We stand up and fight. If nothing else—and believe me, there is more – you have taught me that much.

We met when we were both eleven and, since then, I have marked my years (and fears) by your story. I am almost seventeen now, the same age you were when you defeated Voldemort for the final time. Because of you, because of your wonderful story, and because of what you stand for, I am no longer afraid.

With love, respect, and gratitude,

—Melissa W., 16

Diana, 14, California

Diana

Dear Mr. Potter,

I, Diana Munoz, of San Diego, was proud to say that I was perfectly normal, thank you very much. I was the last person you'd expect to be involved in anything strange or mysterious, because I just didn't hold with such nonsense. Not yet had I known the feeling of wanting to become someone completely different. I now have that spirit. My days are now filled with the daydreams of creating spectacular magic and being a part of the wizarding world. All day, I dream.

—Diana M., 14, California

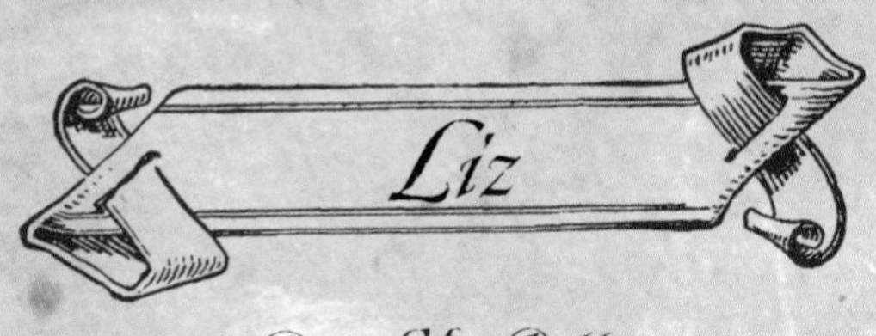

Dear Mr. Potter,

We met when I was six. I followed you to Hogwarts and had the kinds of adventures every child dreams about. I felt your fear during your encounters with Voldemort. I, too, shared your suspicious about Snape. I cried when Sirius, Dumbledore, Hedwig, and Fred died. Whenever you, Ron, and Hermione needed to be brave, I tried to be, too. When it was time to fight, I stood by your side; and I never left.

Seven years after our journey began, I was in Florida, adopting a little sister in whom I planned to instill undying love for the Wizarding World. The last chapter of my magical world came out on the night of my birthday, and I would not rest until I found a tiny little bookstore that was holding a midnight release party. Thousands of miles from home, I feasted on cauldron cakes and pumpkin pasties, sharing something so precious with so many strangers who, for that night, became my friends.

I got back to the hotel that night, clutching the chronicle to my heart, and immediately began to read. Long after everyone had gone to bed, I stayed curled up in the closet, laughing and crying with you for the last first time we would ever have. Hours later, when our story had finally ended, I couldn't bear to close the book. I knew it would mark the end's real presence, and I couldn't let that happen yet.

And so I fell asleep in that tiny closet, my magic still open in my lap, realizing that I was ending this journey where it had all began, in my very own cupboard under the stairs.

All I can say is thank you, and I hope all is still well.

—Liz H.

12/31/10

Dear Mr. Potter,

I remember when I first started to read your story as an eleven year old sixth-grader, struggling to discreetly read the first few chapters of Sorcerer's Stone in English class. I was so very drawn to the realistic characters who would soon become like my friends. I could particularly relate to Hermione, who externally seemed perfectly poised, intelligent and self-assured but who was internally just as self-conscious as us all. My favorite character though, quickly became Ron, whose light-heartedness always cheered me up. Coming from a big family myself, I also sympathized with his struggle to make a name of himself among the many Weasleys. Don't worry though, I love you too, Harry.

Since then you, your loved ones, and your adventures have inspired me in so many ways and I now have memories that will forever remain near and dear to my heart. I remember anxiously waiting for my dad to return from his business trips, bringing me a different translation of your story each time (it is still my goal to acquire all 67 translations). I remember watching Harry Potter documentaries with my sisters. I remember when I lived in the Ivory Coast and watched the first film at the movies even though it was in French and I didn't understand a lick of it. I remember theorizing on if Dumbledore was really dead or not. I remember having competitions with my sister on who could reread the series faster. I remember the first fan fiction I ever wrote. I remember a rap song that me and my sisters wrote for Rupert Grint on his 18th birthday as a joke but never got to send it. I fondly remember numerous arguments which arose from who in my family owned the coveted Harry Potter pajamas. I remember writing in my diary about how I so wished to be in Harry Potter. I also remember the tears that fell as I turned the last page of Deathly Hallows.

Over the years I've also been taught so many lessons. I learned from Dumbledore that "It does not do to dwell on dreams and forget to live." I honestly and sincerely learned to love reading. I aspire to actually attain all the chivalrous qualities of my favorite house, Gryffindor (although to be honest I think I'm more of a Gryffinclaw). Through thick and thin, the best an worst of times, these beloved novels have always served as an escape for me. I learned to cherish my relationships and not be afraid, but fight for what I believed in. I met numerous people that have changed my life through the online Harry Potter fandom. As I grew up and unfortunately departed with so many childhood friends, I found solace in the fact that we would always make sure to reunite and line up together for hours for book releases of midnight movie premieres.

As this phenomenal franchise centered on your life nears it's end, I also prepare for my final year in High School, then University and life after. Saying goodbye to you is like saying good-bye to my childhood and I can't help but feel an overwhelming sense of sadness and nostalgia. I suppose all I want to say really, Harry, is thank you. Thank you for teaching me to be brave, to be strong, and to persevere. Thank you for making my childhood magical in so many ways.

Most importantly though, Harry, I just want you to know that I'm going to miss you more than words can describe.

Your faithful fan,

Rohey T., 16, Gryffindor

Rohey T., 16, Gryffindor

Dear J.K. Rowling,

I hated Severus Snape. End of story.

Nothing could persuade me to think otherwise. He was just another antagonist. Maybe he wasn't evil as He-Who-Must-Not-Be-Named, but he was still someone I greatly disliked. He was an unfair teacher, was a deatheater, held long grudges, and killed Albus Dumbledore (need I say more?).

So when I read chapter 33: The Prince's Tale in the last Harry Potter book, I cried. Who am I kidding? Crying is a complete understatement. I bawled.

I truly did not expect Severus Snape to be in love with Lily Potter nee Evans. His love and devotion to her tugged my heart. It was the most heartbreaking and unanticipated plotline I have read.

Reading that specific chapter opened my eyes. I realized there are two sides to every story. Next time, before I make a final evaluation, I need to look past my preconception. I cannot judge anyone so quickly. Everyone has their own stories and battles.

Thank you so much for writing such a poignant and breathtaking book. i learned so much.

Sincerely,

Tiffany Y

Tiffany Y
Ravenclaw
Age 17

Letícia P.

Arwen S.

Dear Mr. Potter,

The first time I ever read *Harry Potter*, I threw up.

Let me explain.

I got the first *Harry Potter* book right after I turned 11 years old (which meant, sadly, that I spent an entire year waiting for an owl post that never came). My favorite aunt sent it to me with a card saying that this book was "the latest craze." I promptly put it in the pile of boring gifts and clothes.

About a month later, my family took a road trip to Nevada. In my rush to pack fun things to do in the car, I grabbed *Harry Potter and The Sorcerer's Stone* out of the dusty pile in the corner of my room. As we pulled out of the driveway, I opened the book and dove into a world that began in a cupboard under the stairs and ended at Hogwarts School of Witchcraft and Wizardry in an epic battle between good and evil.

I read that book for six hours straight, never putting it down, never looking up, and never paying any mind to the queasiness building up in my little 11-year-old tummy. When I finished the book, I put it down, looked up at my parents, and said, "That was awesome."

Then I threw up.

I learned a lot of things from *Harry Potter* over the years. I learned about love and friendship. I learned that everyone has both good and evil inside them. I learned that not everything is how it seems. I learned that everyone deserves redemption.

But the very first lesson Harry taught me is that I suffer from motion sickness. Go figure.

– Alise M., 20

Kelly S., 16

Elena

Dear Mr. Potter,

I discovered your world the summer before first grade. I was already an avid reader, but never before had I devoured a book so readily. I escaped into your world, where I was happiest, through paper and ink doorways. When the fourth book was released, I had a contest with my first grade teacher to see who would finish it first. I won. When the fifth book came out, I read it in two days, choosing to lock myself in my bedroom for hours above playing with my older and beloved cousins. When Sirius died, I cried so much my mother forced me to spoil the ending for her (she hadn't finished reading it yet) so that she could comfort me. With the sixth book came many theories from my family and friends about Snape's true nature and many tears over the death of our most beloved headmaster.

I waited anxiously for the seventh and final chapter of your life, Mr. Potter, but I also dreaded it. I did not want the magical world I so loved to have its limitations. I knew that when I finished the book, there would be some doors into your world that would not open for me again. I went to the midnight release of *Harry Potter and the Deathly Hallows* and, the moment that beautiful book was placed in my hands, I sat down in the middle of our Barnes and Noble and began to read. I read until five in the morning, when my eyes failed me and I had to sleep. I woke at 11 and finished by one. Seven hours for the seventh book. Seven hours of fear, hope, pain, happiness, loss, and (above all else) love.

I am more emotionally connected to you and your friends, Mr. Potter, than I am to some people in my own life. I have no doubt in my mind that I would not be the same person without your teachings. To those out there who snub the world of *Harry Potter*, I say this: **You'll never know love or friendship like I have. And I feel sorry for you.**

So, my dear Mr. Potter, thank you for eight years of adventure and excitement. Thank you for eight years of happiness and love. You always have been, and always will be, a huge part of my life and my being.

I can't wait to introduce my kids to you someday.

Love forever,

– Elena

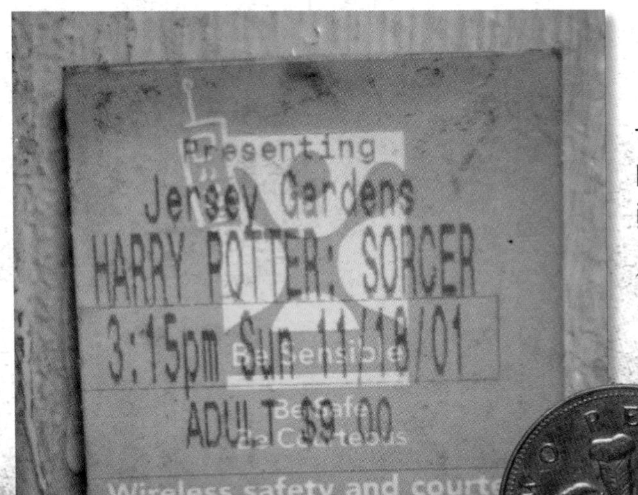

This is the first movie ticket stub I ever kept. It still remains, after a decade, in my *Harry Potter* photo album.

– Lourdes K., 22

Rebekah

Dear Mr. Potter,

Books are a big thing in my life. I could do nothing but read for the rest of my life and never be too sad about it. Obviously, a part of this is because I enjoy reading, but there's more to it than that. I wouldn't say that I was bullied as a child, but I wasn't exactly the most popular of children: a slightly overweight ginger geek who thought she knew everything. I had extremely low confidence and self-esteem, and I still do at times. This isn't meant to sound like a sob story. The scene just needs setting.

I had always been a reader, but at this time I really started to lose myself in books. For me, it was a way to escape the real world and be a fly on the wall in a whole other place where it didn't matter who I was, where I could get lost in the life of someone else. In hindsight, having my head constantly buried in a book didn't exactly make me any more approachable, but I was happy. And then came *Harry Potter*.

I remember the day well. The almost-seven-year-old me had just arrived at my grandparents' house after school, where my

My metaphorical light won't be a letter from Hogwarts, but knowing that one day, I'll find my place in the world. I will be someone. Until then, I'll get by, knowing that I'm so much more than just a boy under a staircase. –Matt O.

mother was waiting. She had three slightly tattered *Harry Potter* paperbacks with her. The books came highly recommended from my godmother and I was more than happy to read anything put in front of me. However, none of us could have predicted quite how fateful a move that would prove to be.

I was hooked, completely and utterly. It was rare that I was found without a *Harry Potter* book in my hands. They were all I could talk about, all I could think about, all I cared about. I remember waiting by the front door for *Goblet of Fire* to arrive, as it wouldn't fit through the letterbox, and finished it that evening – even with a launch party in the middle. The same procedure followed for the next three books.

I turn eighteen this year. I've grown up with these characters, seen myself in them: the family of redheads who find a place they fit in, the know-it-all who learns that it's okay not to know it all sometimes, the overlooked outcast who proves their worth, or the oddball who finds friends who love them for exactly who they are. Perhaps it's overly sentimental or twee. Perhaps it's something I should have outgrown by now. Or perhaps, just perhaps, it was exactly what I needed at exactly the right time.

Joanne Rowling created magic: magic that we can read about and magic in the real world. The kind of magic that can take anybody, regardless of age, race, gender, or social class, and make them feel like they belong to something real. That's what *Harry Potter* means to me.

These aren't characters to me, they're friends. The scenes and settings are the places I see when I close my eyes. The stories are my daydreams. And the author is my hero.

Rebekah P., 17

The Lindenhurst Quidditch League

Dear Mr. Potter,

Thank you for giving this group of high school seniors something to do besides stressing out over college applications, scholarships, and grades. Because of you, we have started our own community Quidditch League and were able to attend both the Quidditch World Cup and the midnight premiere of *Harry Potter and the Deathly Hallows: Part 1* together. We hope that by the time we all go our separate ways next fall, we're at least leaving behind a piece of the *Harry Potter* legacy in our town for generations.

Thanks again, mate.

The Lindenhurst Quidditch League

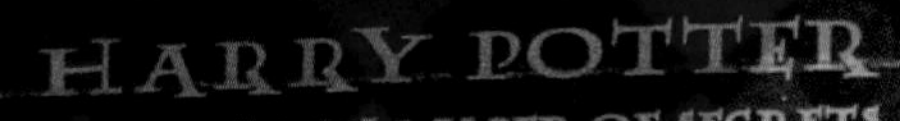

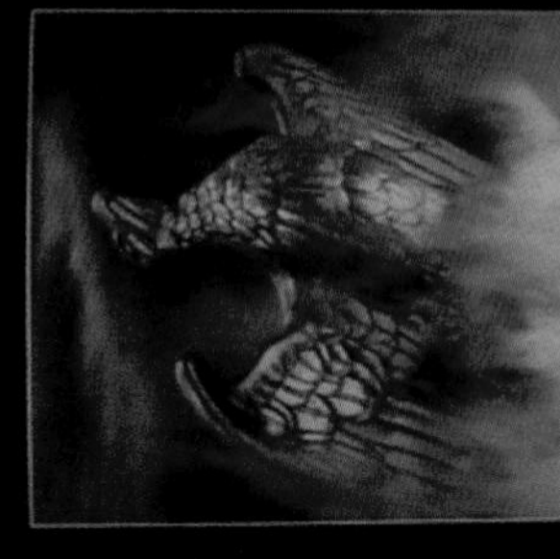

Brittany, 17, Slytherin

John Green

Dear Mr. Potter,

I've been fortunate to have a life shaped by fictional characters—from Nick Carraway to Holden Caulfield—but among them all, you've changed my life the most. There was, of course, your story itself: I was just out of college when my friend Shannon gave me the first two volumes of your life, and I tore through them in a few days. I loved you for your reluctant heroism, for your curiosity, and—although you were 13 and I was 20—our shared inability to figure out how to say the things we wanted to say to girls.

Meanwhile, in New York and London and Moscow and Stockholm, you were changing the world of publishing. People who made and sold books suddenly wanted books for and about teenagers and believed those books could reach broad audiences. *The New York Times* created a bestseller list specifically for children's books because you were dominating the grown-up list, much to the consternation of all those authors who fancied themselves "real writers." Your story paved the way for thousands more: there were plenty of wizard school knock-off novels, yes, but there were also children's and Young Adult writers like M. T. Anderson and Holly Black and Maureen Johnson. And me.

I didn't know it yet, but one day I'd write stories for young people, and you'd make it possible for me to publish them the way I wanted to publish them: for teenagers. I can't imagine what, if anything, my books would be if it weren't for you creating the idea that all kinds of people could enjoy books published for young people, but I know this: they wouldn't be New York Times bestsellers. So thanks for that.

But most of all, thank you for the community you created through your fictional life. When I was reading the first books back in a tiny Chicago apartment, I had no idea that there would be wizard rock and Quidditch tournaments and *Harry Potter* fan conferences. But I happen to have been blessed with a brother who happens to have written a song speculating about your final Hogwartsian adventure, and because of him and that song, I've been pulled into an extraordinary community of people who share an affection for you. Together, we've sent five cargo planes full of aid to Haiti on your behalf and made the last wishes of a dying girl come true. You've given me gifts, dear Mr. Potter, so real and lasting that I can't even really think of you as a fictional character anymore. Like so many other fans, I will carry you with me throughout my life--thinking of you not as a made-up character, but as an uncommonly generous friend.

Best wishes!

–John

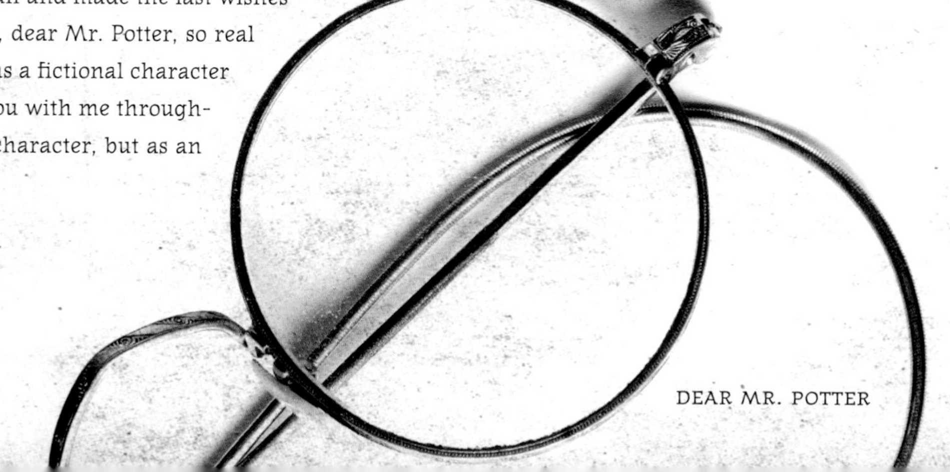

Kate

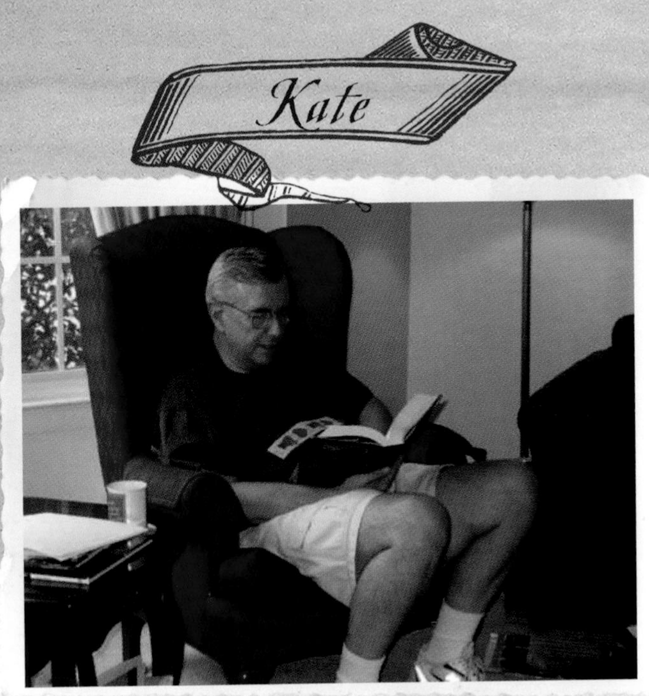

Dear Mr. Potter,

This is my Dad, reading *Harry Potter and the Order of the Phoenix.*

My sister and I are sitting on the couch in the corner. My Dad read aloud to my sister and I as we grew up. We started with stories that Dad would make up out of his imagination. As we grew, we switched to children's books. One year, we started *Harry Potter* and *The Sorcerer's Stone*.

It became tradition for us to sit and listen every night after dinner as Dad read *Harry Potter* aloud. He would come downstairs, getting ready to read, singing "It's *Harry Potter* time!" to the tune of the Howdy-Doody theme song.

Eventually we decided to take turns reading aloud. I will never forget struggling through Dumbledore's death scene, trying to keep reading out loud, but breaking down and crying with each new word. Although we didn't read the final book together, after Dad finished it, he and I spent two hours one afternoon talking about our reaction to the book and how upset we were about all the deaths. My dad was a big softie.

In June of this year, Daddy died of complications from leukemia. One of the quotes that I made sure was used in the funeral was from the great Albus Dumbledore:

"To the well-organized mind, death is but the next great adventure."

That's how I like to think of Dad now: simply on to the next great adventure where, when it is my time, I will join him.

So if you tell me that *Harry Potter* means everything to you, trust me. I understand. *Harry Potter* is a part of my family. It is a part of who I am.

–Kate B.

REST IN PEACE C.J.B, JUNE 24, 2010

Joyce

Dear Mr. Potter,

This is my copy of the *Philosopher's Stone*. I bought it when I was 10, almost 3 years ago. That was also the year I went to my first summer camp. The book was in pristine condition and I had already read the whole series.

Kids go swimming at camp. Swimming means proximity to water. And, since I was rarely without my copy of *Philosopher's Stone*, it got to go swimming, too. Whoops?

My mom suggested buying me new copy this year but I refused. The spine may tearing and the pages may be wrinkled and stained, but that's the beauty of it. My copy has history with it. Harry's been with me through three years of school, friends, and summer camps.

Maybe someday I'll replace it, but for now, my worn copy has a special place on my bookshelf.

–Joyce P., 12

Dear Mr. Potter,
we will never be ashamed to love you.
no matter how old we get.

Lauren A., 20

Camilla

This whole thing is almost over. The final chapter is being sealed. There won't be anything else to look forward to. What you've done for us will never change. Your story will never die.

But I won't know what to do with myself after this.

Sincerely,

–Camilla M., 15, Slytherin

Joyce P., 12

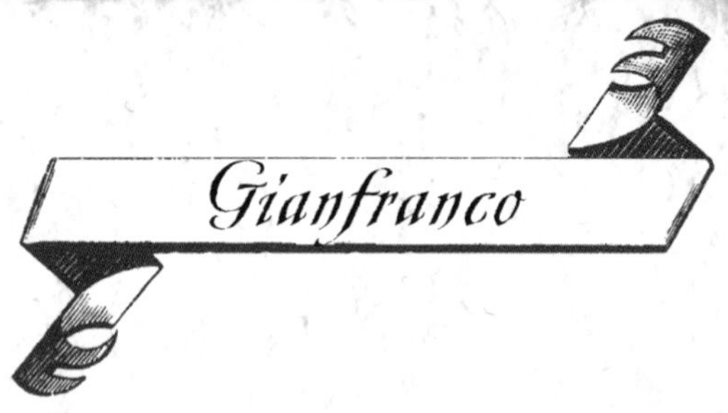

Gianfranco

Dear J.K. Rowling,

If I was to try and express how enormous my love and gratitude to you was, you'd have to use an "engorgio" charm on a skyscraper and doubled its size. Only then would you completely understand the magnitude and complexity of the respect I've held for you these past 11 years. What you gave me wasn't a book, or a series, or movies, or a Halloween costume, or even a theme park. What you gave me was my own personal coping mechanism.

In October of 2000, my father had past away. For a few months after that time, I was lifeless. Dementors had plagued my life, but, of course, I was too young to have realized that. I tried going on with my daily routines, but life as I knew it kept getting harder and harder as I moved to a new house and lost all the people I thought had been my real friends. I was alone. But it was you, Ms. Rowling, who helped me find my Patronus. It was you who helped my 7 year-old-self fight off the Dementors and find my way back in life.

Harry Potter didn't become my "good read," but rather my best friend. I locked myself in my room from dawn till dusk reading and re-reading, only waiting until everyone had gone to bed to find some left-overs in the kitchen. And even after that would I return to my room to commence my research on the Wizarding World. I built encyclopedias of every spell and character I came across, and I even made maps of Hogwarts and all the surrounding areas. I wasn't obsessed; I was dedicated.

Fast-forwarding to this year—my senior year of high school—I began my search for college. With that search came the responsibility of having to explain my life story in an essay for the college admissions. I told them exactly what I'm telling you here today. I told my colleges about how *Harry Potter* saved my life and helped shape my future. I told them how it was you, Ms. Rowling, who helped me discover that what I wanted to do more than anything in life was to write books and help others suffering from Dementors. I told them how it was you who showed me that friends like these in the photo aren't so hard to come by when all you're looking for is a family.

YOU BROUGHT ME BACK TO LIFE, MS. ROWLING, AND FOR THAT, I WILL FOREVER BE ETERNALLY GRATEFUL.

Sincerely,

– Gianfranco L.

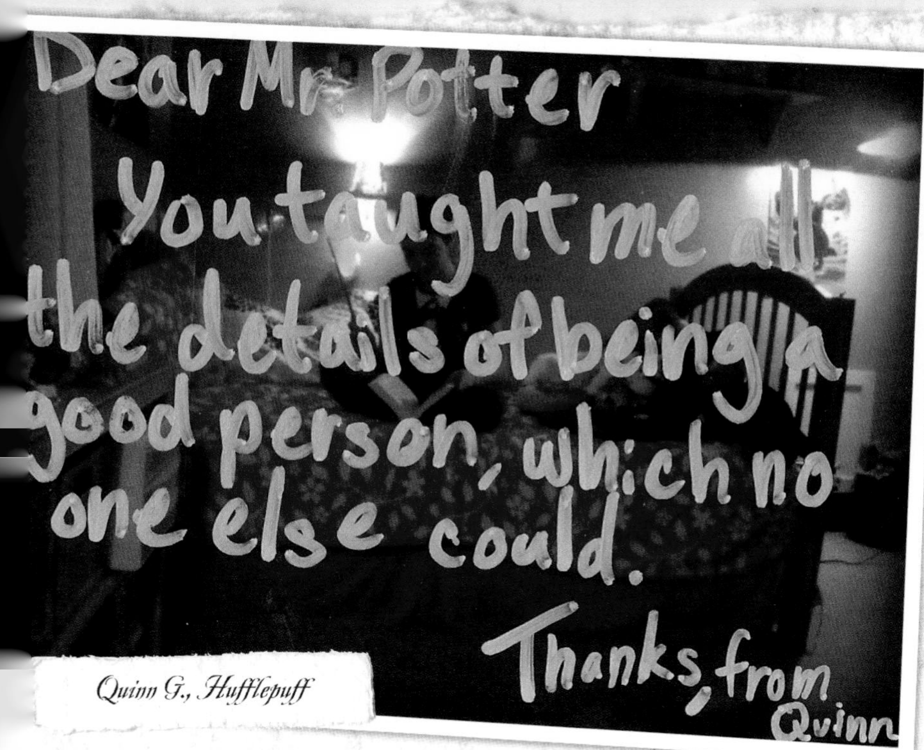

Dear Mr. Potter
You taught me all
the details of being a
good person, which no
one else could.
Thanks, from
Quinn

Quinn G., Hufflepuff

Dear Mr. Potter & Co.,

When I was eighteen, I had a full plate. A drug addicted father, an overworked mother, a closed-off sister, too many bills to pay and not enough money, and a pending court case; the whole world seemed to rest on my shoulders. My best friend persuaded me to read your books, even if only as a means of escape. AND SO I DID.

I was depressed, scared, and nearly friendless, until I began reading. I found in you, Ron, and Hermione something I'd never had before. I found real friends; friends that quarreled and picked at one another, but who were still utterly devoted to each other. My emotions, long since hidden, were now present in every word. When you fell in love, part of me did, too. When you were angry or upset, scared or lonely, I was, too. And when you accepted death, stared your own mortality in the face and embraced it, a tremendous weight lifted from my back. I could do the same as you, couldn't I? I found myself at eighteen years old through a scrawny boy with unkempt hair and glasses. I identified with you; though our struggles differed, we each faced our own brand of evil.

So I want to thank you, Mr. Potter and company, for allowing me to embrace myself, to find my inner Gryffindor and stand unabashedly tall. I believe it was best said in Where the Heart Is: *"We've all got meanness in us, but we've got goodness, too. And the only thing worth livin' for is the good. And that's why we've gotta make sure to pass it on."* So thank you, gang, for allowing me to pass on something good to my future children. I only hope that, despite our late start, we can remain the best of friends.

Sincerely and with Love,

– DeLani R., 19 years old

Dear Mr. Potter,

This is my little brother and I, dressed up for Halloween when I was in second grade. I was Hermione, he was Harry.

– Elena

Dear Mr. Potter,

I first picked up your book when my babysitter offered me a choice between reading you or Captain Underpants. I was grossed out by the first, so I chose you, even though I had always assumed your book was too "weird" for me. I was wrong. I read the first book in about four days and then immediately read *Chamber of Secrets*, *Prisoner of Azkaban*, and *Goblet of Fire*. Your stories immediately made me feel accepted. Here was someone who, like me, felt out of place in the real world. Someone who felt like something inside them was different from other people. I had always felt that way.

Things worked differently for me than for other people. I had extreme mood swings and I changed my opinions and what I liked at the drop of a hat. I found it difficult to form close relationships with people because I always assumed they hated me. I also lied constantly to everyone, including the police and my parents. I admired your bravery and honestly – two traits that I desperately searched for within myself. I couldn't lie to you Harry. You were too good. You were too wonderful.

I saw myself in your books through Bellatrix Lestrange. I don't know how to describe it, but I saw myself becoming like her. I could see myself going crazy and becoming unstable. Maybe it was because everyone had always told me that I was crazy because I was loud and eccentric. I became so fearful that I'd go "bad" and that I'd do something terrible one day. In Bellatrix, I saw the dark parts of myself: the obsessions, instability, temper, and impulsive actions.

One day, I did something very impulsive: I tried to kill myself. After swallowing an entire bottle of Extra Strength Tylenol, I woke up in a hospital bed and I tried to objectively look at my life. Some very famous words from Sirius Black floated into my head, "We've all got both light and dark inside us. What matters is the part we choose to act on. That's who we really are." There was a Bellatrix inside of me, but, in that moment, I realized that there was also a Harry. I cried as I realized that I had to be brave and face my demons the same way Harry faced Voldemort.

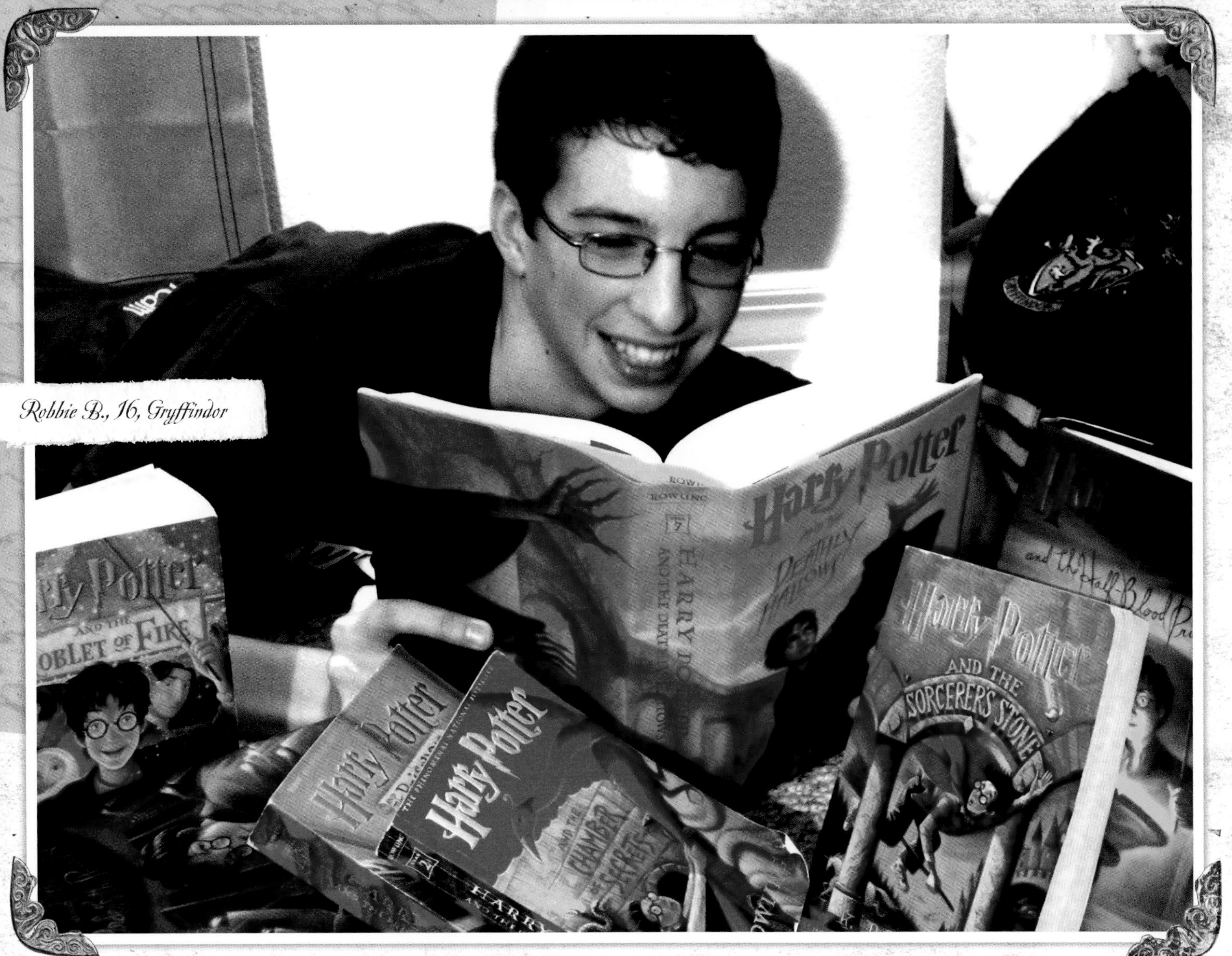

Robbie B., 16, Gryffindor

Since then, I've found that borderline personality disorder was the cause of my differences. I went to therapy and learned how to control and live with my affliction. Now, I face Voldemort every day and I win. I've become the decent, honest, trustworthy, and honorable person that I saw in Harry—the person I thought I was always too damaged to be.

I guess I owe my life to you, Harry. I honestly wouldn't be where I am today without you. When I thought you had to die in order to kill Voldemort, I started crying and had to put the book down. The thought of my brave, honest, trustworthy, and decent Harry having to die totally broke me. I cried even more when Bellatrix, the other part of myself, was killed.

Harry, you taught me something very important. You taught me that there is good in this world and, although we have our problems and our differences, we can all be good people. I am confident that I am a good person now.

Most people are saved by religion or love or change. I was saved by *Harry Potter*.

—Hannah C., 18

WANTED
BY THE MINISTRY OF MAGIC
APPROACH WITH EXTREME CAUTION
REWARD

Alexandra, Kentucky

Harry Potter – the books, movies, and fandom – saved me from a life that would otherwise have been abysmally ordinary. – Ian R.

Jessica L., Ravenclaw

Rachael S., 18

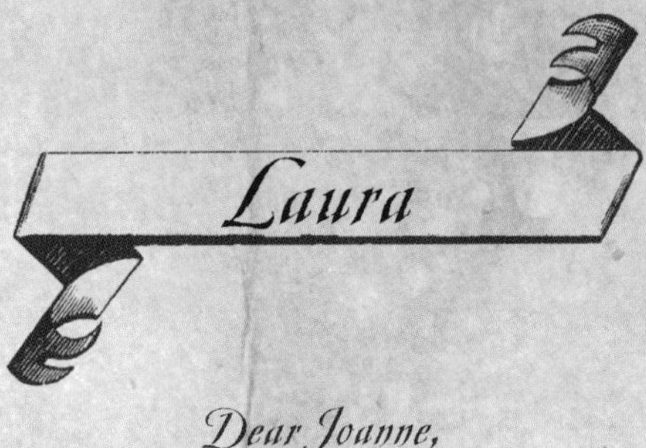

Laura

Dear Joanne,

When you were writing these books, spinning tales and characters in your mind, did you ever think about what kind of impact you would have? Did you ever think things would turn out this way?

There is only one thing you need to know about me, and that is I love to read. As a child, my parents would read to me, and as I grew, I spent more and more time at the library. I brought a book wherever I went.

That's how it began. I received the first three *Harry Potter* books as a set in first grade, the year 2000. I devoured the first book in a matter of days, and the next three followed within a month. I began to live *Harry Potter*. Hogwarts became real to me; Harry, Ron, and Hermione became real. They were my best friends huddled under the blankets with a flashlight late at night. They held my hand when I made scary midnight trips to the bathroom. They were a bridge to meeting and making friends. I breathed *Harry Potter*. I had dreams about being in the *Chamber of Secrets*, running in the maze at the Triwizard Tournament, dancing at the Yule Ball. It didn't matter that the library had new books every month. I read and reread *Harry Potter*.

The weeks before the publication of *Order of the Phoenix* and The *Half-Blood Prince* were agony. I needed to know what happened. It was like I was just another student at Hogwarts, or a bystander in Muggle London who was anxious about what would happen next in her life. When I got my copy of *Deathly Hallows*, it was like a fish in water. I stayed up all night reading it and when I closed the book, I cried. I cried through the deaths and the victories, but when I closed the book, it was like a piece of me went missing.

Harry Potter had become a part of me. It defined me. I was okay with being a bookworm and having slightly larger front teeth. I was okay with spending my time in the library. I grew as Harry and the others grew. I matured as they did. And when the epilogue came, I realized I was lost. They had skipped ahead almost twenty years, but I was still stuck. I reread the series

It is inexplicable, that feeling of being in a theater waiting for the next movie to begin, or in line waiting for the release of one of the books, with hundreds of people who have faced their own battles by embracing the bravery you showed them. It's an instant knowing. The camaraderie of believers from all backgrounds, of all ages, who found the magic in their lives because of your story—it's joy! –*Cait S.*

from start to finish, and I realized something else. This had become a world I lived in. California? That was like a vacation spot. I lived at Hogwarts, I played in Hogsmeade, and the world you have created became a place to which I could escape. When my parents fought, I huddled with the Golden Trio in my room until the quiet came back. Do you know what you have done for me? You've made me a place that I can go to when life gets tough. You've shaped my personality and my values, and you've taught me that not everything is black and white. As you wrote about Harry and the gang, you wrote about me.

A lot of my friends say that magic isn't real. My parents tell me that magic doesn't exist. But to me, the real magic is the way you've opened my mind. The magic is the way you've created something that could affect millions of children and somehow touch the lives of each one, individually. My experiences with your characters may be shared with others, but the outcome could be totally different.

You are my hero. You are my role model. You are the one who's given me hope in this life. I can't, and won't, ever stop thanking you for the magic you brought into my life.

With Love,

–Laura C.

Lisa D., 36

Dear Mr. Potter,

Nerdy girls who dig books and had crazy hair? It was like reading about my own school days, had I only had a wand.

–Lisa D., 36

Dear Mr. Potter,

One of my fondest memories of our time together was when I was fourteen, in a foreign country, crying in a parking lot. I had just finished *Harry Potter and the Order of the Phoenix,* which I began reading in Icelandic and finished in English. When I was younger I loved *Harry Potter*. But being a non-English speaker, I had to wait for each book to be translated, which could take up to a year. I don't know how I waited.

When I was fourteen, *Order of the Phoenix* was published in English and I played the waiting game. The Icelandic translation arrived just days after I departed on a three-week family vacation in England. My best friend, however, received her copy early due to special circumstances. She lent it to me and I tried frantically to finish it before I left, but I couldn't. I had to leave the book.

In England I saw *Harry Potter* posters everywhere, but I was convinced I couldn't possibly finish a whole book in English. Besides, in my head Harry was Icelandic. Imagine your best friend suddenly switching languages. It was too weird. But as the vacation grew longer, I could not contain my anticipation. What was going to happen? Would they rescue Sirius from the Department of Mysteries? At last, my curiosity outgrew my doubts. I bought the book in English and finished it in a supermarket parking lot while my family was inside buying groceries. When Sirius died, I cried. I haven't read a *Harry Potter* book in Icelandic since. As Harry grew, he became irrevocably English to me. But I will always remember that eleven-year-old (Icelandic) boy who just wanted to belong.

I LOVE YOU, HARRY. THANK YOU.

-Gyoa F., 22, Gryffindor

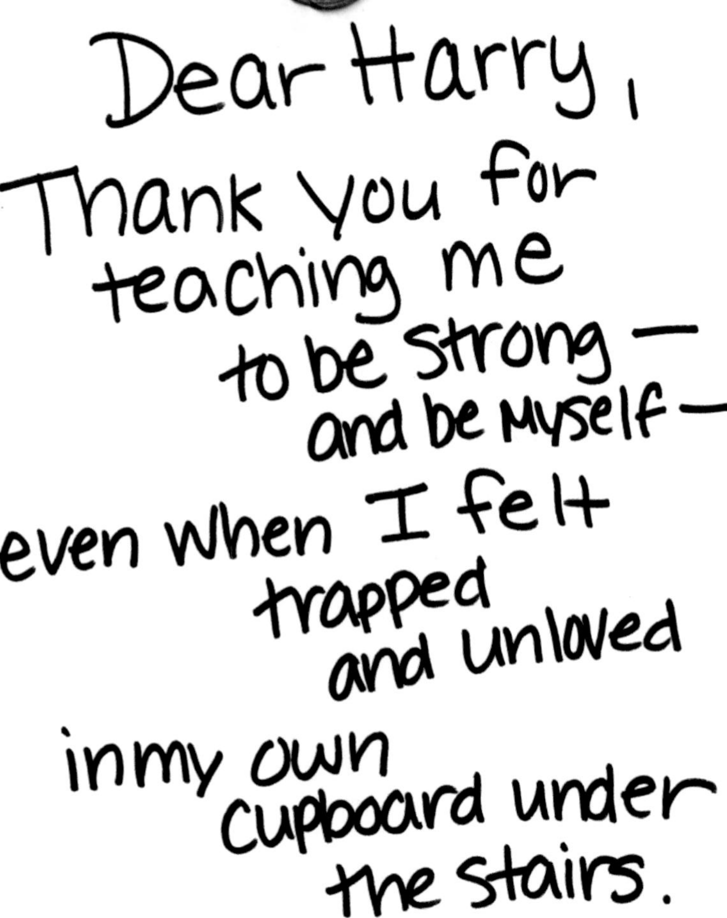

Dear Harry,
Thank you for
teaching me
to be strong —
and be myself —
even when I felt
trapped
and unloved
in my own
cupboard under
the stairs.

Alison R.

Dear Mr. Potter,

When I was young, I believed in adventure. Then I got older, and people told me to be afraid of people and darkness. So I was. I lived years of my life in fear of everything, not really living the way I wanted to.

Then one day, J. K. Rowling told me it was okay. She told me that the darkness was just the unknown and that courage is inside all of us.

Since then, I remembered who I was. I haven't been so scared. I have lived my life the way I want to and not the way people tell me to.

When I was young, I believed in adventure. Then I got older. Now I believe in magic, too.

–Holly W., 14, Gryffindor

Sarah K.

Caitlin O., 17

Dear Mr. Potter,

We are a *Harry Potter* family, and have been since Mum read the first book to me when I was 6. I'm now the eldest of three Potter-obsessed children. I quickly decided she was too slow for me, and read them myself, finishing the first four before seeing the first movie. We have two copies of every book because my sister and I couldn't bare to share. In recent years, my little brother has become as addicted as my sister and I are, and he has bought books of his own as well.

Now I am 17, I take *Harry Potter* with my *Vogue* and reread it whenever I find myself in between other books. You have comforted me for eleven years, and I have no doubt that you shall continue to do so for decades more.

Love Always,

– Caitlin O., 17, Australia

To J K Rowling,

I sit here on Christmas day watching *Harry Potter and the Half-Blood Prince*. I just finished re-reading the beautiful series last night. I'm twenty-one years old and have never been afraid to admit that I am a *Harry Potter* fan through and through. My father has just walked through the living room and exclaimed, rather sarcastically, *"Oh wow, Harry Potter is on! What a surprise!"* All I can say back is, "Of course."

For the past six years I have suffered from nearly crippling depression. Guiding me though the darkest of these times was the companionship I found within the pages of the *Harry Potter* series. Within those pages were battles of dark versus light, the bright spectra of patronuses carrying my favorite heroes to safety, the immense power of friendship, loyalty, and most importantly, love.

Dumbledore spoke the words "HAPPINESS CAN BE FOUND EVEN IN THE DARKEST OF TIMES, IF ONE ONLY REMEMBERS TO TURN ON THE LIGHT." *Harry Potter* is my light. It guided me through the darkest times of my life. I can honestly say that these characters, this world, this brilliant escape saved my life. I am pleased to say that my depression is now at bay, and my love for the world of *Harry Potter* lives on.

I know you weren't planning on saving any lives when you first began writing these novels, but you saved mine. I can only say that I love the gift that you have given me: a new perspective, happiness, a light. THANK YOU, THANK YOU, THANK YOU.

Until the very end,

– Sara S., 21, Gryffindor

Catalina L.

Catalina

Dear Mr. Potter,

I have been part of you since the beginning, when I was an awkward seven year old with no friends. I escaped into your word of magic and Quidditch and saw the true value of friendship that you shared with Ron and Hermione. With this, you took me in and gave me a reason to stand up for myself; if I was a true Gryffindor I had to prove it.

We grew up together, though our lives were so different. I understood your happiness and your pain and you helped me cope with the cruelty of others, the death of a loved one, and the feeling of losing a dream. I sit here today, twelve years since I read about your pain on Privet Drive, and I still remember the overflow of joy when you received your Hogwarts letter. I wish I had gotten one too. In a sense, Harry, I feel we are the same person.

Whether it was dressing up as Hermione, trick or treating as a Dementor, standing in a line with hundreds of others to pick up a book at midnight, wishing I could marry a Weasley, or even dreaming of beating bludgers, *Harry Potter* will always be a part of my life.

– Catalina L.

Nikki G., Gryffindor, 18

Dear Joanne Rowling,

I'd like to start out by thanking you for one amazing childhood. To have the ability to read is a privilege, but to have the ability to enter a world of your own is something different. Thanks to you and your wonderful imagination, I was able to enter the wizarding world at my lowest of lows and even at my highest of highs. I received my first *Harry Potter* book, *Philosopher's Stone,* as an Easter gift back in 1999. For about three months, I could only read the first few pages. It didn't catch my interest. When I saw that there was a second part to this book, I decided to sit myself down and read the book. I was eight years old. I read both books within a day or two. I couldn't put it down. I was always a child who loved to read, it was how I was raised. But these books made me live in a world completely outside of my own. *Harry Potter* and the world he lived in was a very big escape for me growing up. I had tons of problems in my household, and going to my book shelves and grabbing a *Harry Potter* book made it all go away for a few hours. I cannot express how much these books mean to me. You created a world to escape to, created friends who became my best friends, created teachers who became mentors. You have shown me what loyalty, bravery, love and courage is through Harry, Ron and Hermione. You created a lifestyle. Miss Rowling, you inspire me to not only become a better writer, but to never give up. As a struggling single mother with no money to your name, you never gave up. Neither did Harry. I grew up with Harry, Ron and Hermione. They were my getaway and saviors. You have also been a savior. The impact you have made on my life is one of a kind. I am very pleased and proud to say I have stuck with Harry until the end. But it's not the end to some of us who rely on him. Once again, thank you, Jo.

—Nikki G., Gryffindor, 18

Sara & Rosa

Rosa (right): Are you really British?

Conductor: Are you really a Weasley?

Rosa: Touché.

– Sara J., 21, and Rosa C., 20

Sara J., 21, Indiana and Rosa C., 20, UK

Dear Mr. Potter,

My friend Nicole and I, about to board the train used as the Hogwarts Express in the *Harry Potter* movies.

–Jennifer W., 16

Dear Mr. Potter,

When I try to think of a time before *Harry Potter*, what comes to mind is a life full of Muggle things. Everything after Harry is clearer and happier; everything became magical. I first read *Harry Potter* at the suggestion of my older brother. I must have been about seven years old. It was like falling in love, and soon enough I was clinging to midnight release parties and despising SEVERUS SNAPE with the entirety of my soul. Some things have changed, but for the most part, I'm still enamored.

If I had to name one thing that *Harry Potter* did for my life, it was bringing my family together in a way that we never had been before. Not that we hadn't been close, but as the books and the movies came out, we bonded closer and closer together. I remember going to the premiere of *Sorcerer's Stone* all decked out in my homemade Gryffindor scarf, taped glasses pressed into my nose, hand in hand with my grandmother, and I remember going to see *Deathly Hallows* five months after she died. I remember falling asleep at a swim meet because I refused to forego the midnight release of *Prisoner of Azkaban*. I remember taking my little brother and sister to see *Half-Blood Prince* for a birthday gift, and replaying the DVD every single day in our house. I remember so many things, year by year and day by day, and it's so difficult to think that it might one day be over.

What I hope for *Harry Potter* is that it becomes something like Dr. Seuss, known for generations to come. I want to read *Harry Potter* to my littlest sister, to my children. I want my children to read it to their children, and I don't want it to ever stop. Death is simply a horizon, right? It's just a train station, another stop along the way.

Harry Potter has given me my childhood, my adolescence, and my future. It has given me hope, individuality, and the courage to distinguish between what's right and what's wrong. It's given me new ideas about love, besides just fairytale romance. It's reminded me that I'm not perfect, nor is everyone else, and that's okay.

I will always love *Harry Potter*. It's not over until it's over, and by my calculations, that means it never will be.

THANK YOU SO, SO MUCH.

– Anna, 17, Ravenclaw

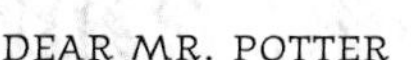

Rachael

Dear Mr. Potter,

This is a photograph from the *Deathly Hallows* midnight release party shortly after the clock struck midnight. After this photograph was taken, I got my copy of *Deathly Hallows* and read about Harry's final adventure. I will never forget this night, nor will I ever forget all of the memories that the *Harry Potter* series has brought me. I have been lucky to have such a positive constant in my life since the age of six. The *Harry Potter* series has brought me so much joy and happiness. I have made so many great friends that share my same love for *Harry Potter*, and these friendships will last a lifetime. I am so thankful for everything you have brought me. Thank you, *Harry Potter*.

WITH LOVE,

Rachael S., 18, Pennsylvania

Victoria & Julie

Dear Mr. Potter,

There once was a girl who loved to read. She read books to escape the mundane and terrible trials of reality. Imagination reigned in her world, and as long as she had books, she was happy.

One day, she went to visit her cousins. The youngest cousin announced, "Guess what, Victoria? I'm a *Harry Potter* nerd!" Victoria wasn't pleased. Oh, she knew what *Harry Potter* was, all right. She saw the thick books at her school library and often ignored them, thinking that maybe they were too much to read at her age. She had nothing against the books, of course. No, the problem was her cousin, Julie. Julie was quite young, and Victoria didn't much like to play with her cousin. She knew that this *Harry Potter* would make Julie less tolerable somehow, and she was right. Julie would constantly brag about the letter that she was going to receive when she turned eleven, about how she was magical and Victoria was a mere Muggle. Victoria wasn't pleased, and her attitude about *Harry Potter* progressed from indifference to dislike.

It was years until Victoria finally picked up a copy of *Harry Potter* and *The Sorcerer's Stone*. She knew she would have done so sooner if she had not made immature assumptions about the books based on her cousin's playful pranks. Victoria adored the books. She loved them so much she couldn't come up with a proper word to sum up her feelings for them. They changed the way she thought about people and the whole world. She used to believe that being smart and getting the highest test scores were the most important things in the world. She was a good student when she was young, and even in elementary school she made a habit of jumping from her seat to answer any question the teacher asked. Naturally, she related the most to Hermione Granger (and was so in tune with this character that Victoria even developed quite a crush on Ron Weasley).

Victoria's way of thinking changed when, in *Harry Potter* and *The Sorcerer's Stone*, Hermione said, "Books! And cleverness! There are

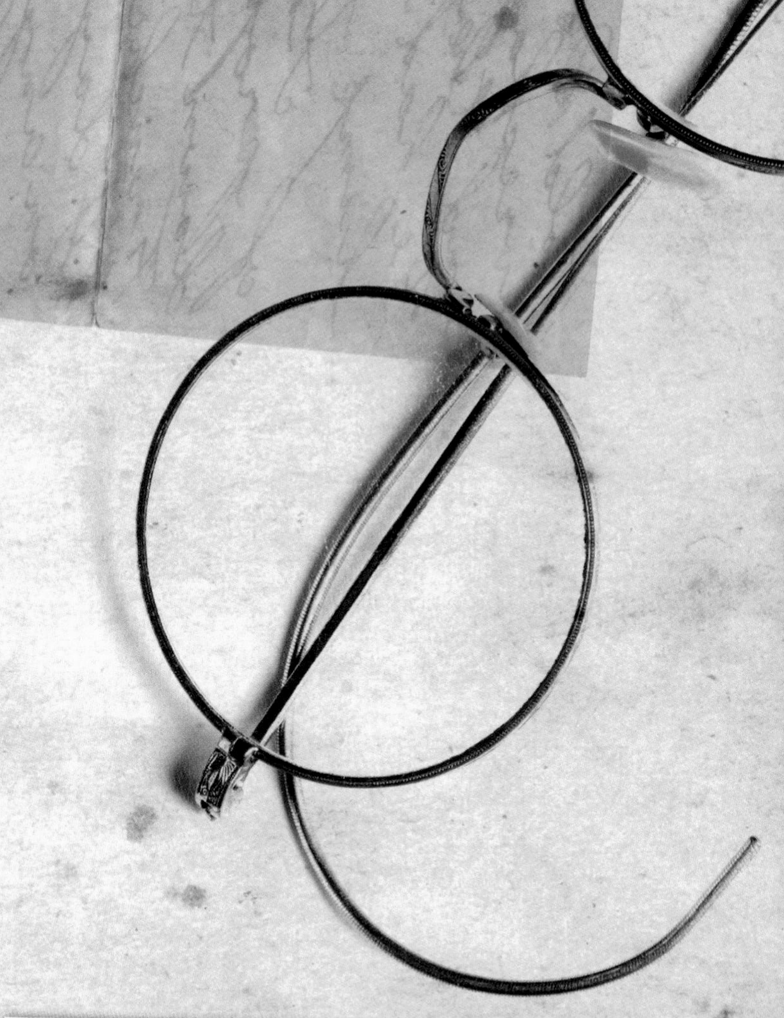

more important things—friendship, and bravery." Victoria thought about what Hermione said for a long time. She came to value friendship and bravery even more than she valued intelligence. However, Victoria never thought of herself as brave. She had absolutely no idea what she would do if a powerful dark wizard tried to kill her, or even what to do if she met a troll in the girls' bathroom.

Two things comforted Victoria. The first was Neville Longbottom, the boy everyone thought they could push around, when he finally showed how worthy he was to be in Gryffindor throughout the series. He stood up to his own friends, insisted on accompanying Harry and his friends to the Department of Mysteries as part of the D.A., and even confronted Lord Voldemort himself in the end. Victoria also put a lot of value in Albus Dumbledore's wise words: "It is our choices, Harry, that show what we truly are, far more than our abilities."

It was through these books that Victoria rediscovered bravery, tolerance, and love. Through this series, Victoria and her cousin Julie bonded and became as close as Harry and Ron did. Both girls grew up with the books, as did millions of other children around the world. They read, discussed, and imagined Hogwarts. The magic that took hold of the readers was real, and it transcended languages and distance and will live on through time.

Looking back at all of this, Victoria feels a strange sadness. She relives the moment when Harry stares at the Hogwarts Express, now carrying his two sons, and realizes something. Victoria, like the rest of the readers, is waving at the train. It used to be that she would board the train along with Harry, Ron, and Hermione. Now, she is watching it as it leaves, bidding farewell to her childhood. She is sad to see it go but immensely happy that after everything, all was well.

Forever Grateful,

—Victoria D. 17, Gryffindor and Julie F. 14, Slytherin

Alexandra M.

"You're a wizard, Harry."
H
"I'm a What?"
Harrington 12

William H.

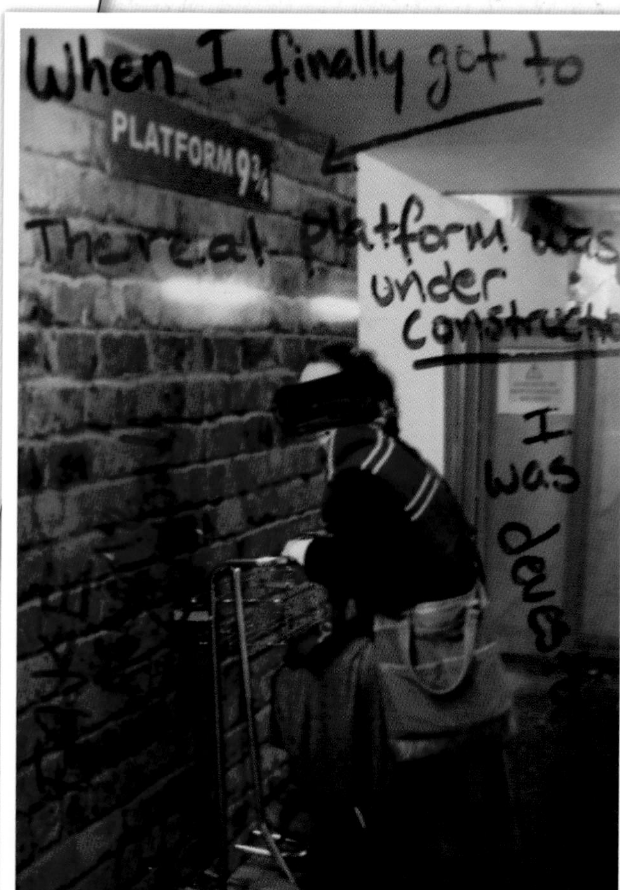
When I finally got to
PLATFORM 9¾
The real platform was
under
I
was

Taylor N., 20

Whenever I meet a man, I mentally compare him to Sirius Black.
–Kaitlyn, 20

Me and my mandrake birthday cake on my 18th.
–Bethany, 18

Morgan

CHUDLEY
CANNONS
RULE!

To a Mister Ronald Weasley,

Every night I fall asleep with Harry Potter and The Deathly Hallows under my pillow as a reminder to always fix what I've broken. It's never too late to apologize. Your strength gives me the courage to face the people I've hurt. Sometimes I wonder how different things would be if you hadn't sat with Harry on the train your first year. Perhaps Harry would've been sorted into a different house. I try really hard not to think about this. You see, had it not been for this small action, I would've never known the kind of person I strive to be every day. The book under my pillow tells me that whenever I feel that things are too difficult or complicated and I just want to bail on the world, that I must always return and mend what I've broken. I promise myself & you that I will always be there for my brothers and sister, even when I'm mad at them for being pricks. I will always be there for my friends even if I'm scared. And I will always see the positive in a negative situation (and if there isn't one, I'll be sarcastic at inappropriate times just to see someone smile.) Ron, you are me. You are me and everything I strive to be every day of my life. And you were always there for me. **THANK YOU.**

-MORGAN S. (Gryffindor Pride)

Farzana

Dear Mr. Potter,

Zoë M., 14

I didn't go to school that day. My sister had given me a book some weeks ago, telling me that it was a bestseller, and I honestly wasn't too interested– a book about a kid with magical powers? I'd read lots of those. No matter. With nothing better to, I picked up the softcover. A thin boy on a broomstick. Striped shirt. Okay.

Unfortunately, halfway into the first chapter, things weren't looking too good. I was bored. Still, I read on. Finally, at the last sentence something happened: "To *Harry Potter*–the boy who lived." A spark. The start of something that I knew, even then, would last for years. From then on, we were inseparable.

I grew up with Harry. We were awkward, lonely children and then angry, angsty teenagers together. When the third book came out and I mourned the loss of our beloved Sirius Black, I was surprised at how much anger and betrayal I felt. Why did it need to be this way? Why couldn't things just be easy for a while? While I wasn't willing to admit it to anyone, this was my life too. Whatever issues I had, I had to deal with alone, just like Harry. Two books later, I cried bitterly at the loss of Albus Dumbledore. Once again, I felt a bond to this boy who existed only on paper. The movies, though loved, could not do him justice. *Harry Potter* will never be as green-eyed, tragic and brave as he was within my nine year old imagination. No Voldemort will be as scary as the one in my head, no trio as loved as the one I grew up with. No moment of triumph as great as when he understands: this is it, I'm leaving.

I was not prepared for the final book. About to enter my last year of high school, I went to the midnight release and spent the next twenty-four hours devouring the book, barely taking the time to breathe. I was not ready for what would happen. He died. Harry Potter made himself the hero one last time and let himself be killed by Voldemort. I put the book down. What was happening? Did he actually just––? He couldn't have. It was impossible. Over eight years in the making, the boy I had befriended almost a decade ago, the first boy I ever fell in love with, died.

We all know what happened next. He, as usual, proved to be far stronger than I and survived the last battle, proved that he couldn't be beaten down. I was breathless too; after all, we had fought through this together for years and years. I was ecstatic and sad. I had been right all along. *Harry Potter* lived.

I will forever be grateful for what I was given. My kids will fall in love with the series, however many years into the future. I'm twenty now. That makes eleven years I have spent fighting and waiting and believing. For all of this, thank you.

– Farzana Z., 20, Gryffindor

Dear Mr. Potter,

Trying to get across exactly how much you have changed my life is hard. I've tried doing it twice already. This time, however, I feel like I actually have something worth saying.

The other night, I began my nightly ritual of knitting. I opened iTunes, found my J. K. Rowling album, went to the last chapter of *Harry Potter* and the *Goblet of Fire* that I had listened to, and began to knit. It suddenly hit me that this is what I feel most proud of accomplishing and this is something that *Harry Potter* was a huge part of.

A few years ago, I was taught to knit and I loved the idea of it. However, I got bored with it easily. I couldn't watch TV and knit because I'd lose track of my stitches and make mistakes and I grew tired of putting music albums on repeat and listening to them while knitting. So my brand new bamboo needles and skeins of yarn were tucked away into a corner of my closet and forgotten for the next few years.

You helped me get out of my cupboard.
—Dana L.

Fast-forward to summer of 2010: I was spending the summer with a friend of mine and her sister, both very into arts and crafts. After seeing her whip up some adorable skirts with her sewing machine and her sister crochet a few adorable little monsters, I decided to try my hand at knitting again. I found a pattern for a scarf online (something way beyond my capabilities at the time), pulled out my size 8 Takumi needles, and decided to turn on my new audiobook of *Harry Potter* and the *Half-Blood Prince*. I had read the books many times at this point, but after hearing a lot of good things about Jim Dale's performance on the audiobooks, I figured I would give it a listen. As the sixth book was my favorite, it was the first one I decided to listen to. Before I knew it, I was on chapter four (just under two hours total) and I was on my way to completing my first scarf. I was so proud when I realized how well I was doing on a pattern that involved more than just one stitch all the way through. Before I knew it, I was learning new techniques and making things I never thought I'd be able to make. All the while, I had the *Harry Potter* audiobooks playing in the background, providing constant entertainment without being a distraction.

At this point, I've completed four scarves and I am now working on another. I've since acquired the rest of the Harry Potter audiobooks to accompany me during my knitting adventures and I've discovered a book from my library called Charmed Knits: Projects for Fans of *Harry Potter*, which includes patterns for things like the Weasley Christmas sweaters, wand cozies, and Dobby's socks. With every new proj ect I attempt, I surprise myself at what a fast learner I've become. The abbreviations in patterns that were once just as meaningless to me as Ancient Runes would be to Harry have become essential and clear. I'm positive that I would never have been able to accomplish what I have had I not had the audiobooks to keep me focused. I always knit longer than I planned to because, despite knowing what will happen next, I'm hooked every time I read, or hear, these books.

Thank you, *Harry Potter*. I'm sure it's not something you've helped a lot of people with, but it's certainly something I'm very grateful for. Thank you for helping me learn how to knit.

– Stephanie F., 20

Amber 20, Hufflepuff

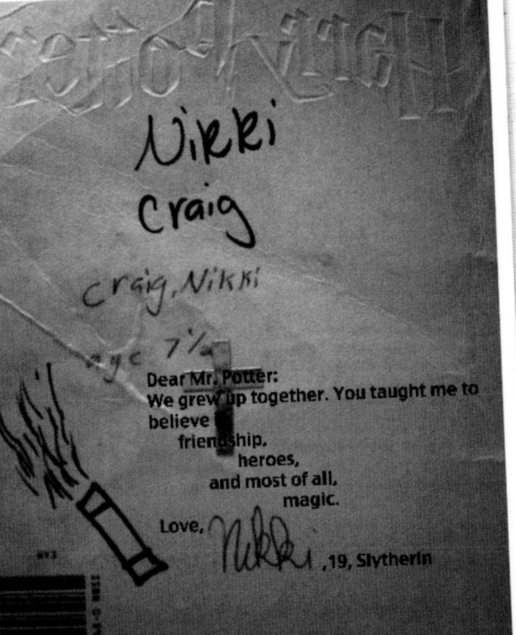

Dear Mr. Potter:
We grew up together. You taught me to
believe
friendship,
heroes,
and most of all,
magic.
Love, Nikki, 19, Slytherin

Lauren

Dear Mr. Potter,

Once upon a time, there was a girl. She was nothing special. She was normal and did normal things. As life went on, she started to read. When she was in third grade, her school wanted to ban a book series. Our girl's mother was called upon to give her opinion. Before making her decision, she asked to read the series.

That was the year our little girl was introduced to the fantastic world of a Mr. H. Potter, who lived in The Cupboard Under the Stairs, 4 Privet Drive, Little Winging, Surrey. This girl and her mother read the first book together. There were scary things and things she didn't understand, but there were also things she loved and connected with.

Fast forward. Once upon another time, there was a girl who was alone. She was made fun of and she felt like everyone was against her. Our girl reread the books. She laughed along with the Weasley twins and she cried when Sirius died. Her heart ached when Hermione fell for Ron and when Harry was pining for Cho. Her favorite characters were Sirius and Lupin, but she was with Harry and Ron and Hermione the entire time. When no one cared about her, she didn't mind, because she always had Hogwarts with her.

We'll hit the fast forward button once more. Now the girl is sixteen. She's left that school where she was ridiculed and she has many friends. She still loves *Harry Potter*. The hardest thing about loving *Harry Potter* is admitting reality. Sometimes, when life is hard, our girl turns to Harry and asks, "Why can't I be with you?" She longs to feel magic at the tip of her wand. She wants to live in a castle and be a part of the story.

But the story has ended. Harry has moved on. Everyone has. Still, Harry will always be a part of this girl's life. She turns to him when life is tough. She feels him every time she runs to her bookcase, grabs a book, picks a chapter, and falls headfirst into the magic that J. K. Rowling has given the world. So don't tell her that it's over. Don't tell her it isn't real. Because, if you do, she'll pick up her book, hit you with it, and say, "This is *Harry Potter*. He has an impact."

I am this girl. *Harry Potter* has held my hand through the toughest years of my life, through things I didn't understand, and through things that scared me. I will never forget him. Don't tell me it isn't real, because sometimes this magic is more real than anything else in the world.

– Lauren D., 16, Hufflepuff

Caroline P.

I remember when I was 8, my grandma brought me downstairs to her room, and she pointed to a top shelf, where there were four Harry Potter books. She told me, 'One day, you're going to read these books, and you're going to fall in love with them, and never forget them.' She was right.
—Yeliz C.

Cristal C.

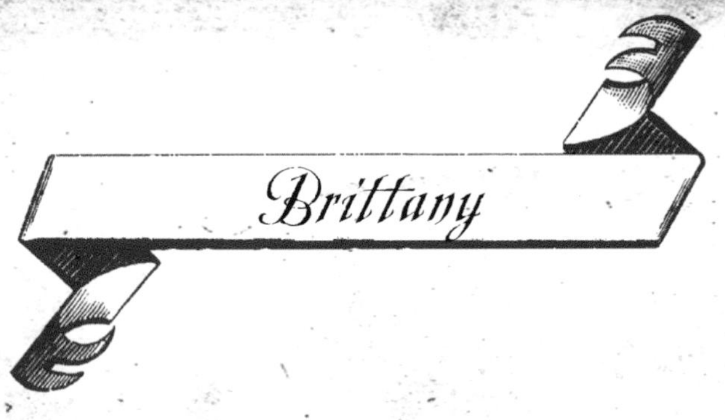

Nupur M.

The Five Stages of Grief– My Love and Loss of Harry Potter

While today nothing could endanger my love for Harry, my uptake of the *Harry Potter* series was slow going. The five stages of grief perfectly reflect my hesitant acceptance and adoration of *Harry Potter*. Not until I let it encompass me completely did I fall into the lovely and magical *Harry Potter* abyss.

1. Denial and Isolation – I first heard about *Harry Potter* when I was in the fifth grade, roughly eight years ago. I suppose my addiction was predestined because the book chose me during a gift exchange (and not the other way around). I was disappointed. The series, in my family's opinion, was a reflection of evil. While my peers gushed over the new books and the upcoming first movie, I chose to stand alone. At some point, whether it was driven by rebellion or boredom, I finally picked up the first book. That is where the adventure began.

2. Anger – At this point, I was in love with the *Harry Potter* series. *Sorcerer's Stone*, *Chamber of Secrets*, and *Prisoner of Azkaban* had swept me off my feet and set me down amongst free house elves, the Shrieking Shack and Grims. I was content. That is, until *Goblet of Fire* was set before me. Throughout its entirety, a vital aspect was missing: Harry and Ron's relationship. My annoyance with this development wasn't an anger that simmered under the radar, but an anger that persuaded me to propel my book across the room. One of the aspects that I value most in the series are its relationships. Even in the midst of war and carnage, love flourished. However, all throughout the fourth book, Harry, Ron, and Hermione's playful banter was lost and, in its place, Harry and I were lonesome in our anxiety. When Harry and Ron's relationship was restored, I was just as relieved as Hermione, if not more so.

3. Bargaining – You can have Neville Longbottom, but don't take Dumbledore! This was my mantra all throughout the sixth book. While I had been forewarned, I refused to believe that the man we had revered, the man we had relied so much upon, could simply perish. However, the *Harry Potter* phenomenon would have been non-existent without the hardships. Couple pain with love, even vengeance, and you have power.

4. Depression – I suppose you could insert my depressed state here – the point at which we have an onslaught of deaths and lives are ripped from our grasp all too quickly. I won't ever get over the nonchalance used when Lupin and Tonk's deaths were mentioned in *Deathly Hallows*. I shed too many tears, and yet not nearly enough, for Dobby, Mad Eye, and the whole lot.

5. Acceptance – I love *Harry Potter*. I've grown with, and have become a part of, the *Harry Potter* generation. The emotions that I feel and have felt for these characters allowed me to become the young adult I am now, accept life's harsh realities, and still enjoy the time that we have been given.

As Harry, Hermione, and Ron's future reflects, life goes on. Although I mourn the end of my beloved series, life will go on. We must take what we've learned from the past and use it to fuel our future. This is what *Harry Potter* has enabled me to do. THANK YOU, JO ROWLING.

–Brittany M.

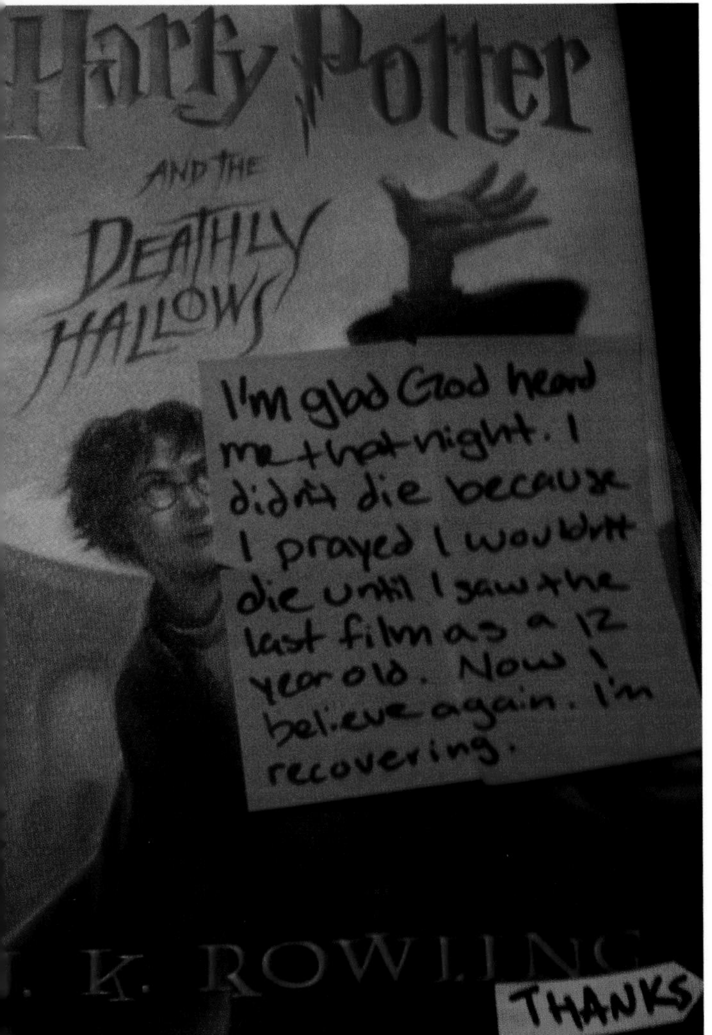

Harry Potter
AND THE
DEATHLY
HALLOWS
I'm glad God heard me that night. I didn't die because I prayed I wouldn't die until I saw the last film as a 12 year old. Now I believe again. I'm recovering.
THANKS

Dear Mr. Potter,

The last two years have revolved around my health. I was diagnosed with kidney failure shortly before *Harry Potter and the Half Blood Prince* came out. I was told that the wait time for a kidney in California could be up to eight years. It was hard to deal with in the beginning. I was constantly sick and did not have the energy to do many things before starting my treatment. I have always loved the *Harry Potter* franchise and some of my best memories include the midnight showings of the fourth and fifth movies, as well as meeting the *Harry Potter* trio at the *Order of the Phoenix* premiere. I made it a personal goal to see all the *Harry Potter* movies no matter how sick I was. I saw *Half-Blood Prince* shortly before I became too sick to do most things.

I was not sure of what my health would be like for the *Deathly Hallows* film (Parts 1 and 2), but my friend and I made plans to see them no matter where I was. I also made it a personal goal that I would travel to London to see all the famous landmarks from *Harry Potter*, if I ever received a kidney transplant.

Earlier this year, a relative stranger stepped up and offered to donate a kidney. I was extremely lucky that she was actually a match. I received a kidney transplant on October 18th, 2010 and was given a few months of recovery. I received strict orders to avoid crowded places for six weeks, but the first part of *Deathly Hallows* would be released prior to that. One of my friends proposed a drive-in theater, and we found one only twenty minutes away. I was able to see Part 1 of *Deathly Hallows* the weekend after Thanksgiving in the safety of a car without endangering my weak immune system.

Receiving a kidney transplant also meant that I could complete my goal of traveling to England. I do have travel restrictions that include no international flying for a year, but I have made plans to travel to London in January 2012. The trip is just in time to celebrate my birthday, as well as the birthday of my friend from London.

The *Harry Potter* books have given me a goal. They have given me a reason to fight for something when all else seemed hopeless and something to look forward to when recovery seemed slow but successful. Thank you, Mr. Potter. I don't think I can properly express how grateful I am that I had you to turn to during the dark times as well as the good.

–J.D.S.

Dear Mr. Potter,

Second grade is a frightening year. You're starting to discover what you're good at and what makes you happy. When I was in second grade, my mother purchased two books that she thought I might enjoy: *Harry Potter and The Sorcerer's Stone* and *Harry Potter and the Chamber of Secrets*. I cracked the spine on *Sorcerer's Stone* only out of boredom on a rainy day. However, the moment I read about Dumbledore, his funny glasses, and his magical gadgets, I was entranced. Imagine my relief when I realized that Harry (older than me, but not by much) was also looking for a place to belong and something to make him truly happy. And, within a hundred pages, we both found happiness. Harry found a love for magic. I found a love for reading.

Harry grew up fast and so did I. *Goblet of Fire* was released between my third and fourth grade years. While Harry was fighting dragons, merpeople, and sphinxes, I was battling loneliness after moving five states away from home. I saw Harry with Ron and Hermione and wondered if I would ever have friends like that. *Half-Blood Prince* arrived just in time for the transition between middle and high school. My fears about school were forgotten as I cried for Dumbledore, the man who had first caught my eye and made me keep reading. Harry had to be strong and so did I. And then, so swiftly, the end came. *Deathly Hallows* was released on the brink of my junior year, a time full of SATs, AP classes, and college visiting. I gazed at the cover and all I could see was our last chance, Harry's and mine, to be together. After this, I had to move on, get a life, and grow up. Reading The *Deathly Hallows* was an experience I will never forget. I laughed so hard that I cried, and cried so hard that I laughed. By the time I closed the cover on the epilogue, I was blinded by tears. Not because I was happy or sad or frightened, but because it was over.

Time went on. My junior year was full of motion and excitement as I prepared for the insane ride that was college application, and this only intensified when I reached my senior year. It was only in June 2009, days after my high school graduation, that I took my battered copy of *The Sorcerer's Stone*, held it like an old friend, and began to read. This time there was no waiting, no interruptions. As I read, watching Harry grow and learn and fall in love and lose people and fight and win, I was overcome with my own memories of friendship and struggle. I had grown up with these books and that is no understatement. Ten years of tears and laughter and loneliness and love are contained in those pages. As I closed the last book for the second time, I realized something that I had not understood before.

I had been looking at the last *Harry Potter* book as a gate closing on my childhood. I was seeing *Harry Potter* as many do: a children's book about a funny little made up school for wizards. But that's not what it is at all. Harry's story is about magic, and not just the magic of wand waving and potions. It's about the magic of friendship and the magic of loyalty. It's about finding a place to belong in the world and finding something that makes you happy. It's about losing people you love and knowing that they're not gone forever. It's about standing up for what is right. But, most importantly, *Harry Potter* is about the magic of love. The love of a parent, more powerful than any other force on earth. The love that holds friends together. Love that binds, love that strengthens, love that protects. *Harry Potter* taught me more about love than any other book I have ever read. No mere children's book could accomplish that.

> IT IS WHAT YOU READ WHEN YOU DON'T HAVE TO THAT DETERMINES WHAT YOU WILL BE WHEN YOU CAN'T HELP IT.
> –OSCAR WILDE

Harry Potter may never be considered classic literature. It may remain overlooked and seen only as a book for children and teenagers. Still, it will always be the book that taught a generation of children to love reading, that bound people together by giving them a world to share. It will always be the book that helped me through some of the hardest times of my life. The greatest thing about *Harry Potter* is that he is timeless. He will help future children conquer their loneliness and their fear of the unknown, just as he helped me with mine. I am nineteen years old and, instead of leaving *Harry Potter* behind with my other childhood relics, I will take him with me, to teach me how to be brave, help me to understand and accept loss, and, above all, to guide my actions so that they are motivated by love, the greatest kind of magic.

– Rachel K., 19

Dear Mr. Potter,

You saved me. Without you I would not be alive. Your story made me happy when it seemed the world had turned its back on me. You have always been there and as I grow into the person I am I know I couldn't have done it without you. For that I am eternally grateful. You are forever a part of my heart.

Love, Royan (16)

Until the very end...

Dear Ms. Rowling,

While the other third, fourth, and fifth grade children read your books, my daughter, the bibliophile, adamantly refused to have anything to do with the Harry Potter series. Why? I do not know. What I do know is that when she was twelve years old and the other mothers overnighted the last book to their daughters at her summer camp, my daughter became intrigued: why were her camp sisters screaming and squealing with excitement while opening up their packages? Why did the camp have a lazy day of no activities in honor of the delivery of these books, allowing the girls to stay up all night long reading them?

Thus began my daughter's love affair with Harry, Ron, Hermione, and Hogwarts. She started at the beginning and read through the series tirelessly within a couple of months. *Harry Potter* took priority; her family, school, and friends played a minor role. From that point on she spent weekends and sick days relishing in the wonders and mysteries of the fabulous world you created.

My daughter could never be bored again: though she loves to read other books, when there are no new ones around, it is Harry to the rescue, always waiting to transport her to her wizarding world. I love that my daughter has be exposed to the exceptional quality of your writing; I do not see her obsession as a bad thing at all. I feel like she has a gift from you that will last her the rest of her life. *Harry Potter* will live in the future, in more ways than you or I can even imagine. I am thrilled that my daughter has discovered the magic of your words and the magical world you have created.

THANK YOU,

–Jodie S., Hufflepuff
(mother of Lindsay, Gryffindor)

Dear Mr. Potter,

For many years, I wondered if I would ever reach a point in my life where I would feel comfortable as a writer. Ever since I was a kid, I spent hours a day stringing words together to tell a story. Whether that story was fabricated in my overactive imagination or I was trying desperately to have my voice heard, there was something cathartic and liberating about those moments of creation. I started off trying to do my best to imitate a lot of the authors I gravitated towards: Edgar Allan Poe. Stephen King. H.P. Lovecraft. Then I read Austen and Conrad and Dostoevsky and Bronte and Alice Munro and Carson McCullers and then I realized I wanted to do this. I wanted to find a way to express myself through the written word.

I entered poetry contests, but I was never particularly good at those. I tried writing speeches, but I felt restricted by length. When I was a junior in high school, I found it intriguing and freeing to take some liberties with an assigned essay and write a stilted, erratic, and experimental piece about the topic given to me: loyalty. By the time I was done, I had written about a painful experience I was going through. I was watching people I thought were my "friends" abandon me because of how different I was. I handed the essay in, expecting that I'd fail. My teacher pulled me aside the next day and told me that she'd never read anything like it. She asked me to write more. She stopped giving me maximum word counts and making me write in the style she was teaching. When I moved on to my senior year, she told my AP Literature teacher to let me be free.

I wrote some awfully contrived and irritating pieces in those two years, but I will always look back on them fondly. I was free. I had found something that made me feel whole. But as the years moved on and my past continued to haunt me, I found that I wrote less and less. College. Dropping out of college. Sixty-hour workweeks. Eviction notices. Depression and death and grief and funerals and relationships soured and I kept all of it inside me.

In May of 2010, I decided to read your story. I expected it to be silly. Disposable. Entertaining, sure, but ultimately disposable. However, as I progressed through the story of your life, gasping at every twist and turn, reveling in the joy of the world of witches and wizards, something happened to me. I felt a kinship I'd not experienced in many years and that spark inside me from years before ignited again. Inspired by the journey in *Order of the Phoenix*, I opened up about the abuse and bullying I'd suffered at the hands of multiple authority figures in my life. Days later, I was frozen with fear, terrified to submit my writing to be analyzed and read and consumed and processed, but I did it. And I experienced the most electrifying jolt of freedom from it.

Mr. Potter, your story has done a lot for me, beyond being entertaining. It has introduced me to friends I hope to have for the rest of my life. It has helped me entertain millions of people around

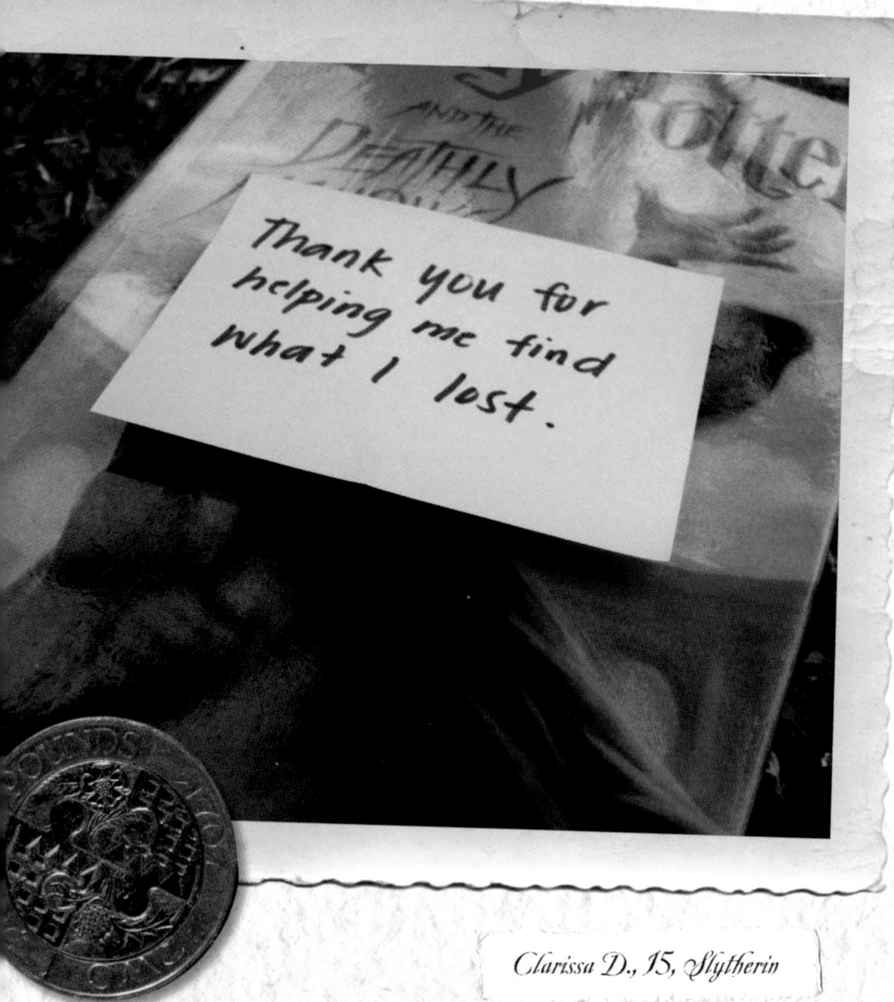

Thank you for helping me find what I lost.

Clarissa D., 15, Slytherin

the globe. It inspired me to create two websites to further my love of analyzing popular media. It has shown me how a good story can completely surround you. Most of all, your story has helped me face things I had kept a secret for far too long. Your story has helped me battle the demons of my past head-on, with hope and courage I may never have found on my own.

THANK YOU, MR. POTTER. I OWE YOU FAR MORE THAN I EVER REALIZED. THANK YOU.

– Mark Oshiro

Author of Mark Reads Harry Potter

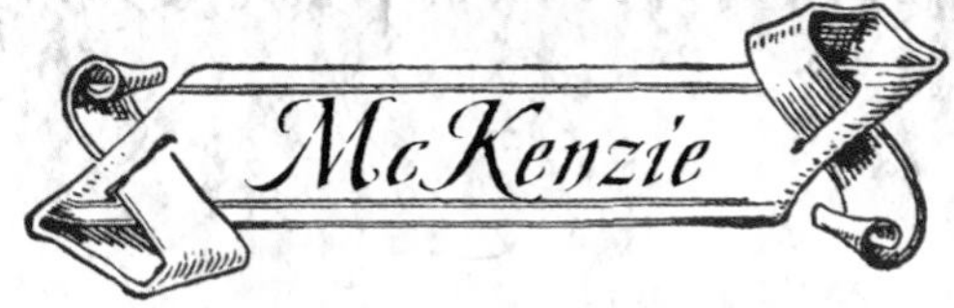

Dear Mr. Potter,

THANK YOU. I write to tell you my story as you shared yours with me. There are those who say that your time is drawing to a close and that your story is ending. I find it difficult to explain how upset this makes me. Stories don't end when the book does. They don't fade away into the background, don't get lost in some endless sea. This is not your story's fate.

When I first met you, I was in second grade. I was a bookish child, even then. I loved you and your world instantly. My home life was a poor. I lived my life in my own cupboard, quite a bit bigger than yours, but no less confining. I didn't have a way out, so I found my escape in you. I grew up with you and, in a way, you raised me more than anything or anyone else. Everything that I am today, everything that makes me strong enough to fight against my struggles, came from your world.

Thank you to Harry, who taught me that you can escape your childhood. To Hermione, who taught me being "the smart girl" was okay. To Lupin, who taught me about beating my inner demons. Hagrid and Luna, who, in a combined effort, made it fine for me to see the world a different way. Severus, who taught me the true meaning of love. And Sirius, who taught me that some things are worth dying for and that some friendships last forever. Thank you all so much for giving me everything I like about myself. In many ways, you've saved my life. You showed me that, if we do what is right, we can change things. We can be amazing. We can be the hero, even when the odds say we can't. You gave me, and so many others, hope. That hope is contagious. In many ways, this is a love letter. I love you, Mr. Potter. You were my first bit of hope. Thank you.

ALWAYS,

–McKenzie K., 17

Ana

Dear Mr. Potter,

Harry Potter was my first true addiction. It wasn't an instantaneous one. I remember when someone offered me my first *Harry Potter* book, *Prisoner of Azkaban*, the day I turned eight or nine. I looked at it, said a weak "thank you" to the cousin that gave it to me, and walked away towards the swings where my friends were playing. At that time, I knew nothing about the magical world of *Harry Potter*. THEN, ONE NIGHT, EVERYTHING CHANGED.

It was a hot summer evening and I was a couple of years older. I didn't feel like watching TV, so I walked to my room and picked up the first book on the shelf. Next thing I knew, I had fallen in love with Ron, couldn't stop rooting for Sirius, and told myself to ask my dad for a hippogriff for my next birthday. It was the first time I ever got lost in a book.

A couple of years ago, I came across my old diaries. By that time, my obsession with *Harry Potter* had dimmed a little. I still loved it, but I had just started high school and, as one can imagine, I had other things on my mind. When I picked up one of those diaries and started reading it, it all came back. When I read my descriptions of how I felt when I got lost in *Harry Potter*, I thought that I had been so very foolish. How could one give up on something that makes them feel so happy? Since reading those diaries, I've never let go of *Harry Potter* again.

– Ana N., 19

Via R., Gryffindor

Return to Hogwarts,
Peoria, Illinois

Hogwarts is real. You-Know-Who just hid my acceptance letter from me because he knew that I'd be so much better at magic at him. Well, maybe not, but a girl can dream, and everyone knows that I'm brilliant at that. –Ashmeen R.

Dear Jo,

When I first picked up *Harry Potter and The Sorcerer's Stone*, I didn't know. I didn't know that *Harry Potter* would effect my life as it has. I never knew that as I turned that first page of the first novel, I would be transported into a world unlike anything I could have ever dreamed of. As I turn that last page of *Harry Potter and the Deathly Hallows* over and over again, I realize what you have done for me, and for millions of others.

I bought the first three books in the *Harry Potter* series in 2004, at the age of eight. My parents divorced when I was twelve years old. My best friend abandoned me. I knew what I wanted to do. I wanted to move to London or New York and become a famous writer. When I was famous, I thought, I wouldn't have any more troubles.

Elle L.

One night, I was alone in my bedroom when I got an email message from a 'mean girl' at my school. She told me that I was fat, and stupid, and that I would never do anything with my life because I was worthless. Being called worthless is the worst thing you can imagine. To think that you literally have no purpose in your life. No one cares, no one will listen. You. Are. Worthless.

That night, I almost took a whole bottle of prescription pills. I didn't, because I glanced over at my bookshelf.

Ms. Rowling, you saved my life that night. If your books had not been sitting there, whispering at me that all was safe, and all would be alright, I don't know what would have happened. *Harry Potter* is a safe house for people like me. We can escape for a while into a world of magic and hope and friendship and in *Harry Potter*, you know that not everything is all right all the time, but it will be. Just turn the page.

Harry Potter is not a character. Hermione Granger is not a character. Ron Weasley, Luna Lovegood, Severus Snape, Draco Malfoy; these are not characters. These are people, little miniature lives carved into normal white pages, and I identify with every one of them. Sometimes when I need to be brave, I'll pretend I'm Harry, with the sword of Gryffindor in my hand and friends by my side. When my life needs a bit of fun, I'm one of the Weasley twins, pranking all my friends and family. Maybe I need to be a bit smarter, so I'll bushy up my hair and be Hermione for a few hours. I live through these people in your stories. I know it sounds crazy, but it helps.

On July 21, 2007, I was at summer camp on the Olympian Peninsula. I had one more day left at my week long overnight camp, and I remember crying a little bit in my bunk because I wasn't there for *Deathly Hallows*. The next day, my parents picked me up and drove me straight to the bookstore. When they set the huge hard-cover copy into my hands, I was afraid.

I was afraid to turn the first page. The first page of that book was the beginning of the end, and I couldn't do that. I had grown up with Harry. We matured together, we lived and cried and fought together. *Harry Potter* was the only place I could truly be myself without having anyone judge me.

That night, I sat in my bed with that book and my hands and I began. I began to read the end.

I'm turning the final page again as I write, and I can't help but shed a tear. That night so long ago, I cried my heart out. I cried for Dobby, for Tonks and Lupin, for Fred and Snape and Moody and everyone who died in the last battle.

But I cried for me, too. I cried because I couldn't handle being alone in the world. When I turned the last page, I thought it was the end of everything. The end of the world you had built with your hands and your mind, the one that had made me feel like I really belonged for once.

I was wrong.

I'm now crying in happiness because I will never be alone in this world. I know that I don't belong here, but I can accept that as long as I have the *Harry Potter* world to live in. Because of you, I feel accepted and loved. You have changed my life as well as saved it. I can never repay you for what you did when you sat down with that pen and that napkin and wrote a story that captured the hearts of misfits around the world. The messages in your books of love, friendship, acceptance and loyalty are ones that I carry with me everywhere I go. I never stop thinking about Harry, and I don't plan to.

Thank you, J.K Rowling. I can never say that enough.

ALL MY LOVE,

– Megan F.

Stacey K., 21, Ravenclaw

Dear Mr. Potter,

I can't imagine my life without your story. Who I would've become, the friends I wouldn't have met, the moments I wouldn't have experienced, I have no idea. Your story has shaped me. For me, being a fan could never be just a phase - I started reading your story when I was 13, the final book came out just shy of my 20th birthday, and now I am still rereading it and loving every minute. Well into my 20s, I have still stuck with you through and through, until the end and beyond.

I first started reading your books because a friend of mine lent hers to me, and that Christmas, I received a set of my very own. I loved reading them, and I like to think that I love reading even more now because of your story.

You hold a special place in my heart. Your courage and selflessness inspires me in my own life, and I can't thank you more for what you have done for me.

Your fan for life,
Tiffany G., 23

Tiffany G., 23

Chelsey O.

Dear Mr Harry Potter,

Because of you I want to change my name to Neddy Potter. My name is Ned.

I like to pretend I am you. I have black hair like you.

Love Ned
age 7 3/4
Australia.

Dear Dan, Rupert, & Emma

I just wanted to tell you guys a few things, because I may never get the chance again. To say that you've inspired is an understatement. You know when you're having a bad day and you just want to go home, crawl into a hole and cry forever? I've had lots of those days. There have been times when I just felt like giving up completely and maybe running away somewhere far where I didn't have to deal with homework and parents and friends who don't care. But then I watch the *Harry Potter* movies, and I read the books, and I feel a lot better. You may never read this, but know that without you, and without the *Harry Potter* series, I don't know where I'd be.

Emma, you've thought me to stand up for what I believe in and not be afraid to be the smart girl. Hermione has shown me that being the nerd isn't bad, and you, Emma, have helped me accept my body and my mind and not try to change it. You've opened the eyes of so many young girls out there who use you as a role model, and honestly, I do too. You're beautiful, and smart, and classy, and you're never mean or rude to your fans. You're the sweetest celebrity I've seen. You make me want to be a better person.

Rupert, my love for you knows no bounds. You're so goofy and hilarious and not afraid of what anybody thinks of you, and that means so much to me. When I was ten, I had a huge crush on you, and I'm not ashamed to admit that. It's your confidence that draws people in, I think, and your orange hair too. A ginger world would be good. I've always wanted to be a ginger. Thanks for making me laugh time and time again.

Dan, thank you. For everything. For showing me that it's okay to do things you're scared of and to step out of your comfort zone. I first saw you in *Philosopher's Stone* in French years ago, along with Rupert and Emma, and you captured my heart instantly. With you in mind, I push myself harder and try new things all the time. I heard you had great taste in music too, and I've always wanted to listen to your iPod. At age twelve, I wrote a letter to you asking what your favourite colour was and if you liked cats or dogs better. I never sent it, but I'll always remember that. (I also wanted to know if Emma liked the Spice Girls and if Rupert had ever felt the need to visit Canada.)

So, merci. Keep being amazing, all three of you, and I'll stay at home, laughing and crying along with you.

– Karolyn A., 16, Ravenclaw, Nova Scotia

Dear Mr. Potter,

I remember being introduced to *Harry Potter*, at the age of eight, by my Nan.

I saw her hardback copy of *Goblet of Fire* on her bedside table and asked her whether I could read it. She explained to me patiently that it was the fourth book in the series, but she could read me the *Philosopher's Stone* if I wanted her to. I let her, and it was the single best decision of my life.

I loved *Harry Potter*. Every Wednesday, when I stayed over at her house, she would read me another chapter with different voices for each character. She would let me read Hermione's bits. We read all four books out at the time, went to the midnight release party for *Order of the Phoenix*, and the midnight releases of all of the films together.

Just after we went to get our copies of The *Deathly Hallows*, my mum told me that my Nan had Alzheimer's. She'd been forgetting tiny things, like how many sugars I had in my tea and what day of the week it was, but I just put that down to her excitement for the last book.

I remember my mum telling me that I couldn't mention it to my Nan because her father had died of the same mental condition a year previously. I read the last *Harry Potter*, with my Nan, and I cried. Not because of the deaths, but at the prospect of my grandmother losing all of the memories that I held on to so dearly.

Months passed, and we went to see The *Deathly Hallows Part I* together. She kept telling me on the way to the cinema that she didn't want me to spoil anything because she hadn't read the last book yet. I went along with it, however much I needed to tell her the truth.

We both enjoyed the film. She thought that both of us were bawling our eyes out at Dobby's death, but I knew that I was crying because by the time the second part would come out, she would probably have forgotten most of the *Harry Potter* experience.

I'm writing this a few days before Christmas. I've bought her a Gryffindor scarf, in hopes that she'll remember *Harry Potter* whenever she sees it. It's my last chance, it's her last chance.

You'll probably be reading this having watched the last film. I hope it's amazing, because it needs to be in order for my Nan to remember those times we had together when I was ten years old and she introduced me to the magical world of *Harry Potter*.

– Bonnie G., England.

Thank you, Mr. Potter, for being my constant.
For being my patch of blue sky amongst the cloudy days, my escape in troubled times, for teaching me that love is everything.
I know I am not the only one; you have taught so many, both Muggle and Magical, to open their hearts.
You have no idea of the families you have brought together, the friendships you have created, the love you have nurtured and the adventures you have inspired.
FOR LOVE IS THE GREATEST ADVENTURE.

Because of you I will fill my life with love and, at the end of it all, greet death as an old friend and go happily, knowing I have lived my greatest adventure.

THANK YOU. FOR EVERYTHING.

Asha-Niketan, 22, Gryffindor. xx

Erika B., 20, Ravenclaw, Kaitlyn P., 20, Gryffindor, and Alyssa H., 20, Ravenclaw

Amanda

Dear Mr. Potter (and friends),

Mr. and Mrs. Dursley, of number four, Privet Drive, were proud to say that they were perfectly normal, thank you very much. They were the last people you'd expect to be involved in anything strange or mysterious, because they just didn't hold with such nonsense."

That is how our story begins. But of course, you knew that already.

My mother bought me a copy of *Harry Potter* and *The Sorcerer's Stone* for my birthday in November of 1999. I was turning 8. I devoured every word on every page. There were some things that I needed explained to me, of course, but I was a fairly intelligent child and didn't need much help. Almost as soon as Harry left Privet Drive, I knew that this was a place that I needed to go with him. I told my mother (and I remember this vividly) "I'm going to keep reading these books til the very end. Even if I'm old. And I hope I will be."

As long as I can remember, I was the brainy, homely girl that everyone got very annoyed with, no matter how much it was meant out of care. I was made fun of mercilessly until high school. Through all of that, I found my identity and managed to stay true to myself because of one Hermione Jean Granger; bushy hair, buck teeth and all. I found love in Ron. Enemies in Slytherin. Freedom in Luna. Everything I could have wanted.

Alas, things do not always end as we hope. July of 2007, I was 15 years old and going through some very tough times in my personal life. I had friends who were abusive and controlling and just, all in all, terrible influences. I was self mutilating, contemplating suicide. I don't remember much of my Freshman year. Again, there were always people there to see me through. Harry, Hermione, Ron, Mrs. Weasley, Lupin, the twins, everyone... and they always would be. Even though this would be the last time I would wait in line at midnight dressed up as Hermione waiting for the book, as I had for the last 3, I could stay up and read the book in one shot as soon as I could and no one could spoil it for me. This feeling

Do you know what you have done for me? You've made me a place that I can go to when life gets tough. You've shaped my personality and my values, and you've taught me that not everything is black and white. As you wrote about Harry and the gang, you wrote about me.

—LAUREN C.

Kimberlee C., 19, New York, Hufflepuff

would never end. As our Hermione didn't leave Harry's side when Ron left, I came to realize that there was no point in losing myself for the sake of anyone else. I am me and there is NOTHING wrong with that.

Throughout my childhood and adolescence, I went through many phases and stages but there was always one thing constant: Hogwarts. It was someplace where I knew that I had friends. I could go flying, mix a potion, battle a dragon... it was MY place. No matter what trouble I had gotten myself in, I could escape there. Hogwarts is and will always be my home, as it was Harry's.

As the movies draw to a close this summer, Harry and the gang will have seen me through every stage of my life; from childhood to adolescence to teenage to adulthood. I can tell you that I could not have done it without the Golden Trio by my side.

So: Harry, thank you for teaching me bravery and loyalty. Hermione, thank you for teaching me to stay true to myself, no matter what the cost. Ron, thank you for teaching me love. Fred and George, thank you for teaching me what it was to laugh and joke. Luna, thank you for teaching me how to dream. Bellatrix, thank you for showing me how wonderful crazy and evil can be. Draco, thank you for teaching me to really see things from other people's perspective. Finally, Jo Rowling, thank you for saving my life and ensuring that for me, too, all can be well.

– Amanda K., 19, Slytherin

12/28/2010

Dear Mr. Potter,

In second grade, I got a note sent home to my parents from my teacher. The note was reprimanding me for not listening to the geography lesson and instead, reading a Harry Potter book under my desk. I apologized, but really, I didn't care. I had more friends in books than I had in real life and that was how I liked it.

There is a line in the <u>Deathly Hallows</u> that reads: "Hogwarts was the first and best home he [Harry] had known. He and Voldemort and Snape, the abandoned boys, had all found home here..." (697).

This is true, not only for Harry, but for me and thousands of other children who found home at Hogwarts, whenever they felt lost or abandoned. Hogwarts will always be my home. And getting in trouble in second grade over Harry Potter was <u>definitely</u> worth it. I finished <u>Goblet of Fire</u> before she caught me.

Thankyou, Harry and everyone else who lives in your fantastic world, and most of all to J.K. Rowling.

Lots of love,

Annie H. (16 & a Gryffindor)

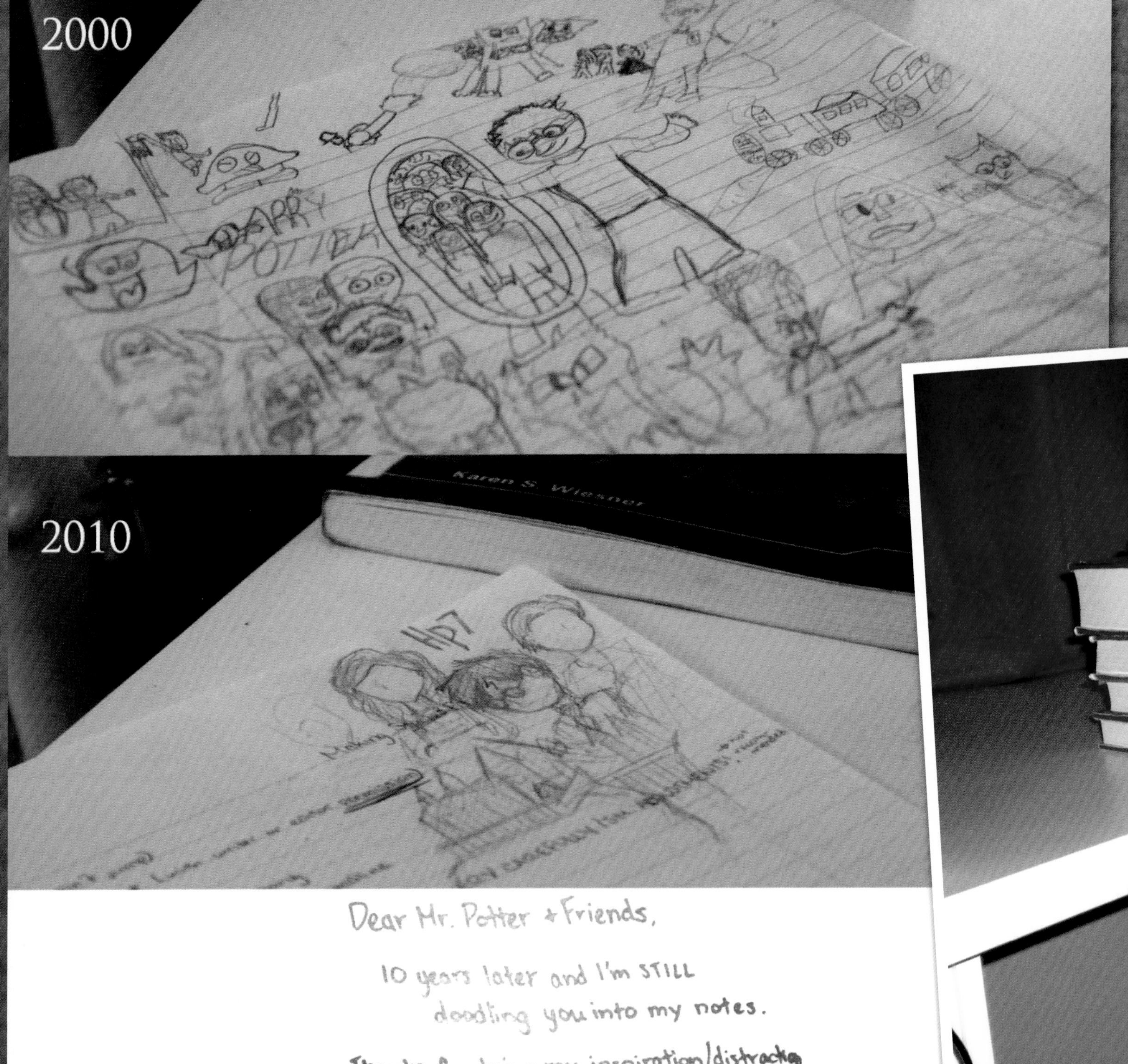

Dear Mr. Potter + Friends,

10 years later and I'm STILL doodling you into my notes.

Thanks for being my inspiration/distraction

Emeline. 19. Ravenclaw.

Harry Potter was a huge part of my childhood – from the second grade until my senior year of high school, where our senior prank was playing Quidditch on the school lawn. – Courtney R.

Therese I., 14, Ravenclaw, Norway

Without you I would not have met such great people.
Molly W, Tonks, Luna & Dobby to name a few.
HARRY POTTER AND T
12:01am Fri 11/19/20
4 PG13
I would not have gone great places
SCHOLASTIC AND SIMON & SCHUSTER/CBS CORPORATION
PRESENT
AN EVENING WITH
HARRY
CARRIE
& GARP
J. K. ROWLING · STEPHEN KING · JOHN IRVING
READ TO BENEFIT DOCTORS WITHOUT BORDERS & THE HAVEN FOUNDATION
AUGUST 1 & 2 · 7:30PM · RADIO CITY MUSIC HALL
ENTER AISLE H FC BENE
A BENEFIT EVENING WITH
HARRY, CARRIE & GARP
AGES 8+ ONLY!
RADIO CITY MUSIC HALL
CHAMPION MORTGAGE SERIES
WED AUG 2, 2006 7:30PM
NO REFUND NO EXCHANGE
WITHOUT YOU,
dear mr. potter,
I would not
be
ME.

Catherine W., Hufflepuff

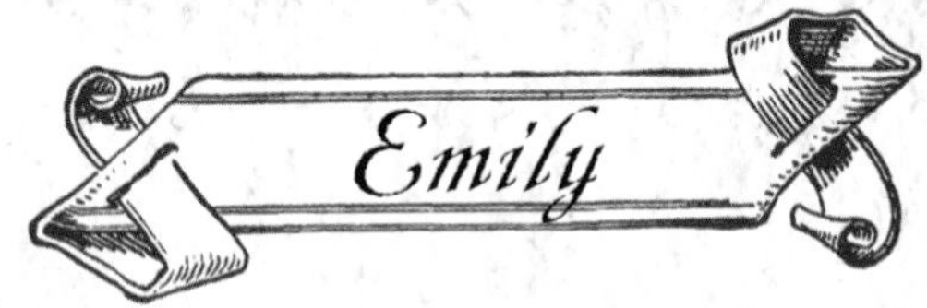

Dear Mr. Potter,

It's been too many years to count since I first was given what would soon become my favorite book. I opened the pages of this strange novel, wondering to myself "Who is *Harry Potter* and what is a *Sorcerer's Stone*?", and soon I was lost in the magic that is your world.

I love these books. Not necessarily because I wanted to be a wizard or witch and save the world from an evil villain, although, I admit that sounds like a nice change in pace. But that's not really my reason for loving these books. I love this series because these books gave me hope.

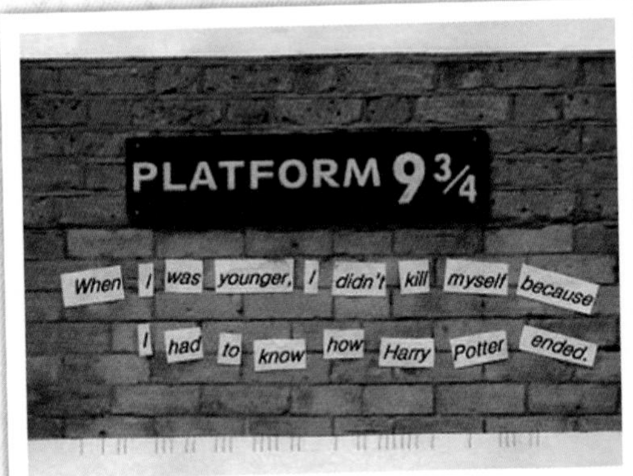

Like you, I was adopted at birth. Like you, I have been told my entire life that my birth parents were worthless and incapable of taking care of me - that they didn't want me. Like you, I am the least desired youngest child of a family that was happy as it was. Like you, I am bullied by an older sibling who is favored by my family.

But unlike you, I have never been whisked away to a magical land where I was suddenly valued and adored. These books - your story - gave me hope. They gave me hope that one day I would not be the lonely friendless little girl sitting in her bed reading of far off lands and magic. That one day perhaps I would find my own Hogwarts, and in a way, become my own "Boy Who Lived". They gave me hope that I don't always have to be lonely. That what people tell you perhaps isn't always true. That the impossible could happen. That your past creates you, but does not have to continue to define you.

You, Mr. Potter, taught me how to grow up and learn about who I am. When you found out your godfather was a killer, my heart ached for you, because I could understand the pain of finally finding a part of who you are—and then having it snatched away. When he died, though you may not have known him too well, I cried with you. I closed my book and could not continue reading until I had cried my eyes out, not only for you and your godfather, but for the symbolic loss of your parents, yet again. When you subsequently lost Dumbledore, and Remus, I was amazed by your tenacity and your strength. It is strength I admire, strength I try to find every day. I empathize with your connection to the Weasleys. I know what it's like to be searching for a family unit because your own just isn't what you need. And more than just sharing a past, I see so many similarities in our personality. I am temperamental; though I try every day to be a little more calm. I am overemotional, and extremely stubborn. I try to be brave; sometimes it fails me, while sometimes I go to the point of recklessness. I am firm in my convictions, though I'm not always sure what they are. I see all of these things in you. I have watched you struggle with them, watched you grow and change as you face these challenges... in many ways, it parallels my own life. In many more, it teaches me about myself. I never thought a children's book could help me grow as a person, but that's what you have done for me.

People laugh at my love for you. For your story. To them, I am a seventeen year old girl with a crazy obsession with a children's book about silly magic stories. But to me, you are so much more than that. I see myself in every page of your books. You have given me so much hope, and through that hope you have helped me grow into the strong, optimistic, and loving woman that I am trying to be.

So thank you, Mr. Potter. For everything.

Love,

– Emily K.

Jessie

Dear Mr. Potter,

My first childhood journal was a spiral bound book with hot air balloons on the cover. It contains only one thing: a poorly written story about *Harry Potter*. So when I look back at my childhood, *Harry Potter* seems a perfectly good place to start. It's like coming full circle.

I've been trying to figure out what it is about *Harry Potter* that pulls me in— why it grabbed me once upon a time (over a decade ago) and why it has yet to let me go. It's a little bit of a mystery, to be totally honest, why a teenaged wizard is such a significant part of my life. But *Harry Potter* was, in a lot of ways, my first love. Although there have been other passing fancies, other loves, somehow I always return to Harry. You never do forget your first love, after all.

What is it about an awkward boy with knobby knees, and the patchwork story that made him an entire world's savior, that keeps me hanging on so long after his fate has been set? His story has been told, his future has been written, and the book of his life has shut with a satisfying crack of the binding. And yet the story of the boy with a lightning bolt scar lingers, like some ethereal backdrop of my life. He's part of my history, of where I come from and where I am going, and our stories connect, just a bit, at the edges. I wonder if I'm fated to forever have Harry in my life with no real reason why.

Sometimes I love Harry's story because his life has played out so much like a fairytale. Others, I remember that the force that should have saved his life—magic—sometimes only causes more hurt. And others still, I'm drawn to the fact that it's not just a story of a boy called *Harry Potter*, but also of the decisions and mistakes of the past that put him on the road as the chosen one.

It's about so much more than most people assume. It's a story of being a good mother. It's about how loving someone, even if that

Dear Mr. Potter (& JK ROWLING)
Because of You
i am a better person.
I Read, Volunteer, Learn, Create, & FIGHT against World Suck!
Without you... I WOULD PROBABLY BE... selfish, obnoxious, self-centered, AND A BIT snobby.
10 years and counting...
THANK YOU FOR LETTING ME GROW UP WITH YOU.
Katie, 18, RAVENCLAW

Sarah A., 14

love is unrequited, defines your life and theirs too. It's about what can come from sacrifice, and how love and sacrifice intertwine to give us a future.

It's about women—women named Lily and Molly, Andromeda and Nymphadora, and even women named Narcissa and Petunia, who give everything to bring their children safely into the world, and try their hardest to keep them there. It's about how family is found and forged through necessity and sometimes pain, and how those relationships are what matter the most.

Harry's story also teaches what it means to live a life with regret, and tells the stories of men who lived with regret. Albus Dumbledore set out on a path that led to greatness, but found only shame in his need for power. Then this humbled but powerful man unknowingly welcomed a future tyrant into his school, and watched helplessly as that boy became a man—and then a monster.

A second man in Harry's story lived with regret. It's the story of a man named Severus Snape, and how his past shaped his future. How the chaos created by that monstrous tyrant is where he found his solace, and how loving a beautiful woman changed his life. And then, and only then, it's about how Severus Snape's greatest regret led to the life of a little boy named *Harry Potter* who was raised in a cupboard under the stairs, who went on to find an ancestry in a world of magic, a world full of friends and love, and people to take care of him. And then it's about how that boy went on to save the world, marry a woman who became a good mother, and live a life free of regret.

At its core, it's the story of the passing of generations, of how mistakes impact the future, and how somehow, no matter what, everything comes full circle.

SO MAYBE I DO KNOW WHY HARRY POTTER HAS PULLED ME IN...

—Jessie W., 23

Dear Mr. Potter,

It's been just over nine years since you officially came into my life, but truthfully, I can't remember ever not knowing your name. Those big "Harry Potter" books sat on the second shelf of the big bookcase downstairs; despite the fact that I had learned how to read in preschool, I was too afraid to read them, as I thought they were just for big girls. Of course, that all changed on November 16, 2001, the day my mom took me out of school early to go see a movie.

Erin C. as Bellatrix & Nicole J. as Angelina Johnson

These past nine years have been crazy to say the least. I've made and lost friends; I've switched schools five times; I've been to seven funerals... but you've stuck with me throughout everything. You were my constant (and sometimes only) companion during my four lonely years of homeschooling. You were my escape when one of my best friends was recovering from self-harm and unloading everything on me. You helped me make new friends, and you're continuing to bring me closer to the friends I have now. Right now, you're helping me get through my sophomore year of high school, and I doubt I'd have been able to manage any of this without you to lean on.

Harry, you're my best and my oldest friend. You know me inside and out, and I know you better than just about anyone else in my life – after all, we watched each other grow up. I laugh every time I reread your snarky comments to Draco, and I'm sure you remember that time I nearly blew my speakers blasting the Prisoner of Azkaban soundtrack. I cried with you when you lost Sirius; you helped me get back on my feet after the death of my uncle. Harry, I know you physically exist only on paper, but you're more real to me than the air I breathe. By teaching me so much about love, sacrifice, friendship, loyalty, and individuality over these years, you've shaped my personality into what it is today. No matter where I am or what I'm doing, you pervade my thoughts and influence my decisions. I love the person I am today, and I owe it all to you, Mr. Potter. You're going to stay with me for the rest of my life, and I'm so proud of that. Thank you for everything.

Emily G., 15, Gryffindor

Shery Mae S., 21, Ravenclaw

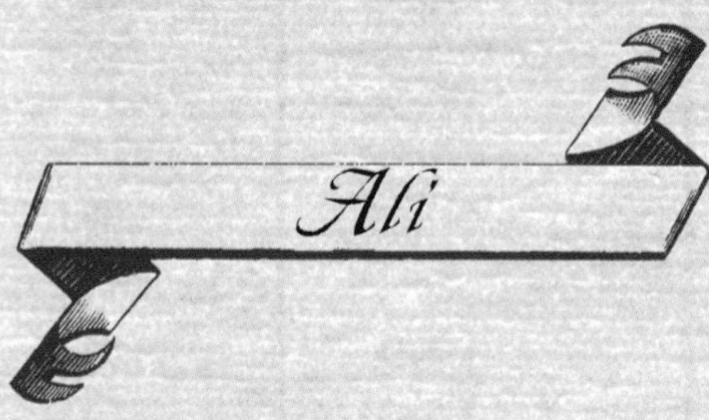

Ali

Dear Mr. Radcliffe,

First and foremost, you gave a face and a voice to my childhood hero. Since I first picked up *Harry Potter and The Sorcerer's Stone* when I was seven years old, I've had dreams of going to Hogwarts, casting spells, and playing Quidditch alongside Harry, and you brought these dreams to life. As soon as you appeared on-screen in the first film, you became *Harry Potter* for me. Gone was the imagined version of Harry in my head, and in its place was a real, live person, and a kid like me. Throughout the next ten years of my life, I continued to watch you and Harry grow on-screen, and I feel like I've grown up with you. I've watched Harry experience some of the same things I've experienced as a high school student—although I haven't been fortunate enough to do it at Hogwarts with a wand at hand.

Ever since you were chosen to play Harry, I felt like I could relate to you not as a famous actor, but as a person. You were a normal boy with a normal life, and you ended up living your dream. You give hope to other normal children like me, because you're living proof that you don't need the fame or the connections to get what you want. It makes me feel like if I have the motivation, I can achieve my dreams, too.

I'm now approaching my eighteenth birthday (making me a seventh year Hogwarts student) and soon I'll be starting the next phase of my life as a college student. Although I'm nervous, it comforts me to know that no matter where I go in life, I'll always have a part of my childhood in *Harry Potter*. Even now, ten years later, my love for Harry and for you has yet to dwindle, and doubt it ever will. The truth is, *Harry Potter* is not just a children's series. It is the one thing in my life of which I'll never tire. Each one of these books and films is timeless, and this is due a great deal to you and the rest of this phenomenal cast. You make these characters real people.

You took *Harry Potter* from being that little boy under the cupboard to the grown man who saved his friends and made his world a better place. By doing that, you make our Muggle world a better place, because you give people hope. Harry gives people hope that good can triumph over evil and that love can save lives. You, Dan, give people hope that with a bit of talent and a lot of drive, you can do great things.

Thank you for allowing me and millions of other kids to grow up alongside you. Thank you for helping me believe in myself. Most importantly, thank you for giving me my childhood.

—Ali M., 17, Ravenclaw, New York

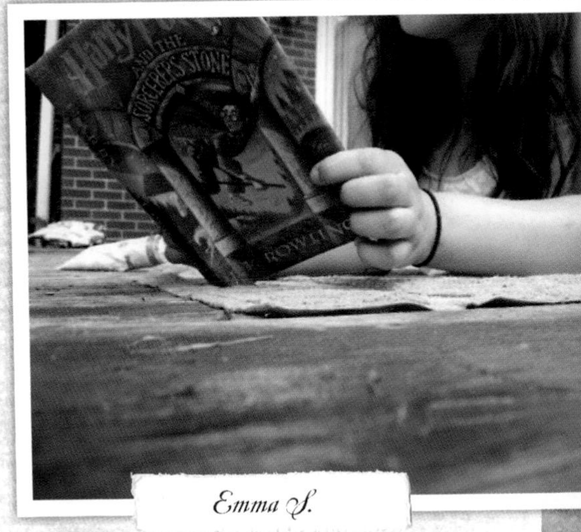

Emma S.

Harry Potter was not a part of my childhood. I watched the movies, I liked them, but I didn't love them. My brother started reading the books in 2000, so I always knew he liked them a lot. He tried to convince me to read them at least 4 times when I was around 8. I don't remember much, but I didn't read them becowse I was simply not interested in books yet. I was too young to be obsessed and I don't regret it. I was just not ready to have my life changed yet.

So, one beautiful winter night, on July 16th, 2006, when I was 11 and 7 months exactly, at around 8:30 pm, I simply decided I wanted to read Harry Potter during my winter vacation. I can't remember what motivated me exactly, but I'm so, extremaly, beyond words, glad. Maybe it was boredom. I don't know. But I'm glad.

Anyway, what can I say about Harry Potter? How can I describe in words the way my life changed after those 7 beautiful books?

I guess mainly my thoughts and feelings about love, death, life, courage, ambition, curiosity, desire, friendship, pity, passion; the good and bad things in life, the things we should seek and the ones we should avoid, have either been severely or entirely affected by JK Rowling. But there's so much more— my love for books, many friendships, other passions and interests would be inexistent if I had never read Harry Potter. If I hadn't been bored on that night of July, 2006.

ϟ Betina P., 15

Lauren, 16 and Paige, 11

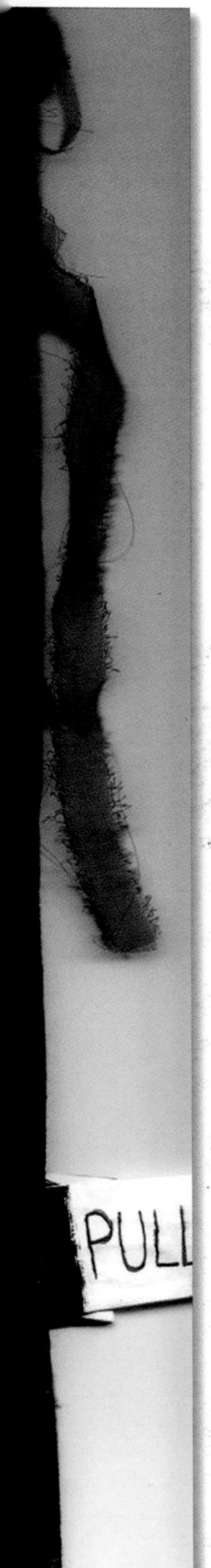

The moment *Harry Potter* came out, I loved it. When the first movie came out, I walked through the store holding that VHS tape until my parents had no choice but to buy it for me. Sadly, as time progressed, *Harry Potter* became less and less important. It was still there, it just was not as big a part of my life as it had been before.

It wasn't until I was about 15 years old that *Harry Potter* reclaimed my life. All around me, everything was crumbling down. My family was falling apart. My parents fought until my dad left. My boyfriend was controlling. I took my best friend's caring as cruelty and we fought all the time. I started cutting; everyday and everywhere. It didn't matter with what or if I was home or at school. I found a way to release all my pain. There was one instance on the shower floor, with the hot water burning my cuts and me with a razor to my throat, when I wanted to end it all.

Something that morning made me get up, though. I'm not sure what it was. So I did. After that I began reading *Harry Potter* again. After that, everything looked better. I knew I had friends at Hogwarts that would always be there for me. The day was brighter. I'm not going to sit here and type that I lived Happily Ever After, because I didn't. There are times now and have been times in the past where I've wanted to go back into that hole and just suffer and end it all. Sadly there have been times where I have even gone back to cutting. Yet, I have stopped and thought, "what would Harry and the gang say if they seen you like this? How would they feel if you missed out on one of their adventures?" So I would cheer up and join them. In those pages, I would be on top of the world: flying through the sky on my Firebolt, sitting in Hagrid's hut, enjoying life. Then Dumbledore would step in and say, "it does not do to dwell on dreams and forget to live" and I would take that as my cue that the fun was over today. I would put my book down and go spend time with my family or go out with my friends. I knew it was important that I was blessed with such a wonderful family that really loves me. My friends and I would come up with our own crazy adventures. *Harry Potter* taught me that love is important, and in the end it conquers evil.

– Anonymous

Mehvish J., 15

Dear J.K Rowling,
Before I read Harry potter & the philosophers Stone, I had given up on all kinds of Magic. Now I know you dont have to make things whizz around the room of their own accord to have magic., picking up a pen & writing is close enough.

- Olivia, 14, Hufflepuff.

Hannah & Nicholas

Dear Mr. Potter,

As a child, I was always easily caught up in my own head. I could spend hours playing somewhere by myself and not have a clue or care about anything else going on around me. I was one of the first kids in my class who could read on my own, although I rarely did. I would much rather make up my own adventures than read about someone else's. All of that changed in 2001, when I was introduced to *Harry Potter*.

I was in fifth grade. After summer break I would start middle school. One of the sixth grade English teachers from the middle school came down and talked to us about the middle school's summer reading program. We had to log a specific number of reading hours and if we succeeded then we would get to go on a field trip to see *Harry Potter and The Sorcerer's Stone* when it came out in the movie theater. I was intrigued, and decided that I would read the *Harry Potter* book to complete my summer reading hours; that way I would be able to follow the movie better.

To say that *Harry Potter* and the world J.K. Rowling created ignited my passion for reading is most certainly an understatement. It was reading *Harry Potter* that made me realize you can still use your own imagination to create the world and characters you are reading about. Even if everything is spelled out in exact detail, every person who reads it makes it their own.

Over the summer I often went on visits to my great Aunt's house. On several of my day visits over the summer I brought my *Harry Potter* book with me. I would sit and read and she would play on the computer for a while. Then, I would tell her all about the part I just read as we ate snacks and watched her soap opera.

On one of my visits she mentioned to me that my cousin Nick, who is three years younger than me, was also reading *Harry Potter* when he came on his visits to her house. This started rivalry between Nick and me. It amused our aunt, and she decided to fuel our rivalry.

Auntie began pre-ordering the *Harry Potter* books as they came out so that Nick and I received them as soon as possible. Then, we would race each other to see who could finish the book first. This went on for years, as the books were released and Auntie always took great joy in being able to give Nick and I something that we'd cherish forever. Yes, we will always be family, but Nick and I bonded so much over our love of *Harry Potter* and spending time with Auntie that we have grown to be something much bigger; best friends.

Sadly, in 2008 Auntie was taken from us unexpectedly. Since then, *Harry Potter* has meant even more to both of us, because the magical world keeps our memories and love of Auntie wrapped up between its pages. When we miss her too terribly we turn to *Harry Potter*, rereading the adventures that brought the three of us so close together; or even just sit, holding the book to our heart, taking in the glorious smell of a good book that now always makes us think of her.

Harry Potter will never end for me and Nick. It taught us so much about life and if nothing else, it will always be in our heart, acting as an unending tie to our aunt.

– Hannah B., 21, and Nicholas F., 18, Ravenclaws.

I was only doing what millions of other eleven year olds were doing – waiting for my Hogwarts letter. I still can't believe it never came. –Sabina F.

Dear Mr. Potter,

In 1999, Lance Armstrong won his first Tour de France, Britney Spears released her first album, and the world population surpassed six billion, but none of that is important to me.That same year, when I was eight, I read *Harry Potter and The Sorcerer's Stone* with my dad. Every day, he and I would take turns reading chapters aloud. He would help me with the big words and correct me on my mispronunciations (like calling prefects "perfects"). Later that year, *The Chamber of Secrets* and *The Prisoner of Azkaban,* my personal favorite, were released to the world.

Let's fast-forward ten years, seven books, and six movies later. I finally convinced another family member, my sister Olivia, to join the wonderful, nerdy, and magical world of Potter fans. Before I talk about her first experience, it is important to explain why this seemingly insignificant event changed our entire relationship.

When Olivia was born in 1994, I was three and overjoyed to become an older sister. However, as we grew older, we also grew apart. Ironically, I once threw a *Harry Potter* book at her head when a fight broke out between us...not one of my finer moments. We were polar opposites. As a kid, I was a shy and reclusive bookworm. My sister was a social butterfly who believed in watching the movie instead of reading the book. I was lost at Hogwarts while Olivia remained distant and in a world of her own.

It was frustrating to watch my sister show affection towards her friends when I couldn't even get a hug from her without being shoved away. I began to shut her out and gain friendships from the characters in my books. Hermione never judged me, Ron was never bitter, and Harry gave me hope. Their friendship was inspiring. They showed me true loyalty and camaraderie. I was an outcast at school and I couldn't stand being fake to impress others. Like Harry, I decided to follow my heart. I was alone, separated from my friends and my sister. I thought of Harry in *Goblet of Fire*. If Harry could endure his classmates' jeers, "Potter Stinks" pins, and the silent treatment from his best friend, I knew that the people I cared about most would eventually come back around.

In 2009, after watching the trailer for *Half-Blood Prince*, my sister decided to come with me to the midnight showing. Waiting in line for six hours, I was finally given the opportunity to connect with my sister. Sixteen years of disagreements ended that night. With our newfound friendship, I eventually persuaded my sister, the girl who hated reading, to give books a chance.

I know it could be much worse. I am blessed with a family that I would do anything for. That's why getting along with Olivia is so important to me. I want her to know that, like the friends in *Harry Potter*, I will always have her back and I will always love her. I am

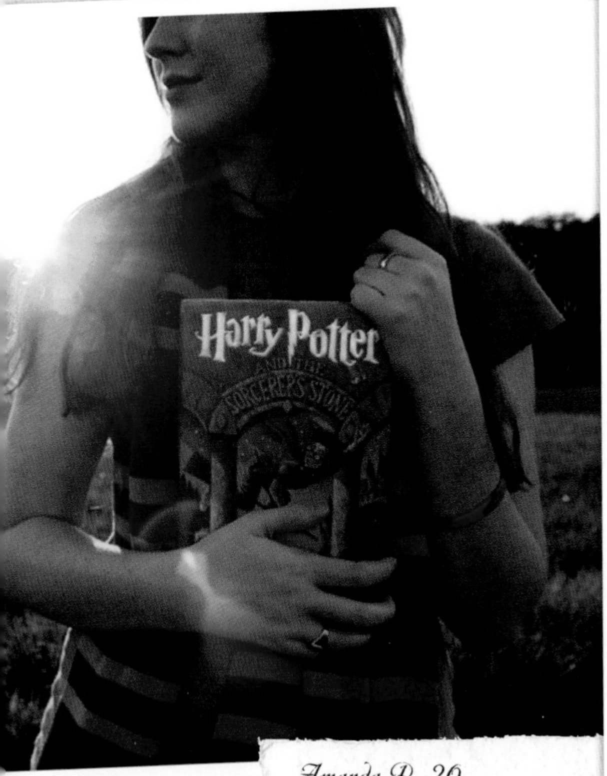

Amanda B., 20

so glad that I can finally bond with my sister. In fact, this last July 31st, we celebrated Harry's 30th birthday with a movie marathon. We even baked a cake like the one in the first movie. Thank you for helping me learn to read chapter books in elementary school, thank you for making reading exciting, and thank you for bringing my family together.

WITH ETERNAL GRATITUDE,

Taylor A., 19

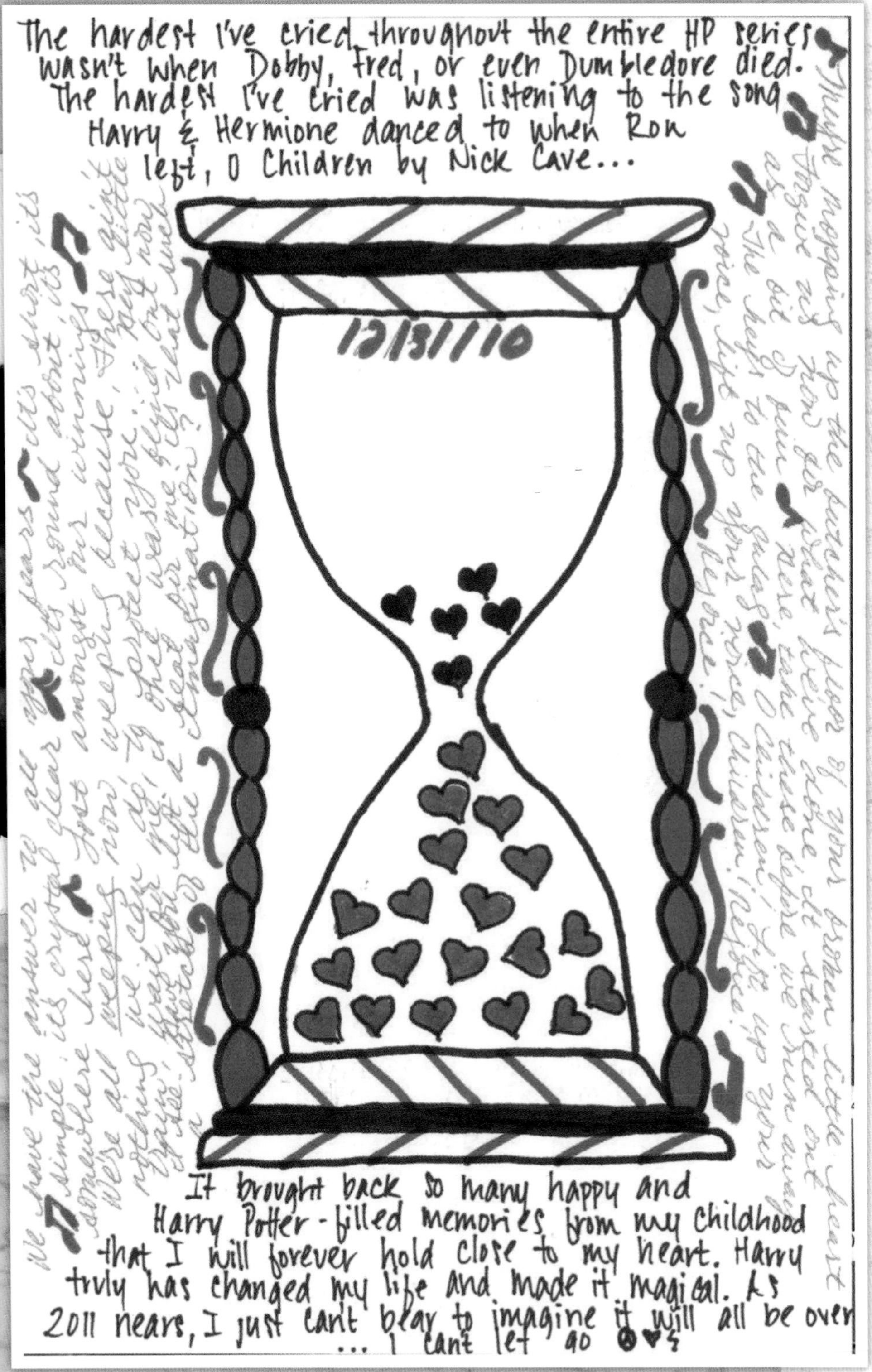

The hardest I've cried throughout the entire HP series wasn't when Dobby, Fred, or even Dumbledore died. The hardest I've cried was listening to the song Harry & Hermione danced to when Ron left, O Children by Nick Cave...

We have the answer to all your fears it's short, it's simple, it's crystal clear it's round about, it's somewhere here lost amongst our winnings We're all weeping now, weeping because there ain't nothing we can do to protect you Hey little train! Wait for me! I once was blind but now I see Have you left a seat for me? Is that such a stretch of the imagination?

They're mopping up the butcher's floor of your broken little hearts Forgive us now for what we've done It started out as a bit of fun Here, take these before we run away The keys to the gulag O Children Lift up your voice, lift up your voice Children Rejoice, rejoice!

12/31/10

It brought back so many happy and Harry Potter-filled memories from my childhood that I will forever hold close to my heart. Harry truly has changed my life and made it magical. As 2011 nears, I just can't bear to imagine it will all be over ... I can't let go ☮♥'s

Sarah-Jane R., 15, Slytherin

Ally M., 18

Daniela

Dear Hermione Granger,

You're my best friend. You are my idol. I'd give anything in the world to spend a day with you because I can relate to you more than anyone else. Ever since I was little, I've been very studious and hard-working. I've always strived to get good grades and I love reading. I've been called a nerd, bookworm, know-it-all, just like you. You never let it get to you, though. Your education is important to you and you don't care what anyone else thinks. You've been a huge inspiration to me. Your knowledge, logic, and cleverness served you, Harry, and Ron countless times throughout your adventures. They wouldn't have "lasted two days without you!" You are the brightest witch of your age, and I admire that infinitely. You've inspired me in so many other ways as well. You are the perfect friend loyal to the very end. You genuinely care about others. You're brave, determined, generous, and respectful of all living creatures. You have strong beliefs and defend them tooth and nail. Even if you're the only one, you won't back down or pretend to be something you're not. I try to emulate you every day. I've never been so inspired by anyone as I have by you. Thank you for giving me the strength to be myself and stand up for myself and what I believe in and never back down. You, a true Gryffindor, have taught me so much about friendship and life.

Much love and respect,

Daniela C., 14, Gryffindor

Philip

Philip, a five-year old boy, shares his experiences with reading the Harry Potter books. Starting March of 2010, he is now almost done with the fourth book. Here is what he has to say about it, as dictated to his mom:

Dear Mr. Potter,

"When I finished book one of *Harry Potter*, I thought that I was going to read it again. I didn't know that there was a *Harry Potter and the Chamber of Secrets*. Then, when I was looking into my father's bookshelf, I saw the books of *Harry Potter*. Then I got the book five and looked inside it. I showed it to my father. Then when I finished the book three, I was excited to be at chapter 16. But then, when I was reading book four, it should have been three champions but there were four and the Hogwarts champion was Cedric Diggory and *Harry Potter*. But there should be one champion in each school. Before I read *Harry Potter*, my father explained about it. When I was at chapter one, book one, I didn't know that the Dursleys didn't like Harry."

– Philip, $5\frac{1}{2}$, Gryffindor

Dear Mr Potter,
You taught me that, no
matter what, the most important
thing to remember is to love.
Thank you.
Ellie
x

I'm off to the best place on earth –Nayeli C., 20

Dear Mr Potter,

You have definitely changed my life tremendously. I can't believe I used to hate you when I was younger... I think I could almost slap myself for that.

When I was eleven, I watched Harry Potter and the Sorcerer's Stone & immediately decided to read the books.

I WAS HOOKED.

More than four years have passed since I first touched a Harry Potter book. I'm VERY sad that this whole magical adventure will come to an end in July 2011 with the release of Harry Potter and the Deathly Hallows Part 2.

You have taught me a lot of things....

LOVE friendship LOYALTY RESPECT humor :) PATIENCE perseverance.

& a lot of other life values.

Your Story is a GREAT one. Our generation is grateful to have been with you in this journey :D We will always LOVE & SUPPORT you!

Regards from
Deepa :)
the deementor!

December 30th, 2010

Dear Mr. Potter,
I actually can't believe that so much time has passed since I opened that first book and started reading about a boy living in a cupboard under the stairs. Ever since then all I dreamed about was to receive the Hogwarts letter, or even just to discover that I had some kind of magical power.
When I was eight, I actually thought that if I believed it with all my heart, it would really happen
When I was eleven I thought that my letter had been lost in the mail.
When I was twelve all I had to do was give up, right wrong.
When I was nine, I believed I would die, if I didn't get my letter.
When I was thirteen I realized it didn't matter. It was like I had received it seven years before, when I first begun reading 'the Philosopher's Stone... and fell in love with it.
The Harry Potter world has been a constant companion throughout my entire life and it made me the person I am today. It's the reason why I love books and writing so much. It gave me the start I needed.
Harry Potter was the beginning of everything.

I loved, I hoped, I dreamed, I cried, I cheered and mourned. And even though other books made me feel that way, none of them meant so much. None of them literally grew up beside me, with me, changing in my view so that I loved them no matter what my age was.
And I'm proud, so proud to be one of those people who stuck with Harry until the very end. One of those people who know... that this kind of things don't fade with time. They only mean more and more as years go by.
This kind of magic just never ends.

LONG LIVE HARRY POTTER!
Serena

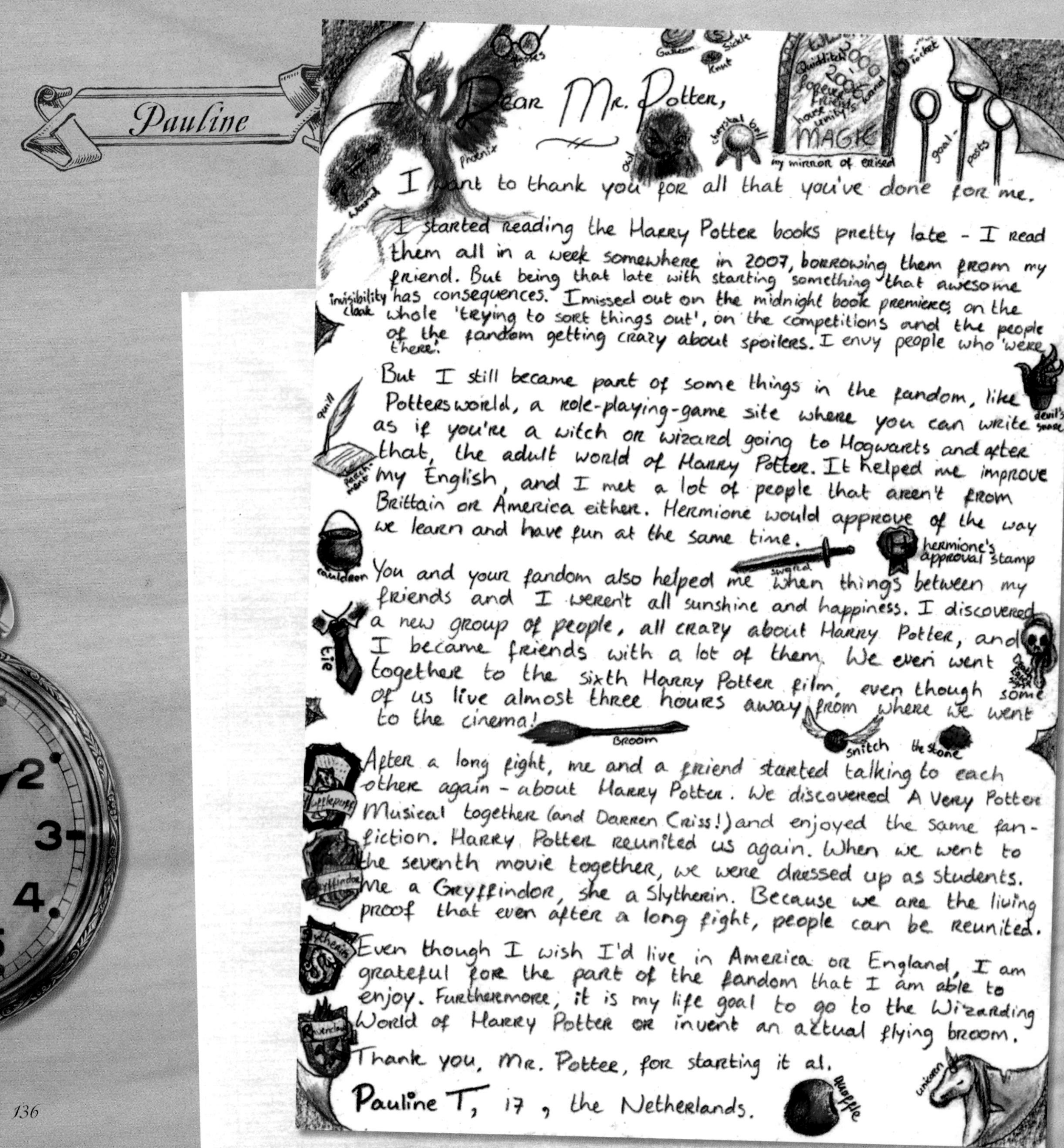

Pauline

Dear Mr. Potter,

I want to thank you for all that you've done for me.

I started reading the Harry Potter books pretty late - I read them all in a week somewhere in 2007, borrowing them from my friend. But being that late with starting something that awesome has consequences. I missed out on the midnight book premieres, on the whole 'trying to sort things out', on the competitions and the people of the fandom getting crazy about spoilers. I envy people who were there!

But I still became part of some things in the fandom, like Pottersworld, a role-playing-game site where you can write as if you're a witch or wizard going to Hogwarts and after that, the adult world of Harry Potter. It helped me improve my English, and I met a lot of people that aren't from Brittain or America either. Hermione would approve of the way we learn and have fun at the same time.

You and your fandom also helped me when things between my friends and I weren't all sunshine and happiness. I discovered a new group of people, all crazy about Harry Potter, and I became friends with a lot of them. We even went together to the sixth Harry Potter film, even though some of us live almost three hours away from where we went to the cinema!

After a long fight, me and a friend started talking to each other again - about Harry Potter. We discovered A Very Potter Musical together (and Darren Criss!) and enjoyed the same fan-fiction. Harry Potter reunited us again. When we went to the seventh movie together, we were dressed up as students. Me a Gryffindor, she a Slytherin. Because we are the living proof that even after a long fight, people can be reunited.

Even though I wish I'd live in America or England, I am grateful for the part of the fandom that I am able to enjoy. Furthermore, it is my life goal to go to the Wizarding World of Harry Potter or invent an actual flying broom.

Thank you, Mr. Potter, for starting it al.

Pauline T, 17, the Netherlands.

Surada, Casey, Elisa, Paula, Courtney, Chelsea, & Morgan

Dear Mr. Potter,

Seven friends, Seven books.

Harry Potter taught us the power of friendship.

– Surada S., Casey D., Elisa T., Paula I., Courtney B., Chelsea M., Morgan D.

Dear Mr. Potter,

The first time I saw the magic, I was only seven-years-old. As I got older, I realized that I did not only see it, but I also felt it, and it was that feeling of euphoria that made me buy all seven books and watch all the movies countless times. I am sixteen now. Although I am sad that everything will come to an end soon, I know that the magic will always live in my heart. Thank you for being such a big part of my life!

- Camille A.

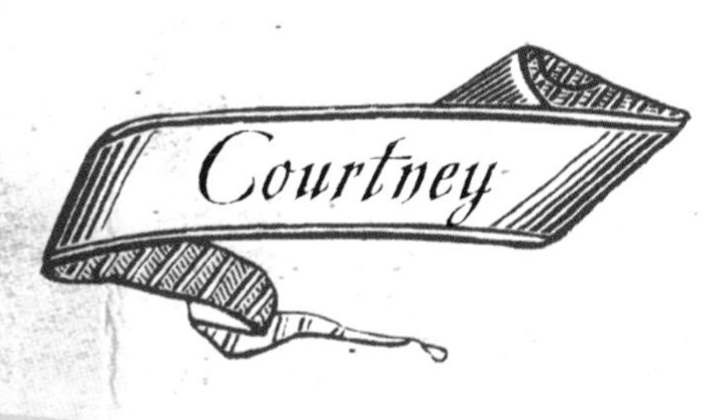

Harry taught me to be brave.
Ron taught me to be loyal.
Hermione taught me it's ok to be clever.
Ginny taught me to stand up for myself.
Fred + George taught me to laugh.
Dumbledore taught me it's ok to make mistakes.
Luna taught me to believe.
Neville taught me it's never too late to become who you were born to be.

I've become who I am today because of **the Boy Who Lived** and his friends.

Thank you for 11 amazing years.

Courtney P., Ravenclaw

Dear Harry,

When you entered my life in 2000 I could never have envisioned the scope of the journey you'd take me on, from the very first page. It was truly a turning point in my life. You've been a friend who I could count on, someone I could take the hand of and travel with into an immersive and vibrant world, somewhere so real for so many of us.

You were there when other friends weren't, when family didn't understand, and when life didn't seem worth living otherwise. I have filled my life with you, I have fallen in love with you over and over, and I have seen and left the places which are unwholesome for the soul.

You are a symbol of hope, courage and perseverence, not just in the wizarding world – you are a symbol of our childhoods and the difficult and intense times after, ever reminding us to value what is good and right, and come out triumphant.

I am one amongst countless others who have walked side by side with you, laughing, grieving, and cheering you on in our hearts. You've given me so many things to look forward to and I never want it to end. I never want to put you back on the shelf, I never want to say goodbye or ever forget the impact you've had on my life.

Your devoted friend,

Amy

www.elder-wand.net

ISU
QUIDDITCH
ISU
QUIDDITCH
ISU
QUIDDITCH
ISU
QUIDDITCH
ISU
QUIDDITCH
ISU
QUIDDITCH

Morgan S., Gryffindor

*"It was the best and the wors
day of my life. The best beca
I have achieved a life long
dream, the worst because I
couldn't get on the platform.
–Bazlina S., Malaysia*

Dear Harry, 12-31-10

I fear it is impossible to fully express how much you have meant to me. You are as much a part of me as the house I grew up in, my birthday or my favorite song. You have been a part of me since our first meeting at number four, Privet Drive. Since then, my connection to you has done naught but grow.

Over the years, I have mourned your losses, celebrated your triumphs and known you as only a very dear friend can.

Though I have grieved over the end of our adventure together, I shall not begrudge your recession from the public eye. As Albus Dumbledore once said, "It does not do to dwell on dreams and forget to live." So, Harry, I will treasure the time we were given, visit you often and remember you always.

Your friend,

Megan S.

Dear Mr. Potter,

When the Harry Potter craze began in the United States around 2001, my entire family jumped on the bandwagon, except for me. My dad read the books to my little brother, who was five at the time. He offered to read them to me too, but I declined, insisting that "books about wizards are lame." Come the arrival of Harry Potter and the Sorcerer's Stone in theatres, I grudgingly went along with my family to see it. After that, I was enchanted. I asked my dad to read me the books at bedtime. Harry Potter soon became something the entire family enjoyed. My brother and I collected the action figures and used them to re-enact scenes and create our own scenes. Our "family fun nights" consisted of Harry Potter trivia board games. When we adopted two giant orange tabby cats, my brother named his Crookshanks and I named mine Ruby, short for Rubeus [Hagrid]. We made going to midnight premieres a family affair, getting dressed up and waiting together outside the theatre for hours. In short, thank you J.K. Rowling and Harry, for giving my family something to unite for.

Angelica, 15, Ravenclaw

← my brother and I with the Lego Hagrid in LegoLand in San Diego, California. August 21, 2004

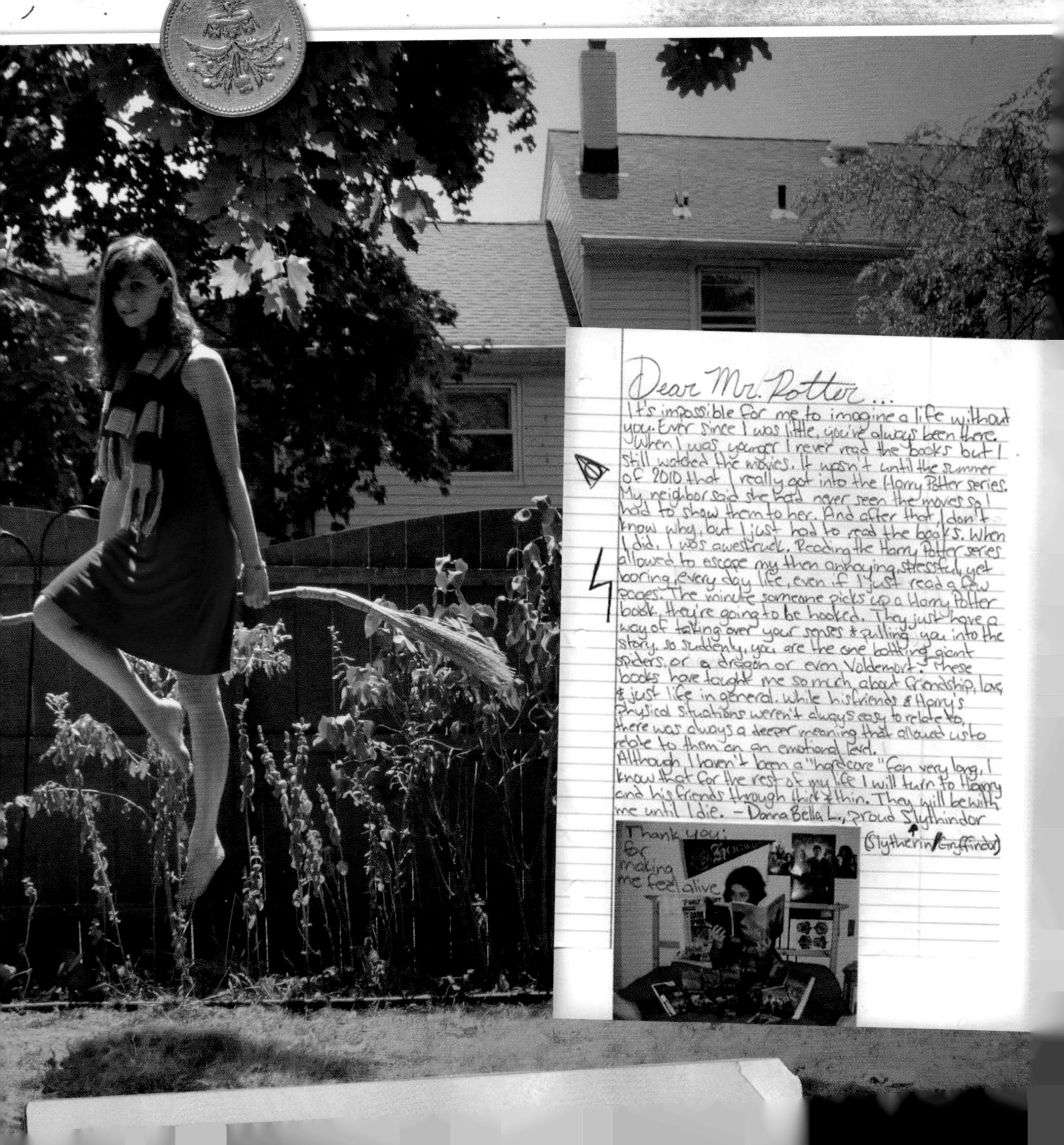

Dear Mr. Potter...

It's impossible for me to imagine a life without you. Ever since I was little, you've always been there. When I was younger I never read the books but I still watched the movies. It wasn't until the summer of 2010 that I really got into the Harry Potter series. My neighbor said she had never seen the movies so I had to show them to her. And after that, I don't know why, but I just had to read the books. When I did, I was awestruck. Reading the Harry Potter series allowed to escape my then annoying, stressful, yet boring, every day life, even if I just read a few pages. The minute someone picks up a Harry Potter book, they're going to be hooked. They just have a way of taking over your senses & pulling you into the story. so suddenly, you are the one battling giant spiders, or a dragon or even Voldemort. These books have taught me so much about friendship, love & just life in general. While his friends & Harry's physical situations weren't always easy to relate to, there was always a deeper meaning that allowed us to relate to them on an emotional level.

Although I haven't been a "hardcore" fan very long, I know that for the rest of my life I will turn to Harry and his friends through thick & thin. They will be with me until I die. – Donna Bella L., proud Slythindor

(Slytherin/Gryffindor)

Thank you:
for
making
me feel alive

Samantha P., 19

Dear Mr. Potter,

We've been best friends for 11 years now. 1999 seems like ages ago, doesn't it? I had just transferred to a new school after the last one was... well let's say it wasn't great socially. You came into my life several months before I really got to know you, and for that I apologize. I wasn't an avid reader, so when I received Sorcerer's Stone for my birthday, I tossed you aside. But I feel like fate brought us together. The nature of the Universe caused me to randomly pick up that book I tossed aside months earlier and read it. Thus begun what would be our 11 plus years of friendship.

If I had to write a book about our history and everything I feel about you, let's just say it'd be as long as Order of the Phoenix. So let me say this **THANK YOU**. I appreciate you, and will always be there just like you've always been there for me. We truly became adults together, and your inspiring story and struggles helped me to overcome my own. Out of all the fandoms I could have been involved in before it became the phenomenon, I am honored it was yours.

Your story is my fantasy. Even as a 24 year old, my friends and I (who also share your friendship) would give everything to be part of your Wizarding World. So since we will never be able to, we live it all we can. We've gone to most midnight showings, most midnight book releases, and read the saga cover to cover once a year. That's just the tip of the iceberg. However, we have yet to visit the Wizarding World of Harry Potter. I know that when we do, we will be very emotional because it will be the closest we will ever get to meeting you.

Our lives, everyone who knows your story, would be so different without you. You've saved people's lives. You've helped people cope with death, hard times, and abuse. Your story is the most powerful of any I've come to know, and your story will live on. I will tell your story to my future children because yours, without a shadow of a doubt, is and will be the greatest story ever told. **ALWAYS**.

Love,

Courtney C., 24

Dear Mr. Potter,

I remember that 3rd grade day, I remember the friends along the way. You are my best friend, my boyfriend, (lol) and my guide. There is going to be nothing in this letter that hasn't already been said, I'm sure. ~~But,~~ I've ~~witnessed~~ how high you are held amongst us children, teenagers, adults - people who are friends, best friends, brothers, sisters, mothers, fathers and perhaps most importantly: strangers (from all over). What a feat! You appeal to both our hearts, our minds and our imagination. Hogwarts is more than a place: it is a feeling. From lessons to life lessons I truly believe in you and the power of good. Thanks for making me laugh, cry and talk about you for hours. and... My, my how we have grown up Mr. Potter. How funny it is that I should meet you at age 9 and finish with you at age 17. No doubt I, and others will show this to my children in hopes we will have some little Harrys, Rons, Hermiones, Lunas, Nevilles and Dumbledores running around (and a Snape!). I could go on but I have a paper for Prof. Binns to do!

Eternally grateful,

Lia J. NJ

a Ravenclaw!

I went there

lol could you imagine baby dumbly?

PS would have done this more neatly had my quill been better, lol.

Kayla (left) and Allie (right)

Emily F., 17

Dear Dumbledore,

I knew. I always knew. Ever since reading the first book when I was nine years old, I knew you were gay. There was just something about the way you carried yourself, something in your charm and your eccentric wit, that let me know. And I was more than fine with it. Actually, I was ecstatic. I had never thought being gay was anything but normal, but then suddenly you came into my life and were extraordinary. You weren't just a wizard or even a good wizard - you were one of the greatest to live. You were the only person You-Know-Who was afraid of.

Now, I've had conversations with many people who think your creator publicly outed you to gain publicity. I can't possibly agree because I knew who you were, but not as a token gay character. She never lied or tried to mislead us as to your nature, although your choice of a celibate life meant most people assumed you were heterosexual (as so many are liable to do when anything other than "straight" isn't explicitly mentioned). She never made you a mouthpiece for anything more than the common good mankind is capable of. She was true to you and recognized that, for a person such as you, in a world such as your own, your sexual preference is a non-issue (I am known to commonly point out Bill and Fleur's gender-neutral wedding vows when making this point). She didn't out you up-front because your sexuality simply had no bearing on your person.

By not making you spout a message of accepting homosexuality, she made the message even more powerful: love is a force that is more powerful than dark magic and that the gender we love simply does not matter. She showed us a glimpse of the wizarding world, where there is no need to fight and defend the right to love in our every moment—although one appreciates the parallels of struggle and prejudice between our world and your world's issue with the purity and blood and the rights of non-human persons.

I had long been "out" and open about my own fluid sexuality when your creator officially opened the proverbial closet door, but to me there never was a closet. To me you had long been a skilled wizard, a kind soul, a friendly eccentric with a sweet tooth, a teacher, a mentor, Supreme Mugwump, Headmaster, and a homosexual. You were brave and kind and brilliant, and one of my heroes.

–Jasper V., 20, Slytherin

Dear Proffeser Dumbledore,

thank you for helping
wen he was Beati
Voldamort.

I hop you a
jn Wi sed He

Say Helo
Dobby and Sna
-ig.

Love from Dar

P.S I can't wai
letter to Hogwar

Samantha

Professor Dumbledore,

I will never know how to eloquently put into words what you have taught me and what you continue to teach me, but I hope that this jumbled up letter might suffice.

I first read about you when I was in grade four, so I would have been around nine years old (two years away from possibly receiving my Hogwarts letter – I did get it eventually, don't worry about the delay). Back then, in my eyes, you were nothing more than the cool Headmaster with exceptional magical abilities. You were somebody that Harry looked up to and, by extension, somebody that I looked up to.

You help everyone and don't expect any sort of thanks or recognition whatsoever. You would let Harry do the stupidest things, then cover for him...I never used to understand why you did that, and I probably still don't entirely, but I have realized that it's because you love. You love your life and everyone in it and, for that, I commend you.

This all seemed to really hit me when I was about sixteen. What you said all those years ago came back to me in one of my darkest of times. I had fallen victim to petty little things that, had I not caught them in time, would have been my undoing. You got through to me. Sometimes, when I would do things, I would stop and ask myself whether or not you would approve of me. Sometimes it was a definite "no" and I would immediately try to right my wrongs and strive to be like you – a loving, caring, and intelligent individual. I still do that today and I think I will forever. In asking myself that one question, I found that I could change and have changed and I now feel that you wouldn't mind me so much. I still have a lot of learning to do, but I don't feel as though I'm being disloyal anymore – to you or to myself.

There isn't a day that goes by where I don't think of something you've said or something you've done. I take a moment, smile, and thank you for being there – for me, for Harry, and for the rest of the world. In the end, I really just want to say thank you for everything. I didn't know back in grade four that you were going to have such an influence on me, but somehow I can't help but feel that it was always going to turn out like this.

You've been asleep for a few years now, but I know you'll wake up someday. You'll never be gone, not from Hogwarts and not from this world. You once said that you would only truly have left when none were loyal to you. You've never left, and you never will, because you will always be in our hearts and our minds.

See you when dawn arrives.

ALL MY LOVE,

– Samantha A., 18

Dear Sirius Black,

You came into my life when I was sixteen years old. I had more in common with you than with any other character I've ever known. Everything I can say about you I can say about myself. We have always been the proverbial lighthouse in a bog, brilliant but seemingly useless. Great things were always expected of us and, to some extent, we usually failed. On our worst days, we can be downright worthless and despondent. Our double standards know no bounds and we actually have the nerve to defend them. We really could have had it all, but we're just too riddled with character flaws. Despite all the bad things, I saw myself through you in ways I'd never imagined and you can't know how much it helped me.

Everything good that can be said about you can be said about me. Because of you, I can see that just because I failed in some ways doesn't mean that I'm garbage. We simply are who we are, how we are, and somebody loves us for it, even when we don't. On our best days, we know how to make the most out of anything and it uplifts those around us. We might have a "do as I say, not as I do" complex, but it's only because we want to protect the people we care about. We are not useless or worthless. Even when we can't do much, our best is, in fact, good enough. Nobody loves stronger or deeper than we do. Turned loose, we would give our all if it came down to it and, in your end, you did.

Your death hurt me a lot more than what was probably normal or healthy, and I was bitter about it for a good while. I can see now that it was a good thing, though. Something about having to accept the finality of your death made me adopt the philosophy that, if I'm upright and breathing, it's a good day. Your fictional life taught me a lot about the right and wrong ways to handle the situations thrown at people like you and me. I still don't always get it right, but maybe my downfalls will make me somebody else's Sirius Black. That's actually a pretty terrifying thought, but if I can do the kind of good in someone else's life that you've done in mine, maybe I'll be equally at peace when it's my time to go.

I'm a 23-year-old woman now. A lot has changed, but at least one very important thing has stayed the same, strange as it feels to admit. You are still one of the biggest influences on who I am as a person, even if no one else knows that. You sat me in front of a mirror and made me accept the good I saw in you as the good in me. I'm a better person because you went ahead of me and made a path for my life.

WITH ALL THE GRATITUDE IN MY HEART,

– Kassandra C.

P.S. It was August for me, but thank you for the wonderful Christmas at Number 12, Grimmauld Place. It's still the best one I've had since I was 14 years old.

Sara S., Gryffindor

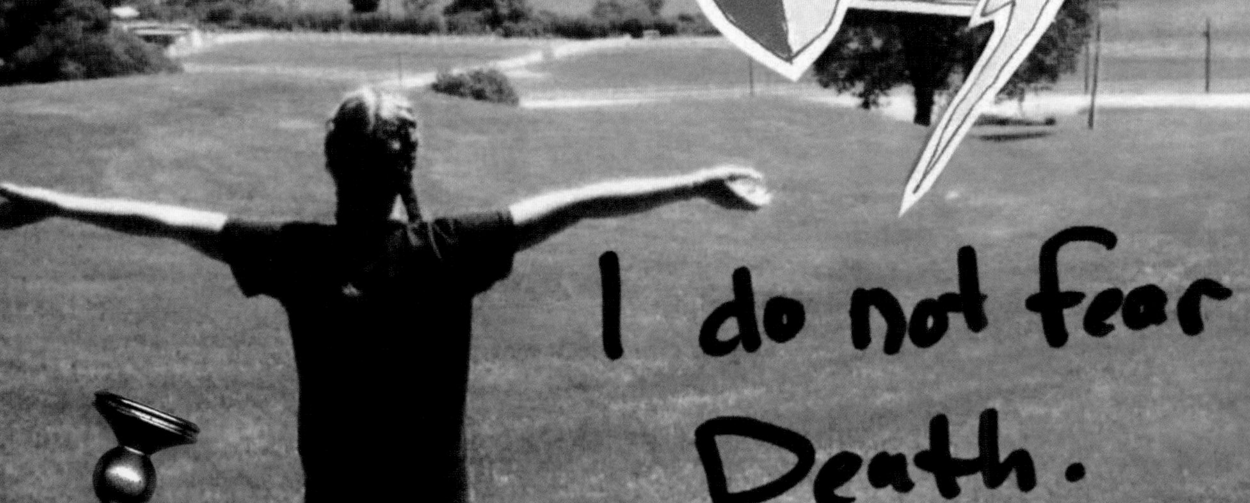
Because of you, Harry Potter,
I do not fear
Death.

Rebecca K, 19

So don't tell her that it's over. Don't tell her it isn't real. Because, if you do, she'll pick up her book, hit you with it, and say, 'This is Harry Potter. He has an impact.'
–Lauren D.

Elizabeth R., Louisiana, 18

Amy E.

Carolyne N.

Evanna Lynch

Dear Luna,

I've procrastinated writing this letter to you for a long time because I'm not sure I'd like you to know who I am. You see, writing to you is like coming to the end of a very long game of hide-and-seek (five and a half years, in fact) in which you are the seeker and I am the hider, and the moment you find me, the moment we meet face-to-face, is the moment I'll finally have to admit to myself that I am not you. I am a mere Muggle, and Luna, that is not an easy fact to face.

My name is Evanna Lynch. If you've ever come across it before, tightly interwoven with yours, it is because I act as you in an internationally renowned film series based on *Harry Potter*'s life at Hogwarts from the years 1995-1998, all the while pretending to be you. It is almost as bizarre to me as it must sound to you, but I can't put it any plainer. I put on the clothes one imagines you wore and I say the things one supposes you said and I do the things modern wizarding history tells us you did. Rather hilariously, I formed a career out of it. However, this letter is not to inform you of the strange and downright bonkers ways Muggles earn their living, but to tell you about the huge and inestimable influence you've had on me and on many thousands of other people of all ages and nationalities. I know you don't need to hear this and you're probably extremely busy working through your recent findings of authentic Heliopath tracks, which is ultimately a great deal more important than the aimless ramblings of one random Muggle girl. And of course I've always admired the way you remain so wholly untouched by other people's observations on you, whether negative or positive, and the way you float above all of that. But I think even you might be surprised and a little bit moved to realise how great an influence you've had on thousands of Muggles and how you've made our world a much brighter place.

On a personal level, I would be a very different person had I never encountered you. It's strange, because nowadays many people believe I am you, but a few years ago I was essentially the opposite of everything you are. I feel I should here explain a certain phase that many young people go through that you will have noticed but, incredibly, seem to have skipped. It's a certain dawning awareness that strikes you when the carelessness of childhood ebbs away and you realise how starkly odd and ill-fitting you are. It's that awkward sensation of not knowing what to do with your hands and feeling simply that you protrude too much. I know you will have felt it sometimes and can understand the excruciating paranoia that dogs young people, but somehow you never succumbed to it and never let it affect you too deeply. As for me, being young, I crumbled under the pressure and let it tell me that I was an incontestable freak. I tried to satiate it for a while with other people's assurances and, when I was about nine years, old I decided that all I needed was a best friend. I felt sure that the feeling of oddness would dissipate immediately when I found someone to hold me hand and say "I'm weird too, let's be weird together." But that didn't work out quite as smoothly as I had planned and I forgot how, at that age, friends weren't ready to make the commitment of lifelong partnership I sought, and that one's best-friend eligibility was based on the size of her My Little Pony collection and the number of Mini Jaffa Cakes contained in her lunchbox. Sorely lacking in both these areas, I soon discovered that people inevitably have a way of making you feel more peculiar than you already felt, and I gave up on the idea of a best friend.

Looking elsewhere, I noticed that people seemed to gain approval and admiration for being exceptionally talented at something, and decided that would be my chosen course of action. Seeing as I had no particular skills and my mother would not agree to give me up to the circus to become a trapeze artist, I joined a drama group and hoped

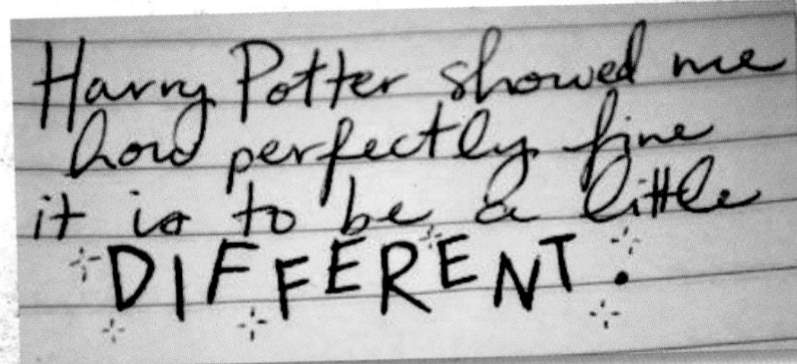
Harry Potter showed me
how perfectly fine
it is to be a little
DIFFERENT.

I could be exceptional at being somebody else. I truly enjoyed these classes and the time spent inhabiting other people's minds, and for a while they gave me some relief. But, of course, there was always someone better and brighter and I realised that drama was probably never going to be my "thing." By this stage in my quest to fit in somewhere, I was feeling despondent with my reliance on other people and I took a very different approach. It happened gradually and as a result of people commenting from time to time on how "small" I was, and the wonderful feeling of uniqueness it gave me. Unique, at the time, was a completely different thing to being "odd." I was small, but I decided I could be exceptionally small, and I began to decrease the amount of food I ate and increase the amount of energy expended. It seems crazy, doesn't it, seeing as being exceptionally small never particularly helped anyone, but for me it was a quick and sure way to find an identity. By this method, I knew I would always be the most exceptionally small out of everyone and, of course, if I wasn't, I could always keep going until I was so small that I was no longer there at all. It felt safe and secure because I was finally great at something and, what's more, people began to notice and worry about me because of it. It didn't matter to me because being "small" and "tiny" and "skinny" had become my identity and I was happy to finally have one. What I failed to recognise, however, was that the path I had taken was one of cowardice. By engaging in a monotonous and physically exhausting routine of food deprivation and exercise, I dulled the feelings of oddness but did not overcome them. I let the cacophonous voice in my head telling me to get smaller become so loud that I could easily ignore the small one telling me I was still odd. But I also dulled the passion for life and hopes for the future and let everything else that used to colour my personality fade away. I thought that I was being strong in my will never to succumb to hunger and physical ache, but in truth I was escaping from devoting my energy to more productive means like art and drama because I was afraid of discovering that I was not very good at them. I achieved nothing creative at all throughout these few painful years because I was too afraid of exposing my inadequacy to even try. Thinking on it now, I see no sense to it at all, but back then in my anxious, paranoid, and fearful eleven-year-old mind, I felt that if I was not the best at one single thing I would be nothing, just an odd and unremarkable young girl who had nothing to offer to the world. That prospect scared me and I became further obsessed with my quest to be extraordinarily small. Admittedly, I became a horrible person in the process. I no longer cared for anything but my incessant daily routine of diet and exercise and I stopped seeing friends at all. I remember one evening, while watching a *Lord of the Rings* film with a family member, she exasperatedly declared that I was just like the character of Gollum. Worse still, I remember looking at his tiny frame and the horrible way his bones protruded from his flesh and feeling slightly pleased that I resembled this level of emaciation. But I also felt a tiny bit sad because I could see other similarities in the way he, once a normal healthy hobbit (or whatever he was), had wasted away to a grey, hunched creature that schemed and shunned and betrayed his friends, lashing out furiously at anyone who threatened to take his "precious" away.

> *Dear Jo,*
> *Do you know how often*
> *I think about Harry Potter?*
> *All the time.*
> *—Bazlina R.*

Eventually this obsession became so great that I was committed to a hospital and put on a programme of "recovery". That's not to say I gave up my selfish struggle to keep shrinking. In fact, the more people tried to "cure" me, the more I resisted their efforts. I had become so heavily identified with my obsession that I was sure that there would be nothing left of me in its absence and I clung to it desperately. It was around this time that you came along. I had been a die-hard Harry Potter fan since I was eight years old because I loved his world and I loved him for being a normal boy trying to accomplish an extraordinary feat. Your world was so unlike ours, in my opinion, so much more fabulous than ours, and yet the same problems and issues ran through your lives. It was a weird and wonderful world to which I longed to belong. But, I suppose, until June 21, 2003 it was also another form of escape from the incessant inner criticism and feelings of guilt that followed me everywhere. As Harry Potter was the only other thing I was passionate about, the doctors gave consent for me to leave the hospital and collect the fifth *Harry Potter* book, *Harry Potter and the Order of the Phoenix,* from the local book shop.

I was so ecstatic to have the book and excited to begin reading it, but there was never any hint of your imminent arrival and the way you would change my life so drastically. Luna, you instantly captivated me. I didn't know why but there was something about you with your upside-down magazine, straggly blonde hair, and the honest, unabashed way you stared at people without blinking that fascinated and perplexed me at once. You laughed hysterically at one of Ron's quips and didn't stop to excuse yourself and feel ashamed when it became clear that everyone thought you strange. Throughout the book, I found myself waiting for your brief appearances and wanting to know more about you and why you were the way you were. You baffled me, not because you were odd (though indeed you were), but because you were...perfect. But it was a different kind of perfect to the perfectly thin, smiling magazine girls I simultaneously idolised and reviled. It was the way you carried your oddness like it was the most natural thing in the world. You didn't market your oddness as your defining feature the way some insecure teenagers do, in guise of confidence and security. And nor were you oblivious to the awkward and uncomfortable feelings your oddness provoked in others. When, unable to comprehend how you wore your oddness so honestly and unashamedly, your peers reverted to mockery and bullying, you recognised this as a reflection of their own deep-seated insecurity and calmly let them carry on, quite above your head. You weren't trying hard to present a certain aspect of yourself that would boldly identify you in the world. And that's when it occurred to me how bizarre and positively ridiculous it was to apply the word "weird" to describe you, when you represented the most natural and unpretentious state possible to be; you were yourself.

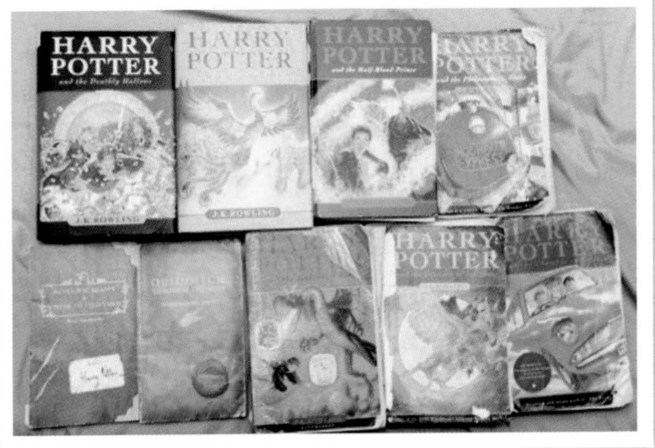

From that day on, I couldn't get you out of my head. Your ubiquitous presence disturbed me greatly. On the one hand, I loved you and felt total relief and joy at having found someone so full of light and love, someone who I knew wouldn't judge me, and someone who, by all appearances, was far more odd than I. At the same time, I couldn't help but feel madly jealous of you for being perfect and everything I was not. Where you were calm and dreamy and let life drift by, unconcerned about where it was taking you, everything about me screamed resistance and control. I began to hate the part of me that was so not you; the anti-Luna. I hated that Gollum-like version of me that surfaced to kick and scream when the nurses threatened to tube-feed me or that glowered back hatefully at the social workers who prescribed further bed rest. You frustrated me, too. For while I suffered and struggled bitterly, starving and depriving and hurting in my quest to be perfect, or even acceptable, all you had to do was sit there, totally wonderful. And though I still told myself I had to resist and tried to ignore the niggling doubts that you had planted in my head, I could not shake the feeling that you were there, sitting on the opposite bed, just calmly watching me with those huge, pale eyes, waiting for me to realise that is was time to change.

There was no sudden flicking on of the light switch or a definitive moment when I decided I was going to be more like you, but very slowly and gradually I let traits of yours filter in and soothe my more aggressive, confrontational ones. It took shape in very small decisions I made

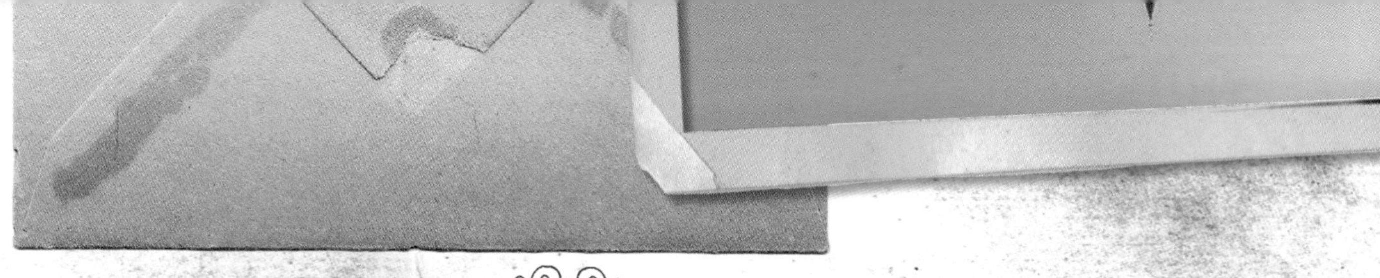

at first, like agreeing to eat that extra yoghurt without a fight or sitting and listening patiently to a well-meaning nurse offering positive words of encouragement without shouting back that they were meaningless. The recovery journey wasn't all upwards and, even with your influence, there were many setbacks. After leaving the hospital there was a period of relapse before I was once again committed to a specialist unit and was given no choice in recovery. The real test came when I returned home from this place and the task of recovering from recovery awaited me. I returned home declared physically "healthy", but determined that I would have to revert to my extraordinarily small state, because I knew no other way to be accepted. But this course of action was disrupted when I began to notice that people liked me more as I was. No longer exhausted and frail and angry with everyone who tried to interrupt my regime, people began to relate and talk to me and acknowledge me as a normal person, not a "sick person" who one needed to tread carefully around. And although it was always tempting to go back to that dark, lonely, secure place, and although there was was still that voice that whispered that I was too odd to risk just being "me", you were always there to remind me that it was okay to be odd, particularly if one did it with aplomb. Through you, Luna, I realised that being odd wasn't really odd at all.

Skip forward two years, and there I was queueing up at an audition in Westminister, London to play your role in the new *Harry Potter* installment. I know not many things perturb you, but I believe you would have found the sight totally bizarre. Hundreds and hundreds of young girls (and three boys, rumour has it) were lining the streets around Westminister, queueing for hours, in the hope of playing you in a movie. I know you're not a vengeful person and hold no grudge against the students who tormented you at Hogwarts, but at that moment, a part of me wished you could have known back then that 15,000 girls (allegedly, but I didn't count them...) would one day want to be you. That day I was nervous, but not very. Facing the chance of a life-changing audition and a chance to play as you in a film against my real-life heroes, I should have been fainting of nervousness...yet I was anything but. For, because of you, I'd never felt more ready for anything in my life. This wasn't an important maths exam that I hadn't studied for. This was the first time I had a chance to shine for being perfectly odd. The *Harry Potter* books, and you, were the only things I knew inside out and had grown up along with. And while I certainly didn't think the part was "in the bag", I knew I had as good a chance as the next girl, and that was why I turned up at all.

I didn't read about your life and I didn't watch your life, I lived through your adventures.
—AJB.

Somehow, miraculously, and in a hazy whirlwind of phone calls and plane flights and childhood heroes addressing me by name, I got the part. I moved to London and added the task of pretending to be you to my daily routine, something I still think on and find unbelievably, hilariously great. But here again, even having secured my childhood dream and being officially employed to pretend to be you, I still relied on you for support. People say you shouldn't meet your childhood heroes, but after this experience I have to say I disagree, and here is why. My heroes were every single actor in the *Harry Potter* film franchise. When I first met them I was rendered utterly speechless for several weeks (I probably shouldn't ever meet you and the gang for real, I would surely have a seizure...). I spent the first few weeks and months in a state of total awe and wonder and an acute terror of putting a foot wrong in their presence. It also gave way to that familiar feeling of inadequacy and a need to please. But this time, it was okay because I knew there was a reason I was there, and that reason was you. People expected me to be you, not some terribly witty, smart, hipster kid that I imagined actors should be. And after a while, over the course of several years and films, I relaxed into my role as a *Harry Potter* cast member and now I feel I belong there. Meeting all these actors and producers was terrifying at first but now, having gotten to know them a little bit, and being considered one of them, I now realise that albeit being

Jessie G., 18

Jessica L., 15, Ravenclaw

brilliant and talented, they are normal and perfectly odd people, too. Meeting them ultimately lowered all the barriers I'd built between me and my dreams and made me realise that, with hard work and dedication, I could be just as capable of accomplishing things my heroes have done, and similarly as other *Harry Potter* fans are easily capable of doing what I've done. There are still moments along this crazy journey where I feel inadequate and out of place. When I'm checked into some five star hotel and stand there amid the gilded mirrors and voice-powered-everything, feeling a little too shabby and Irish, I just remind myself that I'm there because I played you, not because I'm expected to be some glossy-haired, high-heeled celebrity. When we're promoting a film and I step out of a car to lots of screaming *Harry Potter* fans and there's that little voice saying "What are they looking at? You're just a fan too..." I remind myself again it's because I'm the closest thing to a physical representation of you, and they like me for that, nothing more, nothing less.

The films have come to an end now and I'm trying to figure out what to do next. It's been almost a year that I've been apart from your character and it has been a real learning experience. Often, over the course of this year, I've felt lost and confused because there's no one telling me what to do next. In a sense, Luna, you prolonged my childhood by several years by giving me someone to hide behind, someone to lean on, someone to excuse my eccentricities. And now you've left me, feeling a little bit shaky and unsteady but also excited and inspired to find out what comes next. I'm not sure why I've told you ALL this and I'm sorry for going on a fair bit. But at the end of this, all I really want to say is: Thank you for bringing me to this place where I finally feel I can fit in for standing out.

I also want to thank you on behalf of many fans, though perhaps they've written their own letters to you. You really have inspired so many young people to be themselves. I went on Twitter today (a website, a social network, an electronic world that exists in the Muggle world. Actually, don't ask...) to be told "Luna Lovegood is trending." After asking what in the world "trending" meant I was told repeatedly by lots of proud Luna fans "It means that we all love Luna!!". And when I casually suggested we make Lovegoodism a world religion, I found dozens of people already pledging to wear ceremonial yellow robes and erect statues of worship to the Crumple-Horned Snorkack. I also tend to get a lot of letters from people who feel they are social outcasts, eccentrics, and outsiders thanking me for portraying you and making them realise it's cool to be considered odd. They're beautiful, creative, inspiring letters and I am so grateful to get them, but I often wish there was a way of passing them on to you just so you could know. I don't know if you'll read this letter, or that it will get to you across our two worlds, but I hope that on some level, somewhere in your soul, you know there runs a parallel world where you are admired and adored and we truly believe in the Crumple-Horned Snorkack.

With lots of love and continuing awe, your friend,

– Evanna Lynch

P.S. I am enclosing the bright purple jumpsuit I wore throughout the Malfoy Manor cellar scenes of Deathly Hallows: Part I. *Nostalgia aside, I am quite sure I won't miss it. I look on it as a tribute to how much you mean to me that I endured wearing it for several weeks, but I have a feeling that you may actually love it.*

Melissa Anelli

Dear Mr. Potter,

I usually avoid talking to you as though you are a physical person. I'm what people sometimes call a "professional fan," which means my extracurricular life as a devotee has become my full-time vocation. It's a bizarre and oftentimes contradictory calling. There aren't that many like us out there, but let me tell you, as a grown woman I have enough perception battles to fight without everyone in the known world thinking I whisper you my secrets the same way I did to Pudgie the Stuffed Pig in 1984.

My journey with you began in 2000, but truly took off in September of 2001. I had just graduated college and exited the idealistic academic bubble to find life back in New York City was not what it was before we met. My grand expectations of my journalistic career outside college were slowly being reduced to wishes and hopes.

The world had changed. Terror had become more than a faraway spectre: death and blood mixed with ash and cement on the downtown streets of my home.

Yet, as I have on all difficult days for the decade since, I turned to the community that you will never know: the incredible fans. Through their patience, attention and compassion, they made sure that on that day, and every day since, when the world became too real, at least one of my feet was planted firmly in fantasy.

In over a decade we have raised more than a quarter of a million dollars for charity in your name. We have explored and pushed the boundaries of the once-marginalized "fan" label. We have rebranded ourselves as more than passingly passionate, but committed to each other and the world around us. We have sung and celebrated and drawn and danced and partied and blogged and vlogged and talked and listened and written... and we have read. Boy, have we read.

It's not enough to count our achievements, to say that because of you I got a job as a reporter or became a bestselling author. I can't leave it at telling you about the charity work I've gotten to do, the lives I've been able to help save because of you. It doesn't feel like enough enough to say that the people whose hearts have aligned with yours have had their lives fulfilled because of you. Perhaps there are no words to truly encapsulate what it has meant, to be part of a community bigger and more powerful and with more capacity to do good than any one of us, real or fictional.

You may not know me personally but you've been by my side nearly every moment since that fateful New York Tuesday my story began. It is probably time to do away with the formalities.

So, Harry, what can I say? Let's start with this: Thank you, my dear friend. Don't be a stranger.

LOVE,

– *Melissa Anelli*

Carolina

Dear Mr. Potter,

Sometimes the most unexpected things teach you the most valuable lessons in life. It's November 19, 2010, the day *Harry Potter and the Deathly Hallows: Part 1* is released. Today I lost part of myself. Or maybe I found a part that had been missing for almost 11 years. Today I learned that anything is possible with a little magic and love.

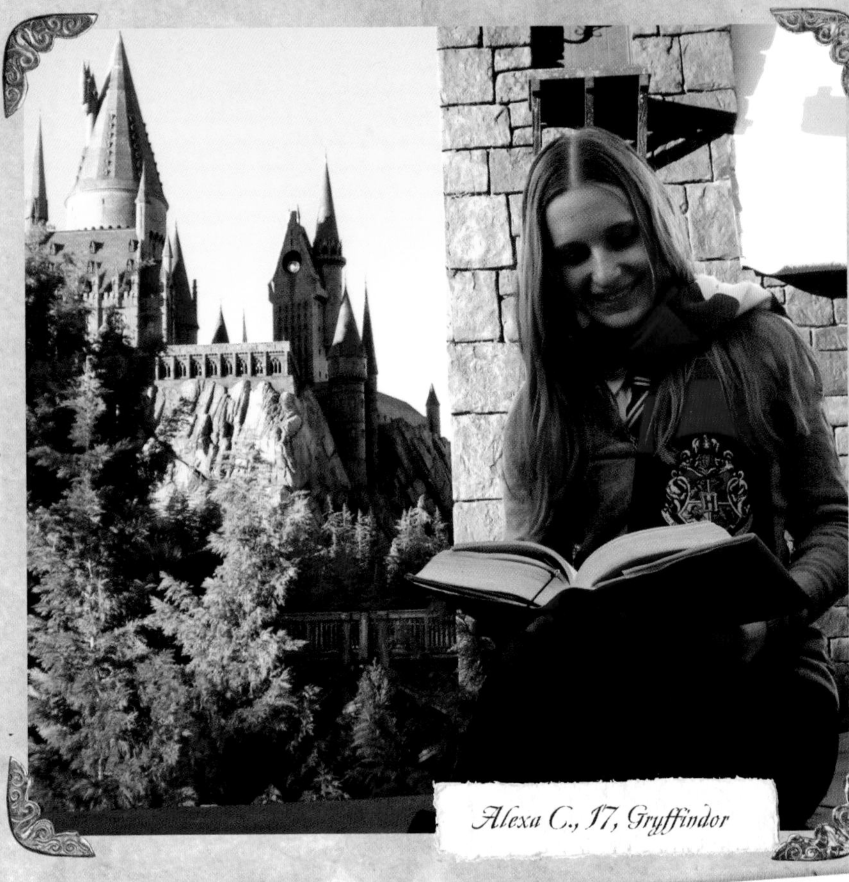

Alexa C., 17, Gryffindor

It's so strange to remember how long ago I embarked on this journey. It feels like yesterday, like I could go back in the blink of an eye and relive the experiences of my childhood. Turn the time turner just a few times and I'd be there, as a wide-eyed little girl of seven sitting in a dark theatre, scared to death of a troll on screen. But what she really had to worry about was time itself. That time could conjure up so many things. That one day she'd wish to go back to that precise moment when she first discovered Harry.

Today, I'm in the same theatre, maybe even the same room. I saw the beginning of the end–the end of the story that started 10 years ago. I grew up in this movie; I cherish these books. And now I'm here. I'm almost at the end. And I loathe it. I despise time, and the distance it put between Harry and I. But what time made me realize is I'm still that same little girl that sat in the theatre so long ago. I still have her in my heart. I will always have this part of my childhood with me. And that boy, he will always live in my heart as well. I can't count the times he changed my life, but I know he did.

Who I am today is in part because of who I was yesterday, and what Harry's story taught me. I don't want it to end. I really don't, but I know it has to. I'll always be able to remind myself of the many reasons why I fell in love with the series that changed my life. Those around me do not realize it. Most people will never grasp or understand how Harry has changed me, and that's okay. I wouldn't have it any other way. This is my own little secret.

I'M A WIZARD IN A WORLD OF MUGGLES.

– Carolina, 16

Carolyn G., Gryffindor

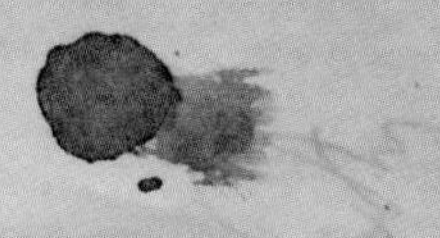

Dear Mr. Potter,

I was in fourth grade at a Catholic school when I was assigned "Harry Potter + the Sorcerer's Stone" for my reading class. Because of that, my life was changed, and shaped, by your story. I waited for my own Hogwarts letter to arrive my 11th year. 10 years later, I'm still waiting. I ended up making my own + pretending that I really was going to Hogwarts, even though I knew a spell would never flow from the tip of the wand I held.

I could go on + on about the impact you've had on my life. But I won't because I know you know how it feels. You know how it feels to find those friends who change your life + make it even more worth living. I found those friends in you, Ron, Hermione, + just about everyone else who played a part in your story. Since first cracking the spine on Book 1, I've found those friends in "real" life as well.

As a kid, I talked about you with my friends, + we discussed what your future might hold for you. At my current age, I still discuss you with my friends— but now we know your fate. Now, it is our own futures that we worry about—final seminar papers + what we're actually going to do with the degrees we are earning. As you grew, so, too, did we. As your problems got more + more complicated, so, too, did ours. We all—you + us—grew up together.

And I feel so lucky... so lucky to have been a part of the Harry Potter Generation: the generation who didn't know where the horcruxes were or what side Snape was really on or whether or not you would make it out alive. The waiting was agonizing, but it heightened the whole experience. It is one that will stay with me forever.

You were my childhood, Harry. I truly believe that I became an imaginative, creative person because of you—one who is capable of making her own magic. The final film installment of your story will be released the summer before my final semester of college. How perfect a way to close one chapter of my life as a new one begins—life as a grown up, the next great adventure. But thanks to you, I will always be able to pick up one of your books + be transported back to that time when I had unruly hair like Hermione + found a childlike wonder, enchantment, + hope in your pages. Those innocent, extraordinary memories will always be just a bookshelf away... always.

With much love + gratitude,

Nicole G., 21, Gryffindor

Nadia R., 20, California

*Harry Potter, you taught me how to use the brooms the **right** way. – Mel R., 18*

Dear Hedwig
Sweet, sweet owl
More than a pet for sure
The best companion to ever be
Caged and afraid no more
Now you fly free.

HERE LIES DOBBY
A FREE ELF
WHO DIED A HERO'S DEATH
FOR HE SACRIFICED HIMSELF

Sirius the Black
Padfoot the Dog
Some think you a baboon
Or an annoying goon
I think you left us way too soon.

To those who choose to bury
Severus
May he rest in peace
He remained always true
Still, I'd like to believe
He resides, happy and tanned, in Greece.

Goodbye Fred
Half of a (w)hole
An ingenious and humorous soul
He would not have wanted
Anyone to mourn —
But we do.

Albus Dumbledore
Eccentric coot
A wise, old hoot
Ambitious, dreaming
Sometimes manipulative and scheming
Yet I speak for all when I say
We love him dearly, anyway.

Farewell Remus (Mr Moony)
Shadowed by lycanthropy
Greatly misunderstood
Wanted so much to be a good man
I know you would if you could.

RIP Tonks
Her vibrancy and cheer
Diminished not by death
She had no fear.

For those unnamed
Do not be appalled
You are not forgotten
Not at all

We salute your loyalty
Your bravery, your fight
Your dedication to what
You believed was right.

PEOPLE DIE STORIES END BUT WE WILL REVISIT THEIR TALE
AND KEEP THEM IN OUR HEARTS AS FAITHFUL FRIENDS
WHO TAUGHT US TO DREAM AND PREVAIL
FOREVER AND AGAIN.

Grace T.

Patty D., Gryffindor

I think that I love Harry, Ron, and Hermione so much because I know that no matter what, they'll always be there, even if nobody else is. –Alex S.

Carolyne N.

Claudia

Dear Mr. Potter,

Had you not come into my life, with your glasses askew and hair untamed, I would not be the person I am today. Claudia the writer, the dreamer, the Ravenclaw, would not exist as she does. For one story to change and mold me like that is an astounding feat, but yours has accomplished it with flying colors.

I suppose we had a rough start. My six year old self was too scared to watch your first movie in theaters, so I opted instead for some frilly cartoon feature. A few months later, when my mother brought your first year home in VHS form, I kicked and screamed before watching it, insisting that I'd have nightmares. Eventually, I met her halfway and agreed to watch the movie in exchange for ice cream. So there I sat, in sickeningly pink pajamas and a scowl worthy of Draco Malfoy on my face. It was not even five minutes into the movie that the scowl faded and I fell in love with your tale.

And that was what started it, those hundred-some minutes in my living room. Not yet old enough to trek through a chapter book, I still picked up that copy of *Harry Potter and the Sorcerer's Stone* and read for days. "That's beyond your reading level," the librarian would say. I nodded and continued to read, too enveloped in the Wizarding World to care. When I finally finished it, I was proud of myself, but hungry for more.

The day I bought *Harry Potter and the Chamber of Secrets* is still fresh in my mind, though I was just seven. I held it in my hands with an unrelenting grip, careful not to let anything at all harm that precious object. Extending my arms to the cashier's counter, I was too short to reach it easily but tall enough to see her muttering things along the lines of "evil book," and "satanic." It crushed me how people could think that such a wonderful tale could be evil.

But that didn't stop me. Nothing did. Your story was like opening up a treasure chest of emotions. I would sob, laugh, grin, and scowl when appropriate. I'd chant during the Quidditch games and pull the covers up a bit higher when Dementors made an appearance. Though often I'd read late into the night, I never felt more awake than while reading your story.

That was the way it was for years, through all the new books and new movies.

And so here I am today, sixteen years old and more a fan than ever. I've devoured every book and inhaled every movie about you. Every minute invested in that has been well worth it.

It's been a decade. Can you believe it? I can't say as much. In my decade-and-a-half life, a decade seems like forever. Though that proportion will soon change, forever will always apply, because forever is composed of nows and you, Mr. Potter, are always a part of mine.

It is because of you, Mr. Potter, that I have any ounce of courage. It is because of Hermione that I strive to learn something everyday, and because of Ron that I try to work humor into most everything. All those who have accompanied you in your journey have instilled something in me, and I would have it no other way.

Because of your story and the eloquent manner in which it is told,

I am inspired every day to pursue my dream of writing. One day, when I finally publish a book— and that day will come, I'm sure of it— it will all be because of you.

At the time of this writing, it has been over three years since the final book in your tale was released. Though that chapter has closed, and this first era quickly approaches its end, I hope you are aware that your influence on all us self-proclaimed Potterheads still lives on, and it will for time through come.

Through your story, I've become a better person; I've regained my faith in the world; I have regained my faith in myself. The morals evident in all seven installments of your tale have been instilled in me. Often, I ask myself, *"What would Harry do?"* Through your story, I have found happiness in the darkest of times. It is you, Mr. Potter, and your friends that remind me to turn on the light, as Professor Dumbledore so beautifully put it. Through your story, I have become who I am today, made the memories that I now call my yesterday, and have made friends, fictional and otherwise, that I will cherish for every single tomorrow.

And that is just a drop in the bucket, to be honest.

To the outsider looking in, I am a little girl lost in a fantasy world. And that may very well be what I am, but your story has impacted my life in a manner that words will never sufficiently express. Your story is compromised not of meaningless words on paper, nor of tedious plots. No. Your story is far more than that; it is something all of us can believe in.

I hope you know, Mr. Potter, that you and your friends have made me who I am today. For these reasons and all those in between, I thank you.

UNTIL THE VERY END,.

– Claudia M., 16

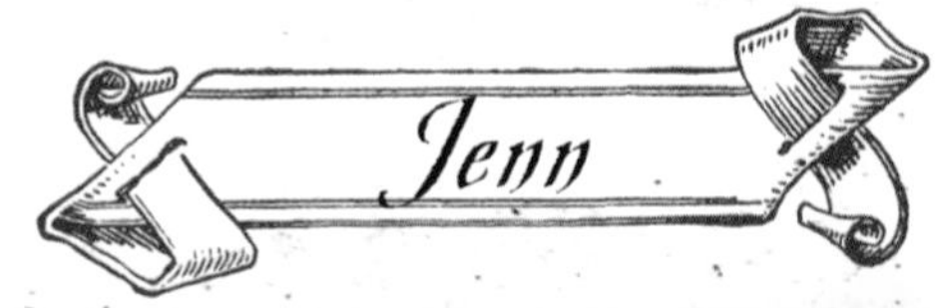

Jenn

Megan B., 17

Dear Mr. Potter,

I've read many letters written to you, full of thanks and admiration, each one heartfelt and inspiring in their own way. I'd like to add my own, if I may. I can't say you changed my childhood, as I was an adult when I made my first journey beside Harry, and I can't say you've inspired me to greatness, as I live a very quiet, unassuming life. But, among all the appreciation, there's one thank you that I believe still remains unsaid.

Thank you for changing the publishing world for the better. *Harry Potter* has changed both young adult and fantasy literature in a way I never thought possible. When I was a kid, most children my age had never heard of Narnia or Middle Earth and the only time most of my peers picked up a book was when it was required reading. Since *Harry Potter*, shelves are now lined with rows of fantasy novels and both adults and children are reading, not because they are told they must, but for the joy of it.

You've opened the door to so many other literary worlds, inspiring the reader (and often the writer) in all of us. You've achieved what so many parents have failed to do, despite years of trying.

In a day where teachers struggle to improve the literacy of our youth, you've made it popular to read.

WITH MY DEEPEST GRATITUDE,

–Jenn Y., 27, Ravenclaw

Kiersten F., 16, Florida

Kathryn

Dear Mr. Potter,

Thank you for your wisdom, support, kindness, love, friendship and hope. I can not adequately articulate how much you mean to me. So once again, thank you for everything you have taught me, everything you continue to teach me, and everything I have yet to learn from you.

LOVE ALWAYS,

– Kathryn S., 18, Gryffindor

Amy

Dear Mr. Potter,

We've been through a lot together. It feels like I've known you forever and, in some respects, you've known me for my entire life.

Our relationship began when I was just a child. I grew up in rural suburbia, much like you did. I don't remember exactly how your story was put into my hands, but I suspect it was one of my cousins - my family is full of voracious readers. From the instant I read the first page of the first chapter, I was hooked. You became the best friend I had been lacking, having just moved to a new state that was completely different from my birthplace. When you got your Hogwarts letter, I shivered in the anticipation of receiving my own letter when I reached age eleven. When you met Ron and Hermione on the train, I imagined myself sitting there with you, eating Chocolate Frogs, getting Bertie Bott's Every Flavor Beans in flavors like vomit, and laughing until we cried.

After you defeated Professor Quirrell and went back to the Dursley's for the summer, I quickly devoured your next three years at school. As the gap in our ages increased, you became a substitute for the older sibling figure that I never had, being the eldest of two. You told me everything you were feeling, and I returned the sentiments. I would read under my desk in elementary school and talk to myself under my breath. The other kids laughed at me but, in my mind, I was talking to you, Harry.

It was round the third or fourth grade that the teasing began. I was called "bookworm" and "teacher's pet" because I was a good student (much like Hermione). Occasionally, the kids got meaner and called me "fat" or "ugly." My self-image, which up until that point had been relatively good, shattered. While the other girls in my class wore tighter, popular brand-name clothes, mine got baggier and more nondescript. Remind you of another eleven-year-old you once knew?

When the fifth book came out, I was ecstatic—surely you would know exactly what to do, having gone through the same ridicule in years past. I began reading immediately—but, to my dismay, Hogwarts was not the same safe, magical home it had been in years previous. There was a darkness in the air, brought by a combination of the destructive forces of that toad Umbridge and your own emotional battles. No one believed you about Voldemort- but I did, Harry. I knew.

And then Cho Chang came along. I want to say that I was above being jealous, but I wasn't. Though I'm sure she never meant to hurt you like she did, in my eyes she was my brother's evil girlfriend. She stole your attention away from what was important, and clouded your judgment. Looking back, I was much too young to fully understand the complexity of the emotions you were feeling as a boy in your mid-teens, as I was still just a child. Your stories had always been my escape from a harsh reality, but now it seemed as if they were beginning to parallel it. In my emotional state, it wasn't something I was able to handle at the time.

So, for the first time, halfway through your fifth year at Hogwarts, I stopped reading. The book sat on my bedroom floor, desolate and lonely, for I don't know how long. Years passed - my middle school years were some of the hardest on me, mentally and emotionally. The teasing I had received in elementary school became full-out bullying and I came home from school many times with my eyes red from crying. I needed someone who had seen it all—fights, teasing, stares—to show me it was going to be okay. I needed you then more than ever.

I still ignored you, leaving you locked in your fifteen-year-old self on a shelf in my bedroom with a bookmark that had begun to go yellow with age. But this all was my fault, Harry—not yours. Don't blame yourself for my mistakes, like you often blame

yourself for everything else. If I know one thing about you, it's that you are incredibly self-sacrificing and self-detrimental (among many other, wonderful things).

I finally came back after the sixth book was released. Even then, though, I was not ready to immerse myself in your world as fully as I once had. I kept myself distant as I read through the battle in the Department of Mysteries, but broke down when Sirius died. We both lost a godfather that day.

When I finished *Order of the Phoenix*, I didn't rush to begin *Half-Blood Prince*. I was beginning high school and my attention was focused elsewhere. I had recently lost several important people in my life and I was not ready to deal with Sirius' loss with you yet. For my cowardice, I'm sorry.

It was not until a few years ago that I finally felt ready to go adventuring with you once more. I had made a new friend who was completely different from me (yet eerily similar), who had encouraged me to make peace with you. He had fought his own demons with you as well, and it made me wonder just how much you'd done since I'd been away. I went home and picked you off my shelf. After the first five chapters, I had already started to cry. We dealt with the loss of Sirius together, and you were my brother once more.

When I met my friend the next day, he saw my face and gave me a big hug. Having spent most of the night before with you at Hogwarts, I quickly realized that this friend was both my Hermione and my Ron. He was even a ginger! For the rest of that summer, he was my liaison between your world and mine—someone who had gone through exactly what I had and was willing to talk, laugh, and cry about it with me.

When I reached *Deathly Hallows* and read through the final, fateful battle at Hogwarts, I cried. So many of the friends that had been both yours and mine were dead, and nothing could be done about it. But when you left to allow yourself to be killed, I had all the faith in the world that this could not—would not—be the end. When you finally defeated Voldemort, I celebrated with the rest of the wizarding world. When you snuck away for some peace of quiet, I was by your side, ready to offer comfort and support, as you had done and continue to do for me.

In the epilogue, I became an aunt to three beautiful children—four, if you include Teddy. When I watched you and Ginny send them off to Hogwarts, I was full to the brim with pride. Nothing in my life has ever felt so real.

Harry, you played so many important roles in my life—friend, brother, protector, partner-in-crime, role model, teacher, comfort, companion. The list goes on. And even though I knew that I was sharing you with millions of other kids across the globe, you still made me feel like what we had was special. You taught me how to grow into my own skin, how to be brave in the face of danger, and how to stand up for what is right.

The era of your story might be coming to a close, but it is a great relief to me to know that our relationship will not end so soon. I have the comfort of reliving your adventures whenever I need them. I will get just as excited now as I did when I was a child. I like to think of our time together as time well spent, and I hope my children will one day accept you and your world into their lives as well.

This is really only the beginning for us, *Harry Potter*. Thank you for every smile, every spell, and every tear.

UNTIL NEXT TIME,

—Amy S., 16

I had been looking at the last *Harry Potter* book as a gate closing on my childhood. I was seeing *Harry Potter* as many do: a children's book about a funny little made up school for wizards. But that's not what it is at all. Harry's story is about magic, and not just the magic of wand waving and potions. It's about the magic of friendship and the magic of loyalty. It's about finding a place to belong in the world and finding something that makes you happy. It's about losing people you love and knowing that they're not gone forever. It's about standing up for what is right. But, most importantly, *Harry Potter* is about the magic of love. The love of a parent, more powerful than any other force on earth. The love that holds friends together. Love that binds, love that strengthens, love that protects. *Harry Potter* taught me more about love than any other book I have ever read. No mere children's book could accomplish that.

—RACHEL K.

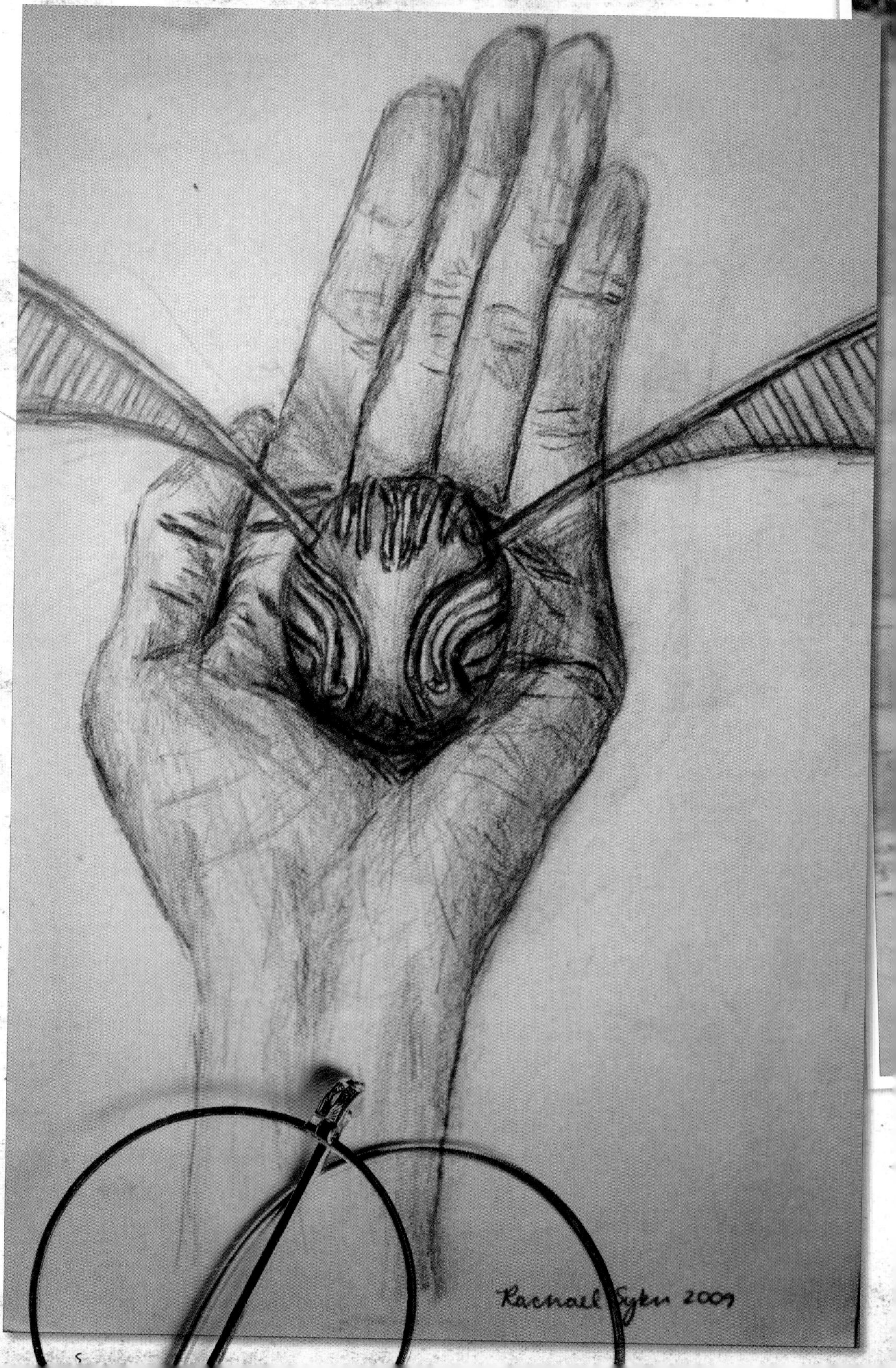

Rachael Sykes 2009

Karima Y., 21, Indonesia

Jacqueline L.

Catherine H., 16

Dear Mr. Potter,

Like many, I have grown up with you. I got your very first story for Christmas when I was 7 years old from the best grandmother in the world. My mum read me *Philosopher's Stone* and then immediately after, *Chamber of Secrets*. I was in love. I couldn't believe I would have to wait to read *Prisoner of Azkaban*. My beloved grandmother bought me every book in the series the day that it came out, and I can never thank her enough for introducing me to your magical universe.

Before the release of *Deathly Hallows*, Nannie was diagnosed with lung cancer. I was heartbroken and even the excitement of the release of the final installment couldn't ease the pain. I had been visiting my Nannie in the hospital almost every day and when I mentioned to her that the last book was coming out, she immediately demanded her purse, took out forty dollars, handed it to me and said, "I don't want to see you in here again until you've read that whole book." And so it was. I read the words of your final story, and boy, was it cathartic. Experiencing your losses with you prepared me in some ways for Nannie's death. A month or so after the book release, Nannie passed away. But before she did, she told me that she was very glad that she was able to buy me the last book. Now every time I flip through the pages of your story, I think of her and I am comforted.

THANK YOU, MR. POTTER.

Sincerely,

– *Kayleigh, 20*

I think Holden Caulfield said it best:

"What really knocks me out is a book, when you're all done reading it, you wished the author that wrote it was a terrific friend of yours and you could call them up on the phone whenever you felt like it." (–J.D. Salinger)

You've done some of the coolest and best things ever with literacy, with creativity and with imagination, Ms. Rowling. Though I may never actually know you, I will always have Harry, and for that I am forever grateful.

THANKS – *Rebecca K., 19*

Dear Mr. Potter,

I grew up with you. I was nine years old and in fourth grade when the first book came out and I first read of you, the boy who lived. When the next two books were released, they were immediately bought and devoured.

When I was in fifth grade, my dad was diagnosed with Non-Hodgkin's Lymphoma. The release date of the fourth book coincided with the day that my dad was put in the Intensive Care Unit of the hospital after a year of fighting a losing battle. I remember my brother and I went to Barnes and Noble and I picked up the book and the book on tape. I would read and my dad would listen or sometimes we'd both listen to your adventures in the Triwizard Tournament. I cried over Cedric and I cried for you, the boy who lived and knew loss. My dad passed a month later. And I was the girl who lived and knew loss.

Harry, I love the books. Not just because each one separately, and the series as a whole, is a beautiful manifestation of the Hero's journey. Not just because they are smartly written. Not just because of the dynamic characters. But because I identified with you, Harry. Together we took on the world and faced adventure despite loss. Your courage made me stronger and helped me find solace in friends and in books. Your books showed me that, while we may lose loved ones, we are not without family. You taught me that anger is normal, though it eats at the soul, and that love is the only salvation.

Harry, you were the symbol of hope, not only to the wizarding world, but to a little girl who found in you the power to overcome grief. Thank you for giving me childhood when the events in my life hastened maturity. Thank you for making growing up an adventure instead of a tragedy.

LOVE YOU ALWAYS,

– Christie F., 20, California

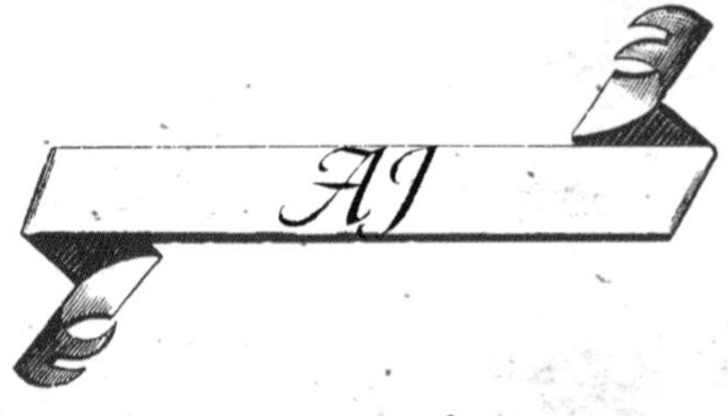

Lauren W., 21, Hufflepuff

I read your stories at the age of six and I can't recall much before that. My big sister was eleven at the time and I wanted to be just like her. She began reading the books and I did as well. Little did I know that my want to conform quickly changed to my need to be different. I went through life not being afraid to do my own thing. I was the child with the amazing imagination. I was the child with such potential. I was the nerd at all times. I was also the one whose *Harry Potter* books taken away in first grade because I read them during math and art. I was okay with it, though, because I learned to always bring another book with you for an incident like this. I grew up with you.

At a young age, I learned the importance of individuality. I began expanding my reading while waiting for the next book. I skipped the children's books and continued to read "big kid's books." While most kids wanted to be a firefighter or police officer, I just wanted to be an author. I still do. My love for reading and writing has become a passion to teach others. I want to be a teacher of English literature and an author. I want to impact the lives of children (and even adults) the same way you impacted mine.

You taught me that it is okay to stand up for what you believe in and to go against the grain. Your good friends taught me that it is okay to be a bookworm and a nerd and that people are often underestimated. I didn't read about your life and I didn't watch your life, I lived through your adventures. I was there with you when you fought the Basilisk. I helped you through the Triwizard Tournament. I pulled pranks with Fred and George. I studied in the library with Hermione. Ron and I pigged out at every feast. I was on the field playing Quidditch. I beat Slytherin in everything. I made enemies in Hogwarts. I mourned over the loss of Sirius, Dumbledore, Fred, and all lives conquered by Voldemort. I helped defeat Voldemort (I even spoke his name). I fought with the D.A. and much more.

With each new book, I went to the midnight release and read the book that night. Your stories inspired me to strive for the best. I was often bullied because I read so much. Classmates would make fun of me because I stayed with you from the very beginning to the end. I am still with you. I will not bore you with my childhood troubles, because they were bearable. I finished the last book within days of getting it. I reread it for the second time on vacation. It was 1:37 in the morning when I finished it for the third time in the hotel room. I remember the time because I stared at that clock, realizing that it was the end. My adventures with you may have been over, but it's time I find others to share adventures with.

It was sad to see you come to an end, but it was time to move forward. No one will ever compare to you. You were there for me when I needed to escape from the world, but now I need to face reality. I am ready. You taught me so much and I will take your lessons and learn more. I face the world with confidence. Because of you, I would do anything for my friends. They often comment on how I am "the best friend," but I hate taking the credit. It was you, Ron, and Hermione that taught me how to be loyal.

I don't know where I would be without you. I don't know who would be my friends. The pain I have dealt with, the bullying, and the shunning might not have happened if I hadn't met you. However, I wouldn't change it for the world. I love the friends I made through you. I love the adventures I went through with you. I love the countless nights of staying up late and discussing, "What Harry's going to do next?" or "What do you think is going to happen?". You changed my life for the better.

I could tell you so much more, but there's not enough time in the world. To sum it all up, I leave you with just this: thank you.

YOUR FAN FOREVER,

–AJ B., 16

"It does not do to dwell on dreams and forget to live"

Sophie M.

When I realized that the people Harry loved – who I loved – were merely people in his life who he had opened his heart to, I realized I could do the same. I could open my heart and love. –Alixandra B.

Sarah-Jane R., 15, Slytherin

Caroline, 13

Shrima

Dear Mr. Potter,

I regret to inform you that although I had been accepted into Hogwarts School of Witchcraft and Wizardry, I had initially declined. This isn't to say that the story of the boy wizard who defied all odds sparked no interest in me. In fact, I remember sitting outside my second grade classroom, scribbling the assignment everyone else had already finished. I recall having to rewrite everything because my tears had dampened my hasty work. My friends were inside, munching on buttered popcorn and avidly watching a half-giant burst through a door. I felt alone and unsuccessful, as if only the elite were rewarded with *Harry Potter and the Sorcerer's Stone.*

As the year of multiplication tables and Judy Blume progressed, so did Harry's story. But when I received my end of the year report card, the pages stopped turning. Third grade brought new books and new adventures and the wizarding world was forgotten.

As years passed, the story of the boy who lived plagued my generation. Every new movie topped the one before it and midnight sales skyrocketed. Surprisingly, none of my closest friends seemed to express interest. Yet, with every new plot point and movie trailer, I found myself inching closer to Platform 9 and ¾. Before I knew it, I had read books one through seven multiple times and often found myself wondering what took me so long. As children, we think words are nothing more than what they claim to be, but I know now that there's more to them than meets the eye. I came to befriend a coalition of like-minded people, whose values stemmed from those magical books. Fantasy taught me a lot about reality because, let's face it, books are far easier to understand than life. I realize now that it is Harry's journey which got me so involved in my own.

– Shrima P., Ravenclaw

Lydia

Dear Mr. Potter,

Were it not for my little brother, I don't think I would have found you. While I was busy trying to cope with the drastic but necessary changes that come with growing up, my little brother was carrying you around wherever he went, his nose often buried in your stories of courage.

Then, one day, when life was going according to plan and I was busy making more plans, I lost my brother. He never woke up that Sunday morning, and on his bedside was the story of how you formed Dumbledore's Army and faced the devastating loss of your own beloved Sirius Black.

In hopes of finding my brother within those pages, in hopes of finding whatever it was that he loved about you, I read your story all the way back to the beginning. And now I understand what he must have found, and I hope everyday that more than anything else he found love, and a triumph over death. For this hope, Mr. Potter, I will be eternally grateful.

BEST REGARDS,

– Lydia B., Gryffindor

Ida V., 18, Ravenclaw, Norway

Ryan

Dear Mr. Potter,

I first found out about you when I was six years old. My earliest memory is of sobbing at the movie theatre, because *Harry Potter and the Philosopher's Stone* was the most frightening thing I had ever seen. Despite that, I was inspired. I picked up the first book and started reading. At that age, I couldn't appreciate your world as well as I would have liked, so I stopped and didn't start again until three years later. At the time, only the first five books were released, but I read them over and over. I could relate to you so much: not really fitting in, having people who you thought were your friends turn on you.

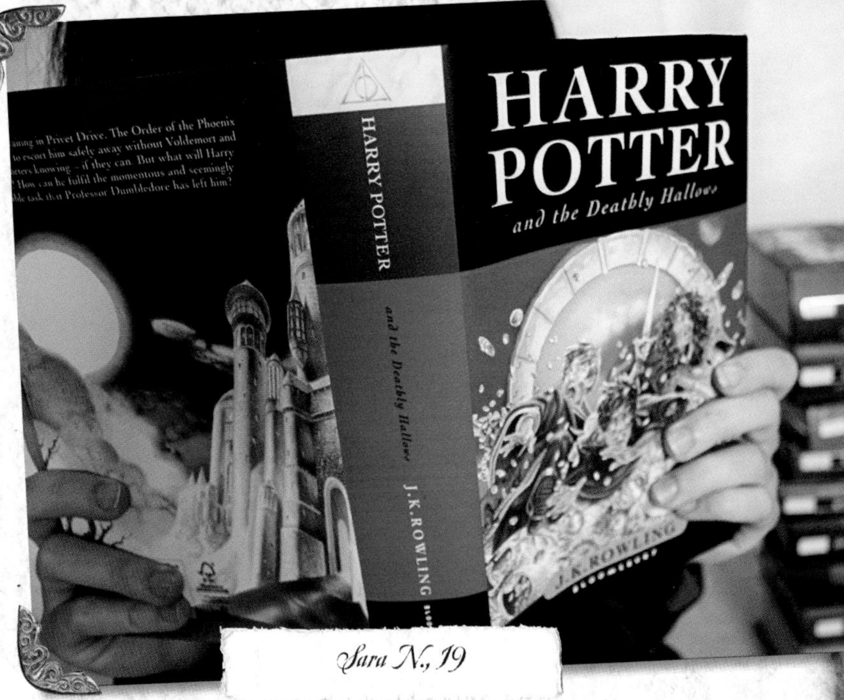

Sara N., 19

Like almost every one of us who fell in love with your world at a young age, I waited for my Hogwarts letter. Two years I waited, and on my eleventh birthday, nothing came in the mail and no owls appeared at my window. I was heartbroken. I felt betrayed. I had truly thought you were real. That was when I left you. I never stopped liking *Harry Potter*, but it was pushed aside as different things took over my focus. I still read the new books and watched the new movies as they came out, but the meaning they had to me was lost. This went on for three years.

When I turned fourteen and started high school, I was put in a private school away from the people I had grown close to. My parents started fighting more and more. My house was never peaceful, school was a horrible place to be, and I had to start taking care of my siblings. Depression took over a once happy person. I had no friends, so I spend most of my school time in the library reading whatever books were recommended.

One day, while taking a book out of the shelf, another one fell out. It was *Harry Potter and the Philosopher's Stone*. I took the book home and started reading what was once the focus of my life. That night I cried and cried, and I realized how I had pushed away what I needed the most. Only at this point did I figure out how my eleven-year-old self was mistaken. You were real, but not in the literal way I thought. Only I could made you real and present in my life. During the next few months, I had probably read all the books over six times. I fell in love again. You had been through so much more than me, and I realized I could conquer this bump in my life, just as you did with the many in yours. You brought me out of my depression, and made me a happy person again. I was proud to call myself a 'Potterhead'.

At fifteen, my parents separated, but it did not affect me as much as I thought it would. Every time I felt like everything was going wrong, I picked up any of your books, opened to a random section, and started reading. Reading your books felt so good, made me feel so much better. Nobody understood why I wasn't behaving how most kids do when their parents separated, but nobody understood that I had you, either. Mr. Potter, you and your friends were with me during the lowest point of my life, and made me a stronger person. I know that with you by my side I can overcome anything.

THANK YOU FOR EVERYTHING,

– Ryan D., Gryffindor

K'lyssa

Dear Mr. Potter,

Once upon a time a scrawny, eleven-year-old boy with jet black hair, green eyes, and a lightning bolt scar on his forehead came into my life and changed it forever. I first met *Harry Potter* in September of 1998, when I was only nine years old. He brought with him fantastic characters, incredible places, and an imaginative story that sucked me in from the very beginning. I was in love with him, his story, and the fantastic Wizarding world that JK Rowling created.

"And I know, it's only a story, but for so many it's more than that.
It's a world all its own where we want to put on the Sorting Hat.
I will miss the train ride in and the pranks pulled by the twins.
And though it's nowhere I've been, I'll keep on smiling from the times I had with them."
– Oliver Boyd and the Remembralls

Each new stage of life that greeted the characters was happening to me at almost the exact same time. I literally grew up with them always in the background. When Harry struggled to fill the void left behind by his parents, I struggled to hold onto the remnants of my relationship with my father. When Harry and Ron were experiencing the ups and downs of their first relationships, so was I. When Hermione wanted the boy she liked to ask her out and he ignored her, I could relate. I learned the value of true friendship from the trio. I learned the value of discipline and bravery and courage. I learned the importance of choice. I learned that you can always find a reason to be happy. I learned that I am a true Gryffindor. I came to understand what it truly means to stand up for something that you believe in. I now realize that no matter what happens, the people we love will never truly leave us.

There are so many key moments of my life that wouldn't be the same if Harry hadn't been there, and there are many more that never would've happened at all. If it wasn't for *Harry Potter*, I would never have started working for MuggleNet. I would never have gone on so many fantastic trips or to so many memorable conventions. I would never have met so many incredibly amazing people that I hope will play a big role in the rest of my life. It was Harry's relationship with Lupin in *Prisoner of Azkaban*, as both a teacher and a friend, that convinced me that being a teacher really was the right choice for me. I graduated from Texas Tech University on December 18, 2010 and am now teaching 2nd grade. I honestly believe that I have J.K. Rowling and the world that she created to thank for my walk across the stage. I've already begun reading the series to my students, with the hope that just one of them will find refuge in the pages of each book.

"This phenomenon is blind to age, gender, race, and location.
So even though we've reached the end, it's not over yet.
We'll still have each other. All the friendships, and all the laughs.
And when it seems dark, we'll all be there with outstretched hands.

Catherine, 16

Kamalie M., 19

Life's a funny thing. It can present you with surprises around every corner.
No one knows what tomorrow will bring, but we can hope that it brings us all a little bit closer."
–Oliver Boyd and the Remembralls

I know that, even as it comes to an end, Harry and Ron and Hermione and the entire series will always be a part of my life. I'll always be able to open one of the books or turn on one of the movies and relive the series and all of the moments that completely defined me as a person as well as my generation. I will never be able to properly thank JK Rowling for everything she gave me when she sat on that train and dreamed up the Boy Who Lived. I will never forget the first time I read each of the books; where I was and who I was with. But most of all, I will never forget *Harry Potter* and what it stands for; love. There have been so many incredible twists and turns in this journey, and I will forever be thankful for each one.

I don't think I will ever be able to put into words exactly how much my life changed the moment Harry walked into it...but I will always cherish every laugh, every smile, every tear, every summer spent theorizing, every midnight showing and every other completely incredible memory that has been created along the way.

"As a great man once said, 'IT DOES NOT DO TO DWELL ON DREAMS AND FORGET TO LIVE.'
We're being given a fresh start.
A new era is fast approaching.
But this time around, we are the storytellers."
- Oliver Boyd and the Remembralls

–K'lyssa S., 22

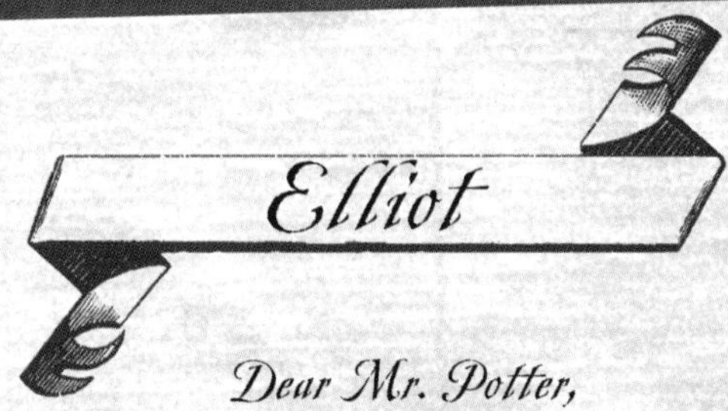

Dear Mr. Potter,

I never had a hard life. We always had money. We always had food. We always traveled and saw beautiful places. My parents and my older sister and I always got on well. We always had love.

We didn't have to worry about getting evicted or losing our cars. We didn't have to worry about paying bills or not being able to buy something nice. When I was four, *Harry Potter and the Philosopher's Sorcerer's Stone* came out. It received rave reviews.

When I was six, my Dad bought it to see how great the book really was. He thought it was so phenomenal that he decided to read this glorious book to his young son.

From the first sentence, I couldn't identify with Harry. I didn't know that life. I didn't know what it was like to have people be stuck with you and despise you. I didn't know people could have that life. I didn't know that people had that life. It seemed impossible; fiction. But I was wrong. People all over the world have that life, feeling unwanted, unappreciated, unloved. I en- joyed the magic and wonder of *Harry Potter*. I loved the characters. All of their funny quirks and what they said always made me giggle and really think. They felt like a second family to me; familiar and welcoming.

As the characters of the *Harry Potter* world grew up, so did I. I began to relate better with Harry, Ron, Hermione... even Snape, sometimes. I knew and felt what they were going through. The characters got deeper and somehow got much more feelings, just like I did.

2001 and 2011; ten years and counting.

Through the years, I grew close to J.K. Rowling's characters. They were my escape. They taught me things I couldn't have guessed at. They were my friends who didn't laugh at or judge me when growing up.

I really can't imagine a world without *Harry Potter*. I can't imagine a world without books. I can't imagine a world with books and people who can't read them. Worst of all, I can't imagine a world without love, but I know that it's there, and no one should live in that world. And yet, some do.

For more than ten years, I've been able to read and love *Harry Potter*; and so should you; the unwanted, unappreciated, unloved person.

If you're reading this, whoever you are, know this: I love you. I love you with all my heart. *Harry Potter* loves you. Hermione Granger loves you. Ron Weasley loves you. Albus Dumbledore loves you. Minerva McGonagall loves you. Severus Snape loves you. J.K. Rowling loves you. Someone loves you.

WITH LOVE,

– Elliott R.

PS: I whole-heartedly plan on reading the Harry Potter *series to my kids, and hope they pass it down through our family, because it is life changing and forever fantastic.*

Dear Mr. Potter,

I was around 13 when I noticed my sister reading your books. I wasn't that interested in books like *Harry Potter*, preferring to read books that explored "real life" stories, and even then I wasn't very interested in reading. I thought fantasy was a bit stupid because it wasn't real, until my sister asked me if I wanted to borrow her copy of *Philosopher's Stone*. There was a film coming out, she told me, but she'd only take me to see it if I read the book first.

I was in love from the very first line. I was amazed that the story could feel so real, despite being about magic and a world that didn't really exist. It was around this time that I started going against the mainstream, liking different music and dressing differently from the people at school. My peers didn't take kindly to different, and everyday was a bit of a battle. The battle against the narrow minded people I met made me love the fantasy world of *Harry Potter* even more. I ignored the people who hated it as much as I could, ditched the friends who thought reading was boring, and started exploring more books and music, deciding I'd be whoever I wanted to be.

When I was 18 my parents moved abroad, leaving me to finish college while living with my sister. That July, *Harry Potter and the Deathly Hallows* came out; we went at midnight and stood in the queue waiting for our copies. It was three a.m. when we got back to the house. We just looked at each other and said "see you when you finish." I went into my room, she went into hers, I stayed up reading the book. That afternoon, I finally finished and walked into her room. It was obvious we had both been crying. She'd finished it before me but waited for me to come to her. We sat there for hours chatting about the book. We've always been close, but that day we were closer than we'd ever been before.

MISCHIEF MANAGED,

– Raimy, 22, Hufflepuff, England

Dear Mr. Dumbledore,

Boys and girls all over the world are turning eleven and aren't getting their letter with that famous dark green ink and dazzling red stamp embolded with the Hogwarts crest. This is an outrage! I recently turned 12. My chance is over. So I'm writing on behalf of all kids not yet over the age limit for their first year at the school of witchcraft and wizardry, to ensure that they are not overcome with the disappointment that I felt when I did not get the letter I earlier described.

Hoping that all still remains well,
William H. 12

It's a Saturday night and I am lying on my couch, flipping though channels. My friend texts me and invites me to a party. Then a commercial comes on advertising *Harry Potter and the Chamber of Secrets* for a showing at 11. I text my friend back saying sorry, but I'm busy. That's the impact *Harry Potter* has had on my life, in a nutshell.

It's not just that *Harry Potter* changed my life. It has been such a big part of my life that I can't imagine where I would be without it. I sort everyone I meet into one of the four houses. I say 'lumos' when I turn on flashlights and 'alohomora' when I open doors. Harry, Hermione, and Ron carried me through days that I couldn't handle on my own. I could always count on the books to be waiting loyally for me, ready to be cracked open. Ready to have tears dropped on them, laughs poured into them. They were never mad when I accidentally let them drop to the floor after my tired eyes just couldn't keep reading.

Harry Potter introduced me to my best friend. Neither of us were big fans of the series or very good friends, but we headed to the movies to see *Chamber of Secrets* (mainly so our parents could get us out of their hair for a while). That movie began our obsession. We came home ranting and raving, creating wands from chopsticks, searching for potion ingredients in our refrigerators, and begging our parents to get us the books. We came home from that movie as best friends.

The next year I moved miles away from my childhood home and from the comfort of my friendship. I was terrified to be moving away from my best friend. *Harry Potter* held us together. We wrote to each other using quills and ink and signed our names as our favorite characters.

Kelsey D., 20

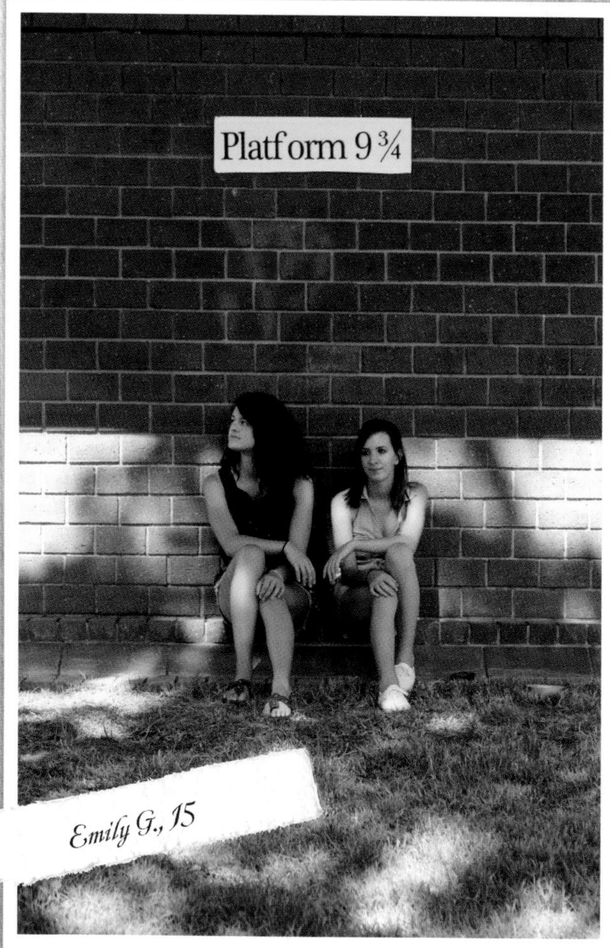

Emily G., 15

Keller High School (Keller, Texas) Quidditch Team

I would pretend that I was on the run from Voldemort or that I was stuck with the Dursley's for the summer. I believed I was surrounded by Muggles, perhaps on an undercover assignment for the Ministry.

After I had finished my homework, I would grab my spell books and study for my OWLS. It seems silly, ridiculous even. I can't help but laugh at my dorkiness. These acts, however, distracted me and kept me hopeful at a time of uncertainty and fear. If I have learned anything from *Harry Potter* it's that hope can always be found and that true friends will always be there for you, no matter how far apart you may be.

Recently, I've been thinking about *Harry Potter* a lot and trying to deal with the fact that it will soon be over. Well, not over, it will never be over, but there will be no more *Harry Potter* things to look forward to. No more sleeping outside of Borders to get the first copy of the next book. No more standing in cluttered lines at the movie's midnight premieres. That part of *Harry Potter* will be over. But *Harry Potter* will never be gone—not so long as those of us who remain are loyal to him.

The *Harry Potter* series was my Hogwarts; it offered me safety from my own death eaters and it introduced me to my best friend. *Harry Potter* taught me how important it is to be courageous, strong, and brave, even when it feels as if the whole world is filled with dementors.

That is why this Saturday night I will be sitting on my couch reciting the lines with the actors, and watching my favorite trio battle the dark arts. So thank you, Mr. Potter. It's impossible to truly express the impact you have had on me.

– Alexandra M., 17, Gryffindor

Kinn

Dear Mr. Potter,

In 2001, I was a shy, awkward seven-year-old who stood out with my severe shortsightedness and thick glasses. I was the kind of little girl who loved to read. Naturally, I was not very popular in school. My only real friend was a girl who lived in my neighbourhood. We took the same bus to school, were in the same class, and sat beside each other. However, the biggest thing we had in common was our love of *Harry Potter*.

We discovered *Harry Potter* sometime during our primary one year. We were both hooked. We spent hours discussing the series and thinking of ways it might continue. We pored over the books, hoping to unearth some clues. We came up with some pretty crazy theories - the later books would prove that we were completely wrong.

We loved *Harry Potter*. We loved *Harry Potter* so much that we actually convinced ourselves that we were witches. We spent about two years in total living in our own fantasy world. Exploring the nooks and crannies of our neighbourhood, we were certain that the cracked granite beside the drain was a sign that a curse took place there. We invented spells and enchantments that protected our fantasy world from our parents and other non-believers. Who knew that, when we were eleven, we would get our letters from Hogwarts.

Of course, we eventually outgrew our childish fantasies and, when we were ten, we fell out and stopped speaking. Soon after that, primary school came to an end and we went our separate ways in different secondary schools. Nevertheless, those stolen hours in corners of our neighbourhood are fond memories. I sometimes wish I could be transported back in time to when I thought that bicycles were secretly operated by magic. In that way, *Harry Potter* made my childhood happier and gave me something to immerse myself in, something I could truly be happy doing. To this day, my only cure for teenage angst, bad grades, or a broken heart is reading *Harry Potter*.

"Happiness can be found, even in the darkest of times, if one only remembers to turn on the light." My light is *Harry Potter* and I am incredibly grateful that Ms. Rowling wrote this series of amazing books. I can only hope that *Harry Potter* brings you as much happiness as it does to me.

–Kinn N., 17

Ever since that winters day in 2000. 10 years and counting. –Jamie P.

Andrew Sims

Nikki G., 18, Gryffindor

Dear Mr. Potter,

Harry Potter changed the direction of my life. I was first introduced to the series in the fourth grade when my teacher read *Harry Potter and the Sorcerer's Stone* to us in class. After she finished, I went to the bookstore one day and found *Chamber of Secrets* on display at the front of the store. I purchased it and started reading right away.

Over the next couple of years, I started developing an interest in computers and the internet. I was particularly interested in creating my own website. The first idea that came to mind was a *Harry Potter* site. I thought it was a perfect idea because it mashed my two interests, *Harry Potter* and the internet, together. I used a Microsoft website creator to make the site. I was 13 years old when I first opened it. There were about 50 people visiting the site every day, so I was pretty happy with how things were going.

At the same time, I noticed other *Harry Potter* fansites. It was clear the biggest site was MuggleNet. I always envied their popularity. About two to three years into running my site, I noticed that MuggleNet had a job opening for a general content creator. I thought that it was a perfect position for me, so I e-mailed them. I was obsessed with getting the job because working for MuggleNet was my dream. I wanted to be a part of a bigger *Harry Potter* site so I could share my passion of web design and Potter with more people. After some serious begging, I finally got in. I was ecstatic. A year or two later, I launched MuggleCast with a few other staff members. That was when I started really getting to know the people who worked on the site on a more personal level since we would Skype with each other every week.

Because of MuggleNet and MuggleCast, I realized my passion for online media. I love going to conferences, premieres, junkets, set visits, and everything else that comes along with it. I love knowing that people rely on MuggleNet and MuggleCast to get their news and entertainment. It's extremely rewarding and I know being in online media is what I want to do for the rest of my life. Not only that, but I've met all of my best friends through the fandom. I wouldn't trade them for any other friends in the world. They are some of the nicest and smartest people that I've met and we're all going to go on to great things. MuggleNet and MuggleCast not only revealed a lot of great friendships, but also great talent. We'll all be working together for a long time.

I'm thankful for *Harry Potter* and the fandom, because I would have been in a completely different place if I didn't have them.

–Andrew Sims, 21

Dear Mr. Potter,

I am up way later than any ten year old should be, but I just can't sleep...not with Hagrid coming. I know that he's on his way right now. My parents can't hide my powers forever. How cruel and lame of them. I glance at the clock. 11:54. Only six more minutes before my eleventh birthday, the most important day for a magical child. I can't wait for him to come bang on my door, confirm what I already know, and take me away to Hogwarts!

Amy E., 2003

11:55. My hands are getting clammy. What if he doesn't come? No, that could never happen. My brother tried to tell me that it wasn't going to, but I knew he wasn't telling the truth. A place as great as Hogwarts has to exist. Something shuffles in my doorway. I get excited but it's just my dog. "Go away, Lexi!" I whisper. "You're gonna ruin it!" 11:58. Oh my gosh, two minutes left. I'm tempted to wake up my brother and rub it in his face when Hagrid comes. Or I'll tell Hagrid to give him a beak or wings or something. That'll show him.

Midnight came and went with no sign of the half-giant. I'm a little worried now. Maybe my brother was right? Maybe I'm not magic? Maybe the magical world doesn't exist at all! The silence is unbearable. I pull the covers up over my face and drift off to sleep...

Nine years after my rather disappointing eleventh birthday, and 12 years since I first picked up *Sorcerer's Stone*, the same rush of emotions still courses through me whenever I open a *Harry Potter* book. I grew up with Harry; he was my childhood. How would I have passed the third grade if I hadn't have done my book report on *Chamber of Secrets*? What if I had never waited in line to see *Deathly Hallows: Part 1* at midnight AND at 3:00am? What books would be taking up my bookshelf right now without *Harry Potter*? I don't know the answers to these questions, but I can say that it's like Christmas morning every time I crack open the spine of a *Harry Potter* book.

Now the books are all published and the movie franchise is coming to an end. But will that be the end of *Harry Potter* in my life? Never. I love these characters, I know their stories, and I share their emotions. A large part of my life has engulfed by *Harry Potter*, and I'm absolutely sure that my love for these books can only grow from here.

– Tyler B., 19

Brigid V.

Karen

Dear Mr. Potter,

The love for the series started with my oldest child. I bought her the books, the movies, the bedroom set, the Legos, anything that I could get my hands on. I thought it was just a childhood phase, something she would grow out of as she grew older. The love only grew stronger, and at times it got annoying. However, despite all of this, I supported her the entire time. I put up with the demands for the newest book or DVD, the excitement for the opening of the Wizarding World of *Harry Potter* at Universal, the overall word vomit of information and characters and the plot that I know nothing about. I brought her to the *Deathly Hallows* midnight premiere even though I had an important work test the following day.

I paid for her to bring her sister to go see *Deathly Hallows* for her birthday, and then the love for the series spread throughout my family. My 16 year old daughter passed it on to my 10 year old daughter, and since then she has begged me to bring her to the library so she could get the books we were missing. They have already started trying to convince me to bring them to the midnight premiere. Recently, I left all four of my daughters home alone, expecting phone calls when there were arguments. My phone was quiet. The next day, I discovered they had spent the night watching the first *Harry Potter* films together until they all fell asleep. The series has united my children and given them a common interest beyond anything else. I have never actually read the books—they haven't convinced me to yet—but I am proud of them because of what the books stand for, and how much they let it influence their lives. Thank you for having such a positive (though at times overwhelming) impact on their lives.

– Karen W.
(proud parent of a Ravenclaw, Slytherin, and two Gryffindors)

Paul DeGeorge

HARRY *and the* POTTERS

Dear Harry Potter, Year 5

For a long time, I've wondered why you haven't joined our band. Are you still moping around over Cho Chang? Too busy with Quidditch? Do you want to talk about any of this stuff? I mean, I've kinda lived through it, so maybe I can help you out. Also, *Harry Potter* Year 4 and I have a tour coming up this summer and could really use some extra help. Any chance you can play drums?

Let me offer you some advice. If it's the Cho Chang thing that's bothering you, you need to channel that energy, dude! All the best love songs aren't about things being happy and perfect. They're about the struggle to get there. I know that date with Cho didn't really go as planned, but there are other witches out there in the wizarding world. You never know when you'll bump into the right one.

But enough about the ladies. You know what they say: snitches before witches. Are we caught up in that old jocks vs. punks personality clash? Is it peer pressure? I know that the Quidditch team would pretty much fall apart without you, especially now that Fred and George seem more invested in their candy business—but then I remembered that you just got kicked off the team by Umbridge! Aren't you full of rage? Isn't now the perfect time to exorcise some of those demons on stage?

No, I haven't forgotten about Dumbledore's Army. How could I? Starting that group is, without question, the coolest thing you've done all year! And it's also why you'd be perfect in our band! Punk rock is not just music: it's a mentality. It's about going out there and doing it for yourself. It's about taking control of your life and giving the finger to people like Umbridge who try to tell you what you can and cannot do.

We have a chance to show people that the world is not an evil and pessimistic place. There is magic—even in the Muggle parts of the world. I've seen it from the stage. I've felt what it's like to be alive and connected to other people. When the voice of the audience rises, I know that Voldemort can hear it because the song is true and it speaks of Love and Friendship and Rock and Roll and he knows that his powers will fail against these weapons. That's why we started this band and that's why we need your help. Plus, we really need a drummer.

PLEASE SAY YES.

Your future self,

—Harry Potter, Year 7

Luna
Thank y
J.K. Ro
for lettin
embra
my inner L

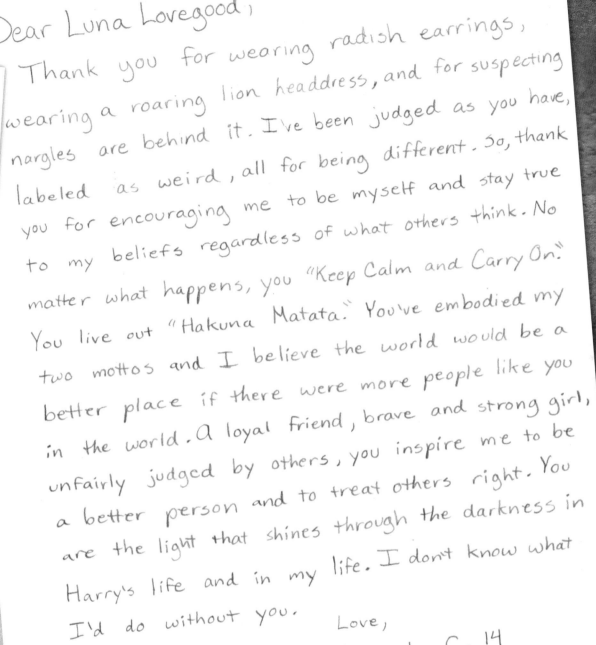

Dear Luna Lovegood,

Thank you for wearing radish earrings, wearing a roaring lion headdress, and for suspecting nargles are behind it. I've been judged as you have, labeled as weird, all for being different. So, thank you for encouraging me to be myself and stay true to my beliefs regardless of what others think. No matter what happens, you "Keep Calm and Carry On." You live out "Hakuna Matata." You've embodied my two mottos and I believe the world would be a better place if there were more people like you in the world. A loyal friend, brave and strong girl, unfairly judged by others, you inspire me to be a better person and to treat others right. You are the light that shines through the darkness in Harry's life and in my life. I don't know what I'd do without you.

Love,

Daniela C., 14

Gryffindor

P.S. You may be in Ravenclaw, but you sure have a lot of Gryffindor in you.

Athyrai

Dear Hermione,

You may be wondering why I am writing to you, Miss Granger, instead of the famous Mr. Potter. I hope that, through this letter, you will see just how much you have impacted my life.

At first, I thought I would identify more with Harry, coming from an abusive home, feeling lonely, having a short fuse, but a good heart. I thought I was like Harry, lonely and angry. Then I thought, no, I'm much more like Ron. I come from an enormous family, the sixteenth in line, with nothing extraordinary to my name. I was insecure and perpetually overshadowed. But then there was you, Miss Granger, an unapologetically hardworking young woman, just like me.

Until reading *Harry Potter and the Philosopher's Stone*, I had never seen the name "Hermione" before. I did not know how to pronounce it until it was spelled out phonetically for Viktor Krum's sake. I guess I should tell you my name. It's Athyrai (pronounced aw-thee-ray). As a child, I was always picked on for my name being different, but here you were: a girl with a different sort of name, just like me, in a book. A prominent figure in this book that appealed to the masses.

In the eleven years I had been reading the series, you grew up and I grew with you. I watched as Draco called you names, like "mudblood," while I went to school and was called "terrorist." I watched as you became involved in SPEW and Dumbledore's Army as I became involved with No One Is Illegal and the Young Liberals of Ontario. In you, Miss Granger, I saw the strength and resolve I needed (and wanted) to be the best person I could possibly be. I saw you change the wizarding world and I want to do my best to change my own.

So here's to you, Miss Granger. Thank you for demonstrating that knowledge truly is power. Thank you for illustrating that even though you are female, you can kick ass just as hard, if not harder, than males. Thank you for showing me how to be loyal to friends in the face of inexplicable danger. Thank you for teaching me the importance of having a cool head, even when the pressure is unbearable. Thank you for showing me that privilege should be used to help others. Thank you for showing me that it does not matter what I am born, but it is what I grow up to be that truly matters. But most of all, thank you for being the best role model a girl like me could have had.

Love Always,

– Athyrai S., 22, Ravenclaw

Dear
HERMIONE G.,
"the brightest witch of her age"
Thank you for showing me:
- smart girls are cool!
- you don't need to be popular
- being friends w/guys doesn't mean you'll be the "damsel in distress", instead, you'll save their butts, time after time
- studying and working hard > crushing over guys
- female power
- how a real role model is like ♡
every little girl needs an intelligent, brave, caring, loyal and friendly role model, like you, to look up to.
Thank you for being my
ROLE MODEL! ♡
(even if you are fictional)
Lena C. 16
Ravenclaw

DEAR MR. POTTER,
I DIDN'T READ THE BOOKS WHEN THEY CAME OUT. ONLY WHEN MY SISTER LEFT FOR COLLEGE, LEAVING ME ALONE, DID I PICK THEM UP AND STA READING THEM BEFORE BED. THANKS TO THE BOOKS, MY SISTER AND HAVE ANOTHER RELATED INTEREST AND I'VE READ MORE LITERATU THESE PAST TWO YEA THAN I HAVE MY ENTIRE LIFE.
THANK YOU, MR. POTTER.
AND ALLIE, IF YOU'RE READI THIS... YOU' THE BEST A I LOVE YOU THAN ANYT CAN'T WAI TO SHARE BUTTERB WITH YO IN SUNN FL THI CHRIST
-KAITL GRAZI

Kaitlyn G., 17

Lauren

Dear Hermione Granger,

From the start, you were always my favourite character. You were a right little know-it-all, the kind of girl who would correct the teacher and read textbooks for fun and always strive to get the top marks. And that was something I could relate to. I was that girl who always seemed to know everything, considered an A- a terrible failure, and read everything in sight.

And yet you were just as brave as Ron and Harry. You held your own, even when they didn't realize the courage you possessed. You were just as determined to defeat Lord Voldemort, or save the world from evil. And I always thought—just maybe—that if Hermione Granger could be loyal and brave, perhaps I could, too. Perhaps I could take down my weaknesses and succeed, even alongside someone like the Chosen One. If Hermione Granger could be a hero, maybe I could, too.

And for that, I thank you. Not just for your inspiration, but for your magic, adventure, and strong sense of what was right. You wouldn't let those house elves be stepped on and oppressed, would you? Of course not. Because you—a "Mudblood"—saw that every single creature had thoughts, opinions, and words.

I cannot express in this letter how much you've inspired me. I can only hope that you already know.

—Lauren R., 12, Ravenclaw

I dressed up as Hermione for Character Day at school. It was great to realize how many Harry Potter fans there are at my school.
—Katie K., 17

Dear Mr. Potter,

From the first time they were mentioned in *The Philosopher's Stone,* I have been in love with the Weasley twins. They are everything that I wish that I could be: mischievous, outspoken, confident, brave, humorous, compassionate, and forgiving.

Though Fred and George did not always apply themselves to their schoolwork, they showed that they were skilled in other ways. Only the most talented wizards could invent products such as Puking Pastilles, Peruvian Instant Darkness Powder, and Wildfire Whiz-Bangs.

My mind often overflows with plans and dreams and things that I want to do and say. However, I do not have enough nerve to do any of these things. I do not take initiative. Fred and George do. When they wanted to fly away from school, they did it. When they wanted to start a business, they did it. When they wanted to do anything, they did it. These are things that I wish I was able to do every single day of my life.

Fred and George have taught me more than any other characters in the series, even Harry Potter himself. I have always been the girl in the background, nearly invisible to the people around her. That is mostly my fault. I am shy, timid, and easily embarrassed. Sometimes I swear that I was born without a backbone. Fred and George are the complete opposite. They are daring. They don't hold back.

There is so much that I love about the Weasley twins and so much that I have learned. As Ginny Weasley learned from her older brothers, I hope to one day fully understand that "anything's possible if you've got enough nerve."

Mischief Never Managed,

– Annica M., 14, Ravenclaw

rry's bravery, Dumbledore's wisdom, the Weasleys kindness, Hermione's intelligence, Neville's loyalty & Luna's acceptance will stay with me until the very end.
King's Cross

Kelly K, 21

DEAR GINNY WEASLEY,

I'M PROUD TO SAY YOU HAVE BEEN ONE OF MY FAVORITES FOR A VERY LONG TIME. IN THE BEGINNING, YOU SEEMED TO BE JUST A NORMAL LITTLE GIRL. BUT THEN YOU PROVED EVERYONE HOW AMAZING YOU ARE. NOT ONLY SMART AND FRIENDLY, BUT ALSO FIERCE, BADASS AND A GREAT WITCH.

I'M PROUD OF <u>YOU</u>. AND THANK YOU FOR THE MESSAGE YOU GAVE US: TO STAND UP FOR OURSELVES, NO MATTER WHAT OTHER MIGHT SAY.

LOTS OF LOVE,

LORENA, 17, GRYFFINDOR – BRAZIL

12-31-10

Dear Harry,

I fear it is impossible to fully express how much you have meant to me. You are as much a part of me as the house I grew up in, my birthday or my favorite song. You have been a part of me since our first meeting at number four, Privet Drive. Since then, my connection to you has done naught but grow.

Over the years, I have mourned your losses, celebrated your triumphs and known you as only a very dear friend can.

Though I have grieved over the end of our adventure together, I shall not begrudge your recession from the public eye. As Albus Dumbledore once said, "It does not do to dwell on dreams and forget to live." So, Harry, I will treasure the time we were given, visit you often and remember you always.

Your friend,

Megan S.

Lori Earl

Esther

Dear lovers of all things Harry Potter:

Harry Potter saved Esther. He filled her world with stories, peopled her life with friends, and magically knit her into a community.

Picture a nine year old girl, flyaway blond hair and freckles framing her sunny disposition, curled up in the backseat of a van on a cross-country trek from Boston to Southern California. There was barely a peep for three days, as she and her sister read the hot-off-the-press *Harry Potter and the Order of the Phoenix*. Buying two hardcover copies was well-spent money! Esther had followed right after big sister Evangeline in her love for all things *Harry Potter*, reading and re-reading each volume, and hours of discussion over their theories and expectations of characters and story-line.

When we moved to France, Esther discovered Harry and the Potters online, and we discovered she had cancer: thyroid, already metastasized to her lungs. Surgery led to treatment, and finally brought us back to Boston and Children's Hospital. In December 2008 we nearly lost her. During the months of recuperation, the internet became her window to the world. She found out about LeakyCon, scheduled for May just a few miles from our house. Esther wanted to be strong enough to go. She got a wig and we mustered resources and chaperones so she could venture, oxygen tank in tow, into the real life world of wizardry, Nerdfighters, youtubers, and the HP Alliance. Her real and online worlds had coalesced!

In *Harry Potter*'s world, evil is tangible and life is about training to fight it. Children can be heroes and their youth never limits them. Obstacles are challenges, and defeat makes us stronger. As the stories unfold, it becomes clear that the darkest battles must be fought within ourselves—and are overcome only as we cling tightly to each other. Esther embraced these truths and filled her days with loving and being loved.

In the end, even Harry's magic couldn't stop Esther's cancer. On August 25, 2010, her tired lungs finally rested. But the stone that rests on the earthly place where we remember our Star shares the message Esther lived for 16 years: "Love is Stronger than Death."

So thank you for your stories, J.K. Rowling. Thank you for teaching us we can be heroes, Harry. And thank you, each and every friend, for loving Esther. You gave her courage and hope and friendship. She gave us back love and light. "Lumos!"

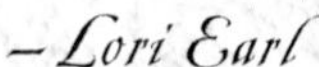
–Lori Earl

Beci M., 16

THESE GUYS ARE

MY

BEST

FRIENDS ANI

WILL BE

ALWAYS

Beci -
16 -

My friend and I traveled to London from California to go to Hogwarts!
– Ali

Francesca R., Ravenclaw

Nina L., Jessica P., Nikki B., Jesse J.

An owl flew into my house when I was eleven. But it didn't bring me a letter.

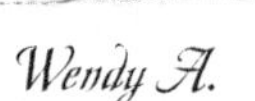

Wendy A.

Bethany

Dear J.K. Rowling,

s I write this letter today to thank you for the gift of Harry, I can no longer remember a time that Hanah and Harry's name were not intertwined together. I cannot look back at a picture without seeing a wand, broom, or tie in Hanah's possession. But, most importantly, I can no longer envision the child who once felt so alone in the world, so isolated. She no longer exists and I will always be indebted to you for giving my daughter the extraordinary gift of the magic, the wizarding world, and Harry.

Hanah was born with two rare chromosomal abnormalities. She had her first two major surgeries by the age of 13 months. She has a g-tube, suffered from a tethered spinal cord, has metal rods in her spine, and now uses a walker to help her get around. She has endured five major surgeries and countless procedures and tests, yet she smiles all the time. She is active in Special Olympics and on her school council. And to this day she continues to sMuggle in her wands to school via her pants legs or coat or arm sleeves....

At the age of six she found *Harry Potter*: a boy who, like herself, was alone in the world. No other person had experienced what he had. She was the only child in the world with her genetic makeup. Separate they were alone, but together they made an unstoppable team. Hanah became Harry, disappearing into his world for hours at a time. She forced us to read and re-read the books until copy after copy had to be replaced. We played Quidditch in the pool, we flew for hours in our backyard, and, most importantly, we read. The geneticists told me that Hanah would have an IQ of 50; she read all of your books! You inspired her to read. She fell in love with reading anything and everything.

The connection to your books allowed her to begin conversations and friendships with other children her age. She dazzled people with her knowledge and collections. She knew more spells than anyone else. As she accepted herself, so did others.

Our lives and her siblings have been deeply influenced by your characters and the choices they made in their own lives. From my three year old son Duncan who picks up sticks and begins to cast spells to our daughter Lillian who just finished reading the first two books as an independent reader. We have met so many wonderful people because of Harry. People who accept our daughter for who she is today.

I can only say thank you, but it is truly from the deepest part of my heart and soul. Thank you.

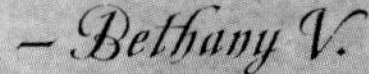

– *Bethany V.*

Ellen H.

This is my brother as Harry Potter in 2001.

Xavier

Dear Mr. Potter,

I was lucky enough to share your birth month and experience growing up with you as a close friend, year after year. You taught me a lot of things, Harry. You taught me what it means to be a true friend; to appreciate family, friends, and life, no matter the circumstances. To say that you have changed the lives of children, teenagers, and adults around the world would not suffice. You have inspired multiple generations to begin reading again. You have created words which have found their way into society and dictionaries. You have spawned a new genre of music, as well as a charity organization that has benefited millions worldwide, and you continue to shape millions of lives with your stories of good morality, love, and friendship. Your lessons will live on in later generations through books, movies, theme parks, music, and the unforgettable stories our generation will tell to those that follow. You've been an amazing friend and I wouldn't be where I am today, doing what I am doing, without you.

–Xavier Austrone

Elizabeth B., 15

Eric Scull

Dear Mr. Potter,

Do you know that there are theme parks about you now? Well, just the one. But there are talks of more. And of expansion. Thanks to the gargantuan number of people across the world who are familiar with your tale—of your struggles, and your triumph over Lord Voldemort—it was thought that a common place to meet and share our love would be a good idea. Oh, and the execution of it! Orlando is quite a bit warmer than the weather at Hogwarts, I assume. It's quite a bit warmer than the places in which I read your stories, that's for sure. All the same, when I visit your Wizarding World with my friends and sit inside the Three Broomsticks drinking a Butterbeer, it takes me back to our first meeting ten long years ago.

I was hesitant, at first, to read your tale. To a twelve year old who did not read, those were big books! My friends, who loved your stories, tried to persuade me, but did not succeed. I suppose I was worried that I could not find a theme I related to in a fantasy world. What did I know?

Later, when a friend's mom insisted I go with my friend and his sister to see the first film adaptation, I finally was introduced to you. The wonder of your world and the endless possibilities of your school and your pure heart and the love for your life would capture me, leading me down the (all-too-familiar, for we who read your stories) path that would eventually lead here, to where we are now.

Thank you, Mr. Potter, for guiding me to find the community of friends that your trials have commanded. Together we shared the highs and the lows of your ongoing quest for peace for your friends. Although you have suffered, you have shown how giving up is insufficient, despite its tender touch. In your world, I found the bravery I lacked to excel in my own. I feel you are responsible for so many things it is not possible for you, me, or the two of us and any one other to know. It cannot be summarized. But it is there: the world created when we decided to endear to you, to follow you, to take the message of your story and spread it far and wide. That world—our world—becomes more and more real every day, and will continue to ad infinitum. I am sure of it.

You must know that you are special. You must know that we will always remember.

-Eric Scull

Ally A., 17

Paul Zalon

Dear Mr. Potter,

I'm Paul; Lily's dad. I read the first book to Lily and her younger sister Annie eleven years ago. Lily was five. This was a "chapter book," so there was a bit of resistance, but it evaporated quickly. Susan and I watched the light switch go on in her head; there was Lily *pre*-Harry and Lily *post*-Harry. At eight years old, she read *Goblet of Fire* on her own—all 734 pages. I read my longest chapter book at 10; *The Hardy Boys: Case of The Secret Panel*—178 double spaced pages. I loved it, but I doubt it was life changing.

Lily's journey into Harry's world was fast and very, very thorough. As Lily says, she really *did* live in Harry's world and only audited ours. This world, in many ways far more interesting than our own Muggle world, seems like it came into being in a miraculous "complete" moment of Rowlian creation; a sort of literary Big Bang.

Harry, Ron, and Hermione were always four years older than Lily. As they became older, stronger, more confused, more fearful, less fearful, more accepting, more loyal, so did she. Through the anticipation of the book releases, movie releases, curly and frizzy Hermione hair, straighter hair, themed birthday parties, trivia games, toys (the Levitation Challenge!), wizard's robes, Ollivander's wands, Time Turners, Marauder's Maps, and standing in line all those times for the midnight releases at Borders, this obsession became magnificent. I watched Lily fall asleep night after night with Jim Dale reading the books to her on her computer. Manually, she read and reread each of the books tens of times; *Harry Potter* was as important to Lily as breathing.

What would Lily be like without Harry? Still an avid reader, but maybe not *as* avid. Where would she have learned that life can be beautiful but often unfair? Would she have learned that it is okay to be a nerd, and to be proud of it? Where would she have learned that all is not black and white, that we all have several facets to our characters'? She usually doesn't listen to her parents, but she will listen to J.K. Rowling, a more than adequate substitute. *Harry Potter* has given Lily a passion, and powerful shared connections with other kids that are based on feelings and the power of writing and imagination. Not on sex, drugs, and rock and roll. Yet.

We went to the traveling *Harry Potter* film exhibit in Boston. Lily has a touch of ADD and is a world-famous multitask-er, but she went through this exhibit like Sherman through Georgia with a single-mindedness I have rarely seen. From left to right there was no detail missed, no caption unread. Tears were in her eyes half the time. We met lots of other kids at the Museum who, identified themselves by their Hogwarts house: "Hey—I'm a Ravenclaw too!" This is the real Dumbledore's Army. We also went to the Wizarding World of *Harry Potter* at Universal Orlando, where there were tears upon entering and even more upon leaving. She looked at Hogwarts Castle with pure openness and love. She was truly in *her* world—which had sprung into physical existence.

Did Harry and Hermione and Ron and Dumbledore and Neville and Snape and McGonagall and the Weasleys and Hagrid (and, yes, even Voldemort) give Lily the courage to take on a project like this at sixteen? *I think they did.* So many people thought she was crazy: "How can you do this while you are thinking about colleges?" or "You're going to do *what*?". Though she started this on her own, Lily learned enough from the books to know when to ask for help. I think I'm most proud of her for that.

– Paul Zalon

ROWLING
HARRY POTTER
AND THE HALF-BLOOD PRINCE
ROWLING
HARRY POTTER
AND THE ORDER OF THE PHOENIX
ROWLING
YEAR 4
HARRY POTTER
AND THE GOBLET OF FIRE
SCHOLASTIC
ROWLING
YEAR 3
HARRY POTTER
SCHOLASTIC
ROWLING
YEAR 2
HARRY POTTER
AND THE CHAMBER OF SECRETS
SCHOLASTIC
ROWLING
YEAR 1
HARRY POTTER

Thank you, Harry, for teaching me bravery + true magic.
Thank
for yo
love +
Rebecca K., 19
HARRY POTTER
I had my high school senior picture t
a Harry Potter book, because that is
mattered to me most in those 4 ye
HOGWARTS
SCHOOL
OF
ITCHCRAFT
AND
IZARDRY
Sharon T.

owling.
of
n.

I am going to take Harry to college with me and then later into marriage and my future family. My children will be raised on magic. Harry will be a part of their lives, and they will grow up with him as I did. That is one thing you can count on.
—Madison G.

Oksana S., 15, Ravenclaw

"After all this time?"

"Always," said Snape.

Loving isn't just while it lasts.

We don't have to let go yet.
We've grown up with these books.
Now let's grow old with them.

*687

Abby M., Ravenclaw

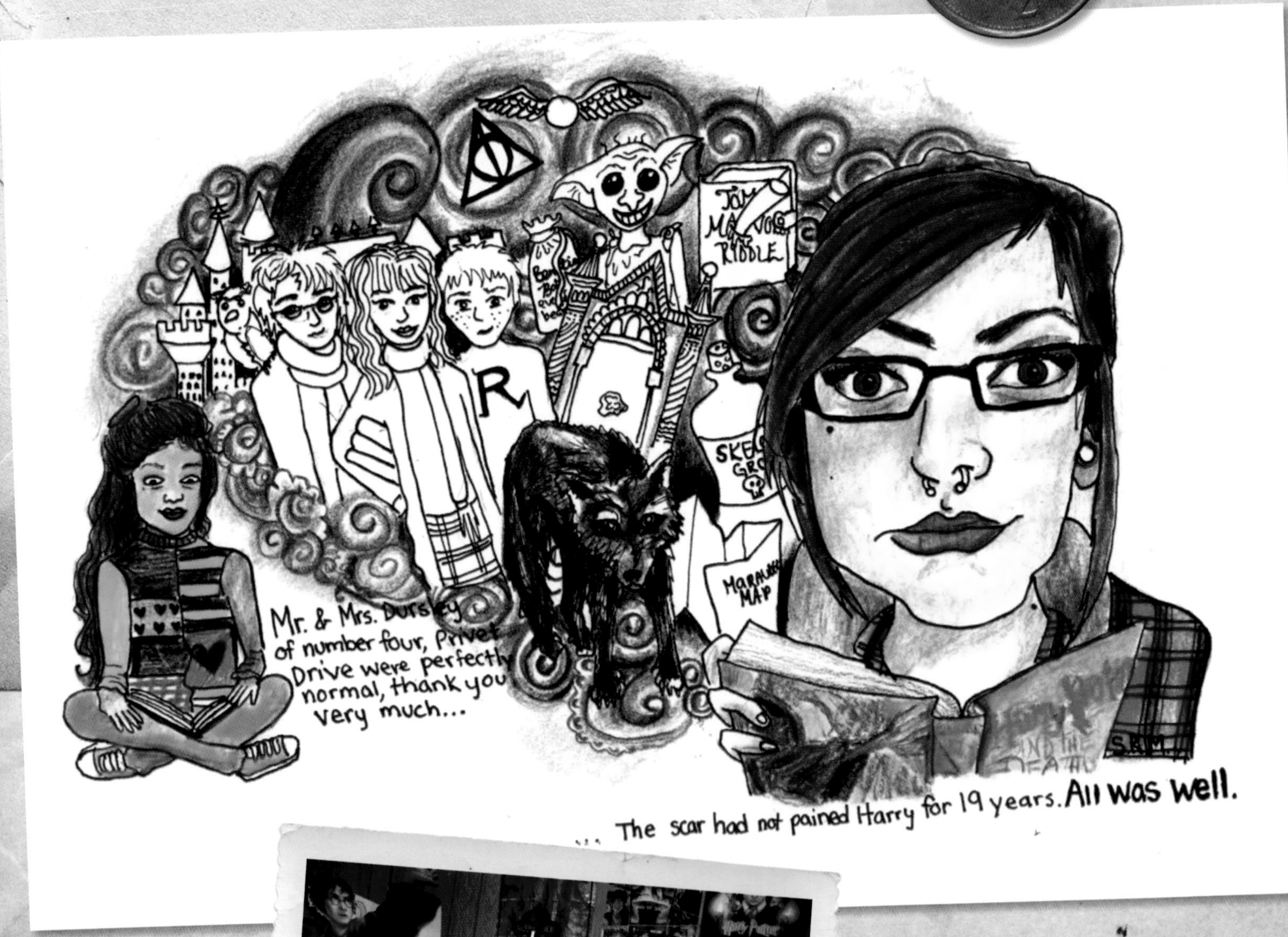

Mr. & Mrs. Dursley of number four, Privet Drive were perfectl normal, thank you very much...

The scar had not pained Harry for 19 years. All was well.

Sammy M., 19, Gryffindor

Jacquelen K, Hufflepuff

Jennifer Dorsey

Dear Hermione,

We could be twins. Well, minus the magic.

When I first met you, I thought I was reading a description of myself. I was 11 and the know-it-all, brown, bushy-haired, book-loving, straight-A student, Muggle version of you. Over the years I too learned to "loosen up" with some help from friends. I too feared failure above almost anything and had a fierce protectiveness for my friends. I shared your fear of getting a bad grade and your joy of making top marks. The likeness was truly uncanny.

Over time reading about you helped me to overcome my own insecurities. And when I was most down or depressed, when things really sucked, I turned to you and your two best friends to reassure and comfort me. To me your story was inspiration and strength.

As I got older, I too fought for the rights of others. Through high school and college I worked for women's rights. My last year of college I co-directed Take Back the Night, a march and vigil against sexual assault, a topic I am unfortunately acquainted with. It was one of my proudest moments.

Now I work for the Harry Potter Alliance and enjoy every minute of combining the two worlds I grew up with—*Harry Potter* and social activism.

So thank you, Hermione. Thank you for teaching me that who I am is nothing to apologize for, that friends and family mean more than appearances and being liked, that being smart is something to be proud of, not ashamed of. Most importantly, thank you for teaching me that fighting for what is right, even when no one else wants to listen, is one of the most admirable things a person can do. Thank you for growing up with me, Hermione, and for helping me to become the woman I am today.

YOUR BUSHY-HAIRED TWIN,

–Jennifer D., 23, Gryffindor

Dear J.K. Rowling,
I am pleased to inform you that you have brought magic into my life thanks to your inspiring and bewitching books. Thank you for letting me be a part of Harry's wondrous world.
Yours sincerely,
Linnie C, Ravenclaw

Lily Zalon

Dear Joanne,

You've changed me. Did you know, all those years ago, sitting in that cafe with your pens and your napkins and your imagination, that what you were doing would have such a huge effect on the millions upon millions of children growing up with Harry? Did you know that you'd alter the life stories of so many of us? That you'd instill in us the values that we hold today, as well as the passion for reading so many of us wouldn't have without you?

I have a terrible memory. I can't remember birthdays, or appointments, or meetings, or homework, or childhood whimsicalities. I can't remember my grandma dying, or my dad losing his job. It's funny, though, how selective a thing memory is. I'll never be able to forget the day you entered my life; beautifully, memorably, and completely irreversibly. I was six. I was sitting in the bathtub. My sister, Annie, and I were furious with our parents, because they didn't let us stay out with the neighbor kids on the street. So my dad read us a book. I still have the copy—a first edition American paperback. It's been destroyed, eaten by time and dozens of re-reads, but it truly is the physical manifestation of not just my childhood, but of myself.

My life isn't measured in years or birthdays. It's measured in the stages of Potter. *Goblet of Fire* was released the year I had my *Harry Potter* themed birthday party—all the adults were required to dress up. My dad was Snape, because of his nose. We ate Bertie Bott's Beans and dressed up as Hogwarts students and played the Levitation Challenge game that was a staple in the lives of young *Harry Potter* fans.

Order of the Phoenix was released the day we drove eight hundred miles in seven hours, rushing to the hospital to try and catch my grandma before she left. I'd been all ready to go to the opening, little nine-year-old me in the Gryffindor colors (all fans are Gryffindors before they decide to go by their actual personalities) and the robe I'd worn for my Hermione Granger costume the year previous.

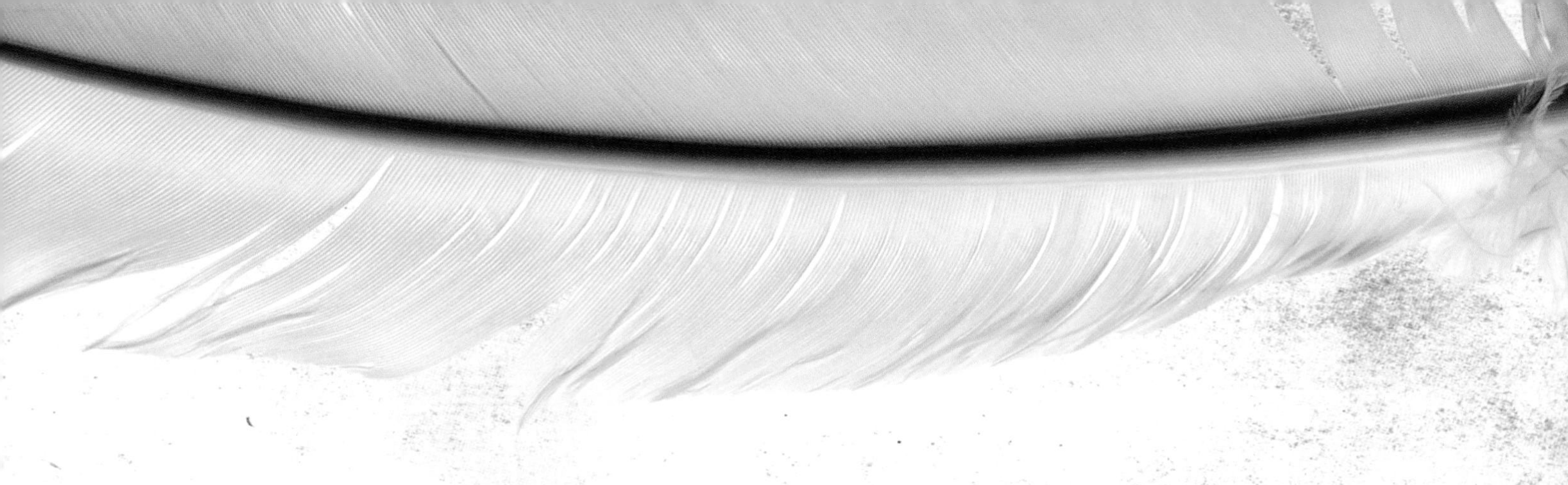

I moved to an unfamiliar school the year *Half-Blood Prince* came out. I had no friends, so I sat on the picnic table at recess and read the first five over and over and over again in anticipation. My fifth grade teacher didn't like that, always telling me to make friends. I had friends, I would tell her, and their names were Harry, Ron, and Hermione. I got to read the sixth book two weeks before its release. My mom was a children's librarian, so they had a copy that early, and she told me that I was lucky enough to get perks. I didn't know what it meant, but I wasn't complaining.

The *Goblet of Fire* movie came out the day someone told me that my bushy hair was ugly. I told them if it was good enough for Hermione, it was good enough for me. Thank you, Jo; you made me stop hating my frizzy, crazy hair because Hermione had it too, and my hatred for my unfitting name disappeared the minute I heard that I shared it with *Harry Potter*'s mother.

July 21, 2007 was the end of my childhood. As Harry aged, I aged also, and as Harry matured, I did too. I was decked out in Ravenclaw colors when I attended this midnight release, and it was the single happiest—and saddest—day of my life. The deaths of Fred, Dobby, Hedwig, Remus, Tonks, and Snape weren't the saddest part, though I did cry. The saddest part for me was the end of the thing that had given me hope and truly kept me alive. I read the book in six hours, starting at midnight and reading all through the night. I was exhausted, but I'd never felt more awake—or alive—in my life.

Harry Potter is not a book, not to me. It's a passion. It's a world that I can be a part of. Inside a *Harry Potter* book is more of a home to me than any house I'll ever inhabit. I live at Hogwarts—I only audit Connecticut. I'm collecting your books in other languages now, Jo. I've got Chinese and British and Latin and Spanish so far. Have you seen the Chinese covers? They're gorgeous. I can only read words here and there, but it's there, it's my *Harry Potter*. It feels good, holding a *Harry Potter* book in my hand. It feels accepting. The messages in your books, of love, and friendship, and acceptance, and loyalty, are ones that I carry with me almost as much as I carry one of your books—that is to say, they never leave my side. I never stop thinking about Harry.

Joanne Rowling, you've changed me. You've dictated my personality as much as you have that of any of your characters. I'll never know what I'd have been like without your magic. I can imagine, though, and I don't like it. I don't think any person alive has had or will have as much of an impact on my life, my values, and my overall morality as you. You've given me a passion, and a love, and an imagination, and a community to be part of, but most of all, you've given me magic, and for that, I'll never stop thanking you.

LOTS OF LOVE,

-*Lily*

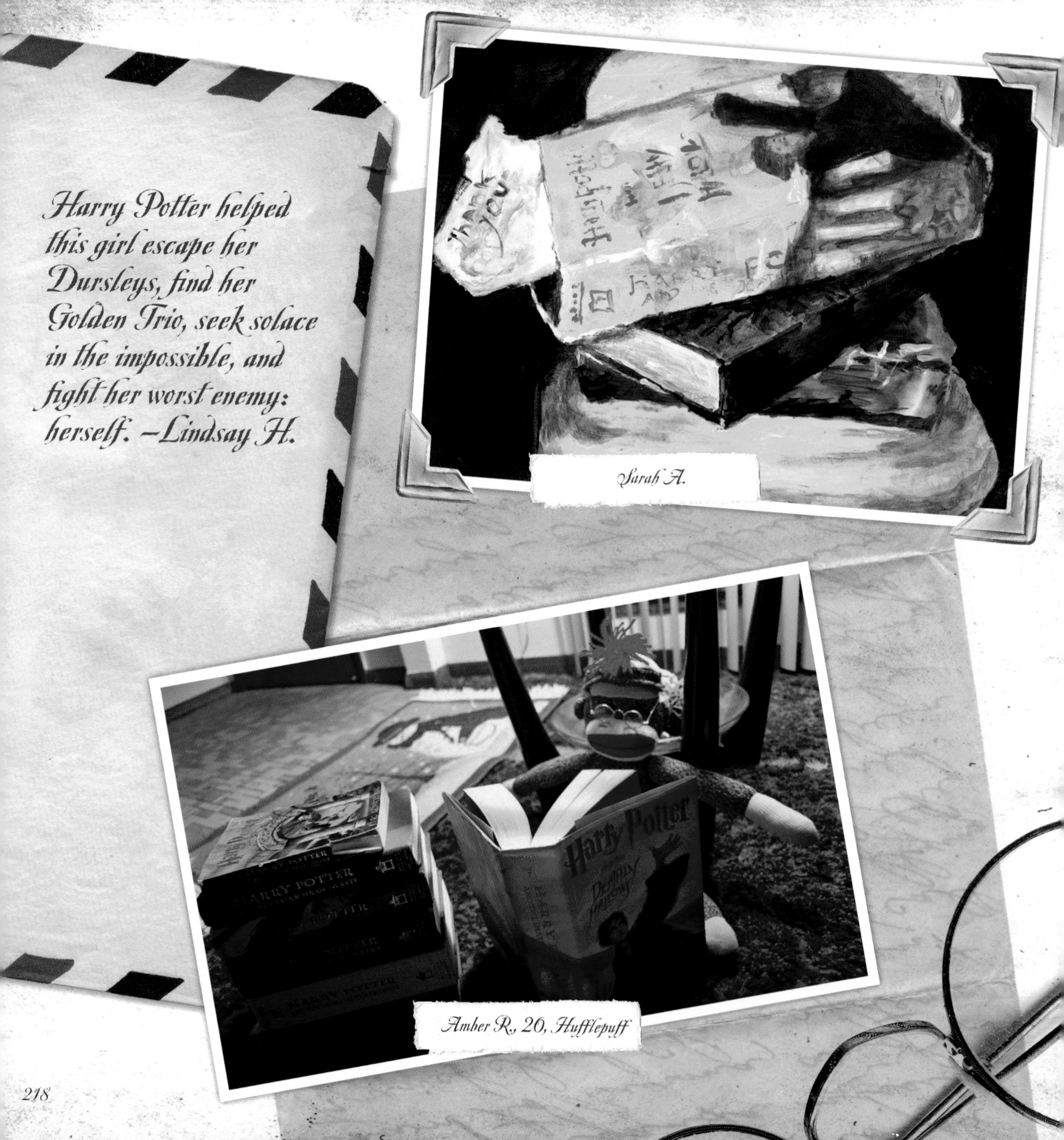

Harry Potter helped this girl escape her Dursleys, find her Golden Trio, seek solace in the impossible, and fight her worst enemy: herself. –Lindsay H.

Sarah A.

Amber R., 20, Hufflepuff

I must not tell lies
I will not tell lies
DETENTION WITH DOLORES
THE HOGWARTS HIGH INQUISITOR

Brittany R., 16

Julia H., 15, Maryland

Dear Mr. Potter

Love, ______________________________